From
the Library
of
IAN BRYSON

B213 © APCo

Corporate Failure
Prediction, panacea and prevention

Corporate Failure
Prediction, panacea and prevention

O. P. Kharbanda

E. A. Stallworthy

McGRAW-HILL Book Company (UK) Limited

London · New York · St Louis · San Francisco · Auckland
Bogotá · Guatemala · Hamburg · Johannesburg · Lisbon · Madrid
Mexico · Montreal · New Delhi · Panama · Paris · San Juan
São Paulo · Singapore · Sydney · Tokyo · Toronto

Published by
McGRAW-HILL Book Company (UK) Limited
MAIDENHEAD · BERKSHIRE · ENGLAND

British Library Cataloguing in Publication Data
Kharbanda, O.P.
    Corporate failure: prediction, panacea and
    prevention.
    1. Crisis management 2. Bankruptcy 3. Corporate
    reorganizations
    I. Title II. Stallworthy, E.A.
    658.4   HD49

    ISBN 0-07-084794-0

Library of Congress Cataloging in Publication Data
Kharbanda, Om Prakash.
    Corporate failure.
    Includes bibliographies and indexes.
    1. Business mortality. 2. Business mortality—
    Case studies. 3. Corporate planning.
    4. Corporate planning—Case studies.
    I. Stallworthy, E. A. (Ernest A.) II. Title.
HD2747.K48 1985   658.4   85-18060
ISBN 0-07-084794-0

12345   WL865

Typeset by Styleset Limited, Warminster, Wiltshire, and
printed and bound in Great Britain by Whitstable Litho Ltd., Whitstable, Kent

To Dorothy,
Sudershan, Vivek, Madhu and Sunil
For their unflinching understanding as this book was written

Contents

Preface

Man is so obsessed with succeeding that his failures are just filed away. Management literature is replete with success stories, but failures are usually ignored. In the corporate world a common result of failure is bankruptcy but while the number of such failures has been on the increase the subject remained largely neglected until the late 1960s. A serious study of corporate failure then began and is now gathering momentum. The subject is no longer taboo but is debated in public and has attracted some reputable consultants who specialize in the subject. It has even become a popular subject for seminars! This is all to the good since half the solution to any problem — and corporate failure is a serious problem indeed — lies in recognizing that a problem exists.

Our own contribution to the subject has been a highlighting of some of the major project disasters in the recent past, but our approach has been constructive. We have sought to draw lessons from those disasters, hence the title of our book *How to Learn from Project Disasters — True Life Stories with a Moral for Management.* The projects covered included a 'heavy water' plant in Canada, a pipeline in Alaska, a refinery in the UK, an LNG plant in Algeria, a fertilizer plant in India, nuclear power plants in the US, the Sydney Opera House in Australia and the world-famous airplane Concorde — a technical triumph but a commercial disaster.

In this book we extend our study from the individual project to the corporation. A project disaster may be one of a number of factors leading to corporate failure and ultimately to collapse. The book has been divided into five major parts:

Basic concepts
Back from the brink?
Prediction is possible
Panacea is better
Prevention is best

Part Two presents a wide range of case histories, from the well-documented classics Penn Central and Rolls-Royce to contemporary examples such as the De Lorean débâcle, the failure of Laker Airways and Carrian Holdings of Hong Kong. We have also studied a number of turnarounds and the techniques of the chief executive who saved the day.

A corporation can well be likened to a human body. Corporate collapse is usually dramatized in the media as a sudden occurrence, but this is almost never the case. The first symptoms appear in minor form, much as does the common cold in the case of man – perhaps preventable but not having a real cure.

We are reminded at this point of the popular saying that you can get over the common cold in 48 hours using medicine, or in two days without medicine – take your choice! If the ailment persists, however, the doctor is called in. If a cure still eludes both doctor and patient, complications may set in and the patient is hospitalized. If his condition continues to deteriorate he will be moved to the intensive care unit. Yet, despite the very best in medical advice, a battery of doctors, consultants and nurses, the patient can continue to fail and finally, despite all the care he has been given, he dies. Then the undertaker moves in. The parallels to the corporate scene may be drawn thus:

Conception	Conception
Pre-natal care	Feasibility Report
Birth	Company start-up
Healthy man	Healthy corporation
Patient	Corporation with a problem
Cold	A problem, usually financial
Doctor (GP)	Management Consultant
Specialist	Consultants technical and financial
Hospital	Bank or other financial institution
Intensive care	No more advances: intensive efforts made for repayment
Death	Failure or collapse
Undertaker	Receiver

We noted earlier that corporate failure, though appearing to be sudden, is seldom so. There is usually ample warning of impending death. But the man – and the corporation – not only ignore the warning signals but even try to hide the sickness. The first visible signs occur when the corporation is in arrears in interest and loan repayment, there is delay in payment to suppliers, there is a shoddy look to the office and the staff are not being paid on time.

The man analogy is consistent at all stages. Corporations are so concerned about the health and welfare of their executives that they insist upon and pay for their regular annual medical checkup. Yet management is totally oblivious when it comes to its own checkup! The Annual Report is supposed to serve this purpose, but such reports can hide more than they show, thanks to 'creative accounting'. The report may well fulfil the statutory obligation, but even that is only done after a fashion. Even if the Annual Report does give warning, this will usually be far too late for really effective action to be taken. The Annual Report pictures yesterday, while what is required is an indicator today for use tomorrow. We therefore advocate methods of analysis and assess-ment to avert disaster.

Our review of cases in Part Two may be likened to a post mortem, although not all corporations 'died'. Many would have done had they not been rescued by a company 'doctor' or bailed out by either government or the banks. That should not have been necessary. In our view prevention is best, but only possible through prediction, the theme of Part Three. Here we study the various tech-niques that are now available to assess the health of a company and determine whether it is in danger of collapse. This leads us to assess the possibility of a panacea (Part Four) only to discover that what is really needed is good manage-ment, a corporate strategy and a resolute chief executive. If these are brought to bear, then crisis should be prevented, as we see in Part Five.

Bankruptcy is what one might describe as a 'growth industry' at present, with more and more companies in trouble every year, almost wherever we look in the world. It is evident from research that the bankruptcy rate is largely independent of the state of the economy. Its causes are still not clearly under-stood, but the growth of techniques for the prediction of potential bankruptcy should help. The emphasis so far has been on prediction, largely with a view to protecting investors and suppliers, but we advocate the use of the predictive techniques to avert rather than forecast disaster.

The academician delights in the theory, the journalist delights in the drama. We have sought to develop a middle-of-the-road, practical, down-to-earth approach to the subject. For us, prevention is what matters, not prediction. We see the ability to predict as a tool to be used by those in management to ensure that their company never gets into trouble. We have chosen not to enter into the legal aspects of receivership and bankruptcy and the question of fraud, since these are already well covered in the current literature. We also exclude failures due to environmental considerations, such as that of Johns Manville and other asbestos-handling firms, or due to accident arising from human error, such as at the Bhopal pesticide plant of Union Carbide. This latter has been described as the world's worst industrial accident ever. We shall be dealing with these examples of failure in another sequel to our earlier book on project disasters, *Management Disaster – and How to Prevent Them.*

In some developing countries, of which India is typical, companies are not allowed to collapse, even though they may be 'sick'. While in a free economy the law of the 'survival of the fittest' prevails, in a controlled economy the over-riding factor is the policy of maintaining employment at all costs. Companies are propped up by a continuous injection of funds, as if the only problem were lack of finance. Dare we liken this to the indiscriminate use in hospital of the life support machine – now under serious debate?

Unfortunately, while lack of finance may well be a problem, it is rarely the only or even the principal one. So, unless it is supplemented by others, more drastic treatment, the company will just drag on in meaningless existence and good money may well be sent after bad. We dare to ask whether in both cases — man and corporation — euthanasia is not justified. This is defined in the Concise Oxford Dictionary as 'gentle and easy death: bringing this about, especially in the case of incurable, painful disease'. If this were done, not only would the patient/corporation cease to suffer but all those expending so much effort and expense to keep it alive could devote themselves to worthier causes.

This leads us to the question: Who is responsible for detecting potential failure and taking action? The auditor and the accountant may well have a role to play, but their influence is inevitably very limited. By the time they become aware of what is happening it is probably already too late. The bank or other financial body is in a much better position to be the watchdog. Since their money is at risk, they can try and establish direct contact with management at the highest level. They are well placed to spot the early warning signals long before they show up in the Annual Report — if only they will keep their eyes and ears open and act. That is where we believe that we can help and have ventured to offer guidance. If we are to learn from the past, we must listen. Thus our closing chapter has a title with the plea: 'Let's listen now'. It is most difficult to get people to listen, let alone learn. It is our sincere hope that this present work will help. We have likened the corporation to a human body. The parallel continues: If you take care of it, it will take care of you!

Our spread of interest, background and location, while it has added materially to the difficulties inherent in completing this book, has nevertheless contributed substantially, we feel, to both its scope and flavour.

O. P. Kharbanda, Bombay
E. A. Stallworthy, Coventry

Acknowledgements

We must acknowledge our dependence upon the wide range of books, papers and articles relating to our subject which we have studied and used while writing this book. As far as possible we have given credit to our sources, listing the major references at the end of each chapter. This also allows our readers to follow up any aspect of the subject matter on which they may need more background.

We would also like to mention the advice and encouragement we have received from Dr R. J. Taffler and Mr John Argenti, exponents of two very different approaches to the problem of forecasting impending company failure. Mr A. J. S. Buchanan of Performance Analysis Services Limited of London was also very helpful in giving us an insight into the commercial application of forecasting techniques. The Centre for Monitoring Indian Economy, of Bombay, founded and carefully nurtured by the late Dr Narottam Shah and an island of excellence in an ocean of mediocrity, to which we have had free access, has also provided much valuable data.

O.P.K.
E.A.S.

PART ONE
Basic concepts

1 What is corporate failure?

Corporate failure is the term we use to describe the collapse or failure of a company, which can well result in its disappearance. The failure could be failure to operate successfully in the marketplace, or in the legal sense when a company is liquidated or goes bankrupt. This is never a pleasant subject, yet it is one that deserves the most serious study. Company failure affects not only those most immediately concerned, those employed by and trading with the company, but also industry in general, the overall economy and the well-being of the country or countries where the company operates. There are many repercussions, often hidden. Naturally those directly concerned, particularly the company management and its workers, suffer most. They are not only the first to experience the hardship that results, but are usually in that position well before the final, formal failure. They are likely to suffer the delayed payment of wages, poor housekeeping in the offices, a general decline in morale at the workplace, all signs of impending failure. At this stage we speak of 'corporate financial distress', another term often met within the literature on this subject.[1] Poor communication between management and employees may well add a serious and most unpleasant dimension when rumour takes over, filling the vacuum created by lack of reliable and official information from management.

It's a fact of life

In our Preface we likened the company or corporation to the human body. Both are born and both, ultimately, die. Death is the inevitable consequence of life, but the lifespan can vary considerably. Infant mortality has its parallel in the companies that never get going, even though they sometimes have a lifespan of a few years. Death occurs before they are able to stand on their own two feet. It is also well-known in the corporate world that the ranking of companies in the 'big league' (say with a turnover of US$10 billion or more) is constantly changing. So even the largest of companies can be in jeopardy. This fact was driven home in the early 1970s by the failure of Penn Central and Rolls-Royce, the two classic cases of company failure that we take up in Chapter 5.

Bankruptcy is but one indicator of failure

Not all companies that are in distress go bankrupt. Many of the smaller companies, particularly when family-owned, just cease to exist. Thus bankruptcy is only *one*

3

indicator of failure and to count bankruptcies is to get but a partial assessment of failure in the business world. However, in most countries bankruptcy is the only official indicator available, and hence the only yardstick of what is happening.

'Bankruptcy' is a legal term denoting insolvency. The individual or company declared bankrupt is unable to pay its debts. A representative (called the Receiver) is appointed by the Bankruptcy Court to distribute the remaining assets of the company for the benefit of its creditors. There are many good, instructive texts on the subject of bankruptcy and we do not propose to deal here with the legal aspects.[2]

Bankruptcy statistics are available from a variety of agencies, such as Dun and Bradstreet in the UK and the US, the Department of Trade and Industry, also in the UK, Tokyo Shoko in Japan and the Federal Statistics Office in West Germany. The information published by Dun and Bradstreet is probably the most comprehensive. This company publishes weekly, monthly and quarterly business reports, analysed into various categories. For instance, their monthly report for the US covers 39 lines of business, in 5 liability size groups, presented by region, state, large cities and Federal Reserve districts. Comment and interpretation of the published information is also given. The quarterly report gives trend indicators and assesses the liability of failure in individual lines of business. A business failure is a business that has ceased operation following assignment or bankruptcy, ceased with loss to creditors after actions such as execution for closure or attachment, closed voluntarily leaving unpaid obligations, or has been involved in court actions such as receivership, reorganization or arrangement, or has voluntarily compromised with its creditors out of court. This is the definition of failure which we will use.

The number of bankruptcies has been increasing almost everywhere. Figure 1.1 shows the number of bankruptcies since 1972 for four of the major developed countries. For the sake of comparison we present in Fig. 1.2 the new business incorporations for two countries, the UK and the US. Bankruptcies in the US are currently running at around 100 per day and the rate is increasing. There seems to be no direct connection between the state of the economy and the rate at which bankruptcy occurs, as shown by an examination of the four graphs in Fig. 1.1 The US economy began to pick up in 1983 yet the bankruptcy rate was maintained, whereas in West Germany, still in recession, it declined.

Bankruptcies are best assessed either in relation to the number of companies in business, or to the total GNP of the country one is looking at. If we compare the US and Britain, the ratio between those two countries in GNP is 6.5, while the ratio for bankruptcies is 2.4. Thus one could say that there are at least twice as many bankruptcies in the UK as in the US, in relation to business activity. Measured in this way, one could use the bankruptcy rate as an indicator — but what does it indicate? Relative business acumen? A superabundance of 'sunset' industries? Or an upsurge of young unproven companies in a new field?

Bankruptcy was a neglected subject till the mid-1960s, reserved for the legal

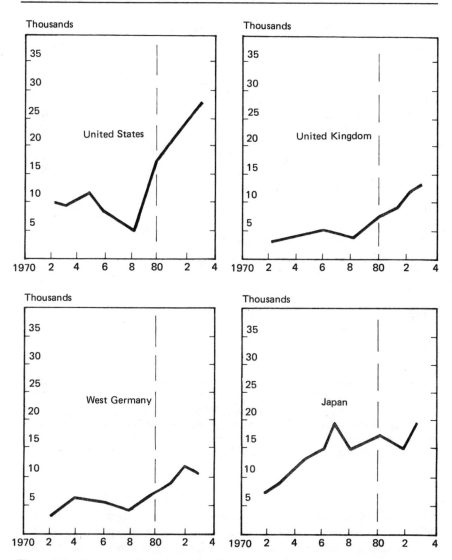

Figure 1.1 Company bankruptcies. *Number of bankruptcies over a four-year period for four major developed countries.* (Sources: *Tokyo Shoko, Dun and Bradstreet, Department of Trade and Industry, Federal Statistics Office.)*

experts, but now it is attracting the attention of academicians in many countries. This interest has been aroused by the realization that a study of the history of bankrupt companies can lead to the development of techniques to forecast impending disaster and failure. Management experts and company 'doctors' are busy developing ever more refined ways and means of reviving or rehabilitating

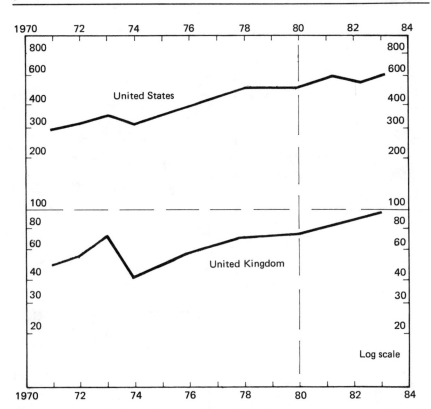

Figure 1.2   New business incorporations. *This plot of new businesses shows that the growth rate is comparable. Hence one factor that could bring disparity – since a percentage of new businesses will always fail – is seen not to apply.* (Sources: *Federal Statistics Office and Department of Trade and Industry.)*

failing companies and industries. Another group uses similar techniques to detect companies on the road to failure, as a guide for potential investors. In a world where the failure rate is steadily increasing, the subject becomes ever more important.

Bankruptcy laws differ from country to country

We do not intend to deal with the legal aspect of bankruptcy, but it should be noted that while the bankruptcy laws vary from country to country, they have one common feature. They do not do justice to the shareholders, workers and creditors, who are always the hardest hit as a consequence of company failure. Current bankruptcy law is under review in several countries, largely because of widespread abuse of the process. The intention of any change would be to make life harder for the rogue businessman, out to defraud.

The insolvency laws in West Germany are strict. Indeed, so strict that few companies apply for *Vergleich* (bankruptcy). The government is seeking to make it easier for companies to apply for bankruptcy, but the bankers and other creditors do not favour the idea, having done so badly out of the few *Vergleich* cases that have occurred. Typical of these is the case of AEG-Telefunken, a conglomerate that faced crisis some two years ago and applied for *Vergleich*. It has now come through, having shed 60 per cent of its debt, and may soon be operating profitably. The shareholders have suffered, but the shares have become popular following a five-fold rise in price since the insolvency plea, made in August 1982. It was the West German banks who lost out.

Lessons from Japan

Japan, too, needs to revise its bankruptcy laws. At the first sign of trouble either the holding company or the bank steps in, making management changes and propping up the company with additional loans.[3] As a final step, especially where national considerations are involved, the government may come to the rescue, as in the US, UK, India and elsewhere. The existing Japanese laws were drafted in line with American practice at the time of the American occupation of Japan after the Second World War and are completely irrelevant in the context of present-day business practice in Japan.

Despite the protective role of the banks in Japan, corporate bankruptcy is on the increase, just as it is in the rest of the world. In 1983 some 19000 firms collapsed, 2000 more than the previous year.[4] There are two possible explanations for this. The growth of their economy has slowed down, being now 4 per cent per year, rather than 10 per cent. Perhaps many firms have been unable to cope with the rapid change in the type of business being done – from heavy industry to electronics. If we look for financial factors, we see that internal financing is low in Japan, being only 38 per cent of total corporate funding during the past few years, whereas in other industrialized countries it is nearly twice that. However, such comparisons between countries can be misleading. If the figures were corrected for possible under-evaluation of capital assets, special tax reserves and other financial conventions peculiar to Japan, then the disparity might well be much less. All this re-emphasizes the point we made earlier, that comparison between bankruptcy rates in various countries is of little value.

When a company is better 'dead'

This is the headline to an article presenting a practical, realistic approach to the problem of companies in distress. Voluntary liquidations not involving bankruptcy are rare, but they may be in the best interests of both management and shareholders. We think that a company in trouble should sell part of its assets piecemeal and distribute the cash. Admission of failure is hard and unpleasant, but acceptance of the fact that a company would be better dead than alive could well be the best for all concerned.

A number of companies have been pursuing this course with a measure of success. UV Industries in the US is a case in point. The market analysts had been valuing its assets at US$30–40 per share, yet the market value was less than half that. The proposed sale of their largest subsidiary, Federal Pacific Electric Co., for US$345 million spurred the company on to consider total liquidation, with the sale of its other businesses and distribution of the proceeds to their shareholders. The success of the operation has encouraged other companies to follow a similar course, since 'by doing this they will realise more than if they were to operate every asset they have. And the market seems to agree.' Voluntary liquidation seems to be easier for the smaller company, especially if they have 'hard' assets, such as land, or diverse operations which can be sold off as a package without disturbing the rest of the business. For major companies, however, the operation can be both complex and time-consuming: the liquidation of the giant Kaiser Industries Corporation, with interest in aluminium, steel, cement, broadcasting, the aerospace industry and engineering, has already taken four to five years.

Some features of failure

When we look at business failures worldwide over the past few years we see no common factor. One writer listing 10 major business failures over the past hundred years or so, found them in businesses as diverse as newspapers, banking, transport, retailing and insurance as well as general manufacturing, thus demonstrating that failure can occur in any type of business, anywhere. Altman, in his study of the subject (1983), takes all his cases from the US, but once again they differ widely both in size and character.[1] The number of bankruptcies in the US in 1982 totalled about 80 000, of which a quarter were business failures (using the Dun and Bradstreet definition). The failure rate in the US has been as follows:

Year	1950	1960	1970	1980	1982
Failure rate (per 10 000 firms)	34	57	44	42	88

Altman has established that nearly half of all failures occur within the first two to five years of operation (see Fig. 1.3). But once we appreciate this fact, we realize that the growing failure rate is not necessarily an indicator of increasing economic hardship, but perhaps an indicator of increasing prosperity. For instance, a large number of new businesses were formed between 1977 and 1979, so we should expect failures to peak over the years 1980 to 1984, irrespective of economic conditions. Failure thus becomes related to the frequency of formation of new companies!

Evidently the context of failure is changing, although the reasons have yet to be determined. Before 1970 businesses with assets greater than US$25 million hardly ever failed, but since then at least 35 non-financial companies with assets greater than US$125 million have collapsed.[6] In a free economy, such as the US and the UK, the law of the 'survival of the fittest' usually prevails; yet this is not *always* the case: the Chrysler Corporation in the US was bailed out by the government to the tune of some US$12 billion, while the UK government did much the same for British Leyland, for a mixture of political, social and economic reasons. This type of action is much more prevalent in controlled economies, such as those of Israel and India. It is also a predominant factor in Japan, as noted earlier. In Fig. 1.3 we saw that failure was most likely in the

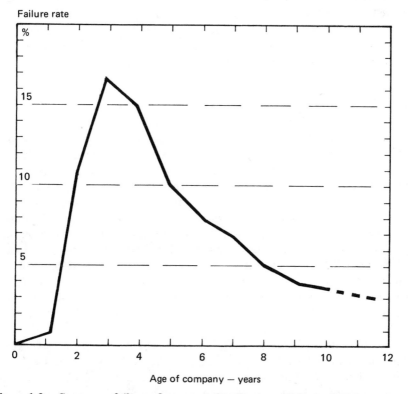

Figure 1.3 Company failures frequency distribution. *This graph demonstrates that most failures occur in the early years.* (Source: *Derived from data presented by Altman.*)

early years of a company's life. If we now compare this factor for several different
countries, we get the following results:[6]

Country	UK	USA	Israel	Japan
Average age at failure (years)	5–7	5–7	9–13	31
Failure rate (per year, as %)	1–2	0.5–0.7	0.2–0.7	0.5

Have we learnt anything? We doubt it. Tamari finds that the pattern of corporate
financial failure is independent of the social, political and cultural factors pre-
vailing in the four very different economies illustrated above and then goes on
to conclude that the theories and techniques established for one economy can be
directly applied in another, but we cannot agree. Seeking to explain the ab-
normally low figure for Japan above, we discover that there the banks protect
and consolidate the financial resources of the companies with which they are
involved. Thus a study of failure there leads us nowhere – there are so few
failures to study! Only where there are bankruptcies that have occurred in 'free'
conditions can we develop techniques that will allow us to forecast pending
disaster and establish ways to avoid it.

Learning from failure

Failure is not something to be ashamed of. You cannot have success without
failure: they are two sides of the same coin. The decisions one takes can be right
or wrong and that will not be known till much later. Those who are best at
decision-making still make mistakes, but when they know that they have made a
mistake they have the courage to admit it and the resolution to do something
about it. General Johnson, the founder of Johnson and Johnson, confessed:
'If I wasn't making mistakes, I wasn't making decisions.'[7] Is it any wonder that
one of the tenets of the company he founded is 'you've got to be willing to fail'.
Toleration of failure is an essential part of any successful company's growth and
that concept should come right from the top. Successful business executives
have to choose between alternatives, and can sometimes make a decision that
leads to failure. But one should learn from failure – that is the theme of one of
our books.[8]

Once the role of failure is recognized, there should be greater readiness to
admit failure when it occurs. Failure can never be hidden, so surely it is better
to first admit it and then take positive action to deal with it. Concealment only
prolongs the agony. Rumours proliferate, the situation is likely to be dramatized
and distorted. Our advice to the chief executive faced with such a situation is:
make a frank, honest, factual statement of the situation and set about resolving it.

Coping with crisis

How? First one faces the crisis, then it has to be dealt with. A whole body of knowledge has accumulated on this (see Chapter 12) and management journals are now beginning to pay serious attention to the subject. For instance, in the spring of 1984 the journal *Management Science* devoted an entire issue to the 'state of the art' in risk management in certain selected areas.

The most practical approach can be embodied in the well-known proverb: offence is the best defence. We will enlarge on this theme later in this book. For now let us recognize that much lies in the hand of the chief executive. He is the 'head' of the body, the corporation, and he is also an integral part of that body. If he acts, he can avert the crisis (see Chapter 4). If he ignores the warning signals, the body suffers and he will suffer with it. Klein, drawing similar, homely lessons, quotes Pogo: 'We have met the enemy and he is us!'[9]

References

1. Altman, E. I., *Corporate Financial Distress – A Complete Guide to Predicting, Avoiding and Dealing with Bankruptcy*, Wiley, 1983.
2. Chivers, D. and P. Shewell, *Receivership Manual*, Tolley, (2nd ed.) 1983; Kosel, P., *Bankruptcy: Do It Yourself*, Addison-Wesley, 1981.
3. Hoshino, Y., 'An analysis of corporate bankruptcies in Japan', *Management International Review*, **24**, 70–7, 2 Nov. 1984.
4. Saito, T., 'Japan's Economy – Need for a Two-prong Policy', *Fuji Bank Bulletin*, July–Aug. 1984, p. 3.
5. Deeson, A. F. L., *Great Company Crashes*, W. Goulsham & Co., Amersham, 1972.
6. Tamari, M., *Some International Comparisons of Industrial Financing*, Technicopy, 1977.
7. Peters, T. J. and R. H. Waterman, Jr., *In Search of Excellence – Lessons from America's Best-Run Companies*, Harper & Row, 1982.
8. Kharbanda, O. P. and E. A. Stallworthy, *How to Learn from Project Disasters – True-Life Stories with a Moral for Management*, Gower, 1983.
9. Klein, H. J., *Stop – You're Killing The Business*, Leviathan House, 1974.

2 Failure - the why and how

There are as many reasons as symptoms for business failure – the reasons bringing us the 'why' and the symptoms being the 'how'. Perhaps as many as there are failures, since at first sight each failure seems unique. Let us begin by looking at a few failures. We dare not describe them as typical at this point, but they are certainly illustrative.

Illustrative failures

A long-established family construction company in the UK, Cornes Tideswell, failed as a result of labour disputes and rapidly escalating costs. Diagnosis revealed that the company had failed to come to terms with modern construction practices, which could have brought considerable savings and so maintained the competitiveness of the company in the marketplace. Crossing the Atlantic, we see a young Canadian company, also in the construction field. Stirling Homex, specialists in house building, started operations in 1967, expanded considerably in 1968, yet collapsed four years later, perhaps as a result of overambitious expansion. More recently a major American contractor running a joint venture, Carlson Al Saudia, with a local partner in Saudi Arabia is reported to have abandoned its operations there because of heavy losses resulting from appalling cost overruns, late payments and bureaucratic delays. In the allied field of construction equipment Europe's largest company, IBH Holdings in West Germany, failed as a result of too fast growth in the midst of a worldwide recession.[1]

We have confined our attention here to construction companies because they all have one thing in common: their capital base is small in relation to their annual turnover. With all such companies, the turnover/capital ratio lies between 10 and 20, whereas with manufacturing companies the ratio is a tenth of that: between 1 and 2. Such companies could therefore be considered to be more vulnerable. One major contract that goes sour can then bring about the failure of companies long established in this field. We have chronicled elsewhere the history and failure of a major American construction company, Chemico, who disappeared in the middle of a major project in Algeria.[2]

12

Experience brings no certainty

Two leaders in the chemical and pharmaceutical industries worldwide, Ciba-Geigy of Switzerland and Bayer of West Germany, set up a joint venture in West Germany, Schelde Chemie Brunsbeuttel, to manufacture anthraquinone. The joint venture started in 1973 with a total investment by the two partners of some DM1 billion (US$330 million), of which DM260 million was the investment in the anthraquinone plant itself. The management decided in 1982 to cease operations, because the technology is now obsolete and market prospects have changed. In anticipation of this decision Bayer absorbed a loss of DM20 million in 1983 and the balance was written off in 1984. At least they had the wisdom and the courage to 'cut their losses', but what a surprising result with two such well-known companies, leaders in the field.

The literature on the subject

With such a confusing picture, let us see whether the experts can offer clarification. Our question is: Why do companies fail? Two management experts, Ross and Kami, conclude that bad management is to blame.[3] For them, bad management is breaking one or more of the 'ten commandments' below:

There must be a strategy
There must be controls, including cost control
The board must participate actively
No one-man rule
Management must have depth
Management must know of and respond to change
The customer is king
Avoid the misuse of computers
Do not manipulate the accounts
The organization structure must meet people's needs.

The above list is commendable and very good advice, but the arguments are not convincing. No proof is presented that bad management is at the root of failure and collapse. Ross and Kami maintain, for instance, that IBM has not collapsed because it has a strategy, whereas Rolls-Royce, who did collapse, had no strategy. But Lockheed, who also failed, were said to have a *faulty strategy*, which is very different to *no strategy*.

Barmash considers a total of 15 case histories in the business world and then concludes: the basic cause of the business disaster is greed, human greed, simple and unadulterated. In most cases, the greed crossed over the line into corruption.[4] There seems to be no limit to this greed! Even people in high office are not immune. But is it at the root of company failure?

Next we can take the views of journalist R. A. Smith.[5] Having analysed several failures he comes up with these reasons for failure:

The autocrat*
Resistance to change*
Overdiversification
Bad luck
Lack of control*
Decentralization

At least three of the above reasons, those we have starred, echo the Ross and Kami commandments, but we believe it is not these factors as such which lead to failure, but either too much or too little of each of the factors listed. But what is too much? Or too little?

Of the more recent books on this subject, a comprehensive guidance manual for those setting up their own business (the self-employed) points out that the death of such a business may be either quick and merciful, or long drawn out and agonizing.[6] Surely that could be true of the demise of any business, of any size, anywhere? Smith suggests that when you start up your own business, the odds are heavily weighted against success, but no proof is offered.

We propose to deal only with the economic and managerial aspects of company distress and failure, but a book dealing with the political and institutional aspects and covering the six major OECD countries points out that industrial crisis was accelerated by the 'oil shocks' of 1973–4 and 1979–80.[7] The central role of management, bankers, public officials and even political parties is emphasized and good crisis management is seen as a combination of four factors:

Close collaboration between the parties noted above
The retention of production resources (knowledge, plant and workforce)
Maintenance or increase of efficiency
Equitable distribution of the costs of adjustment

External circumstances certainly can create crisis that could lead to failure, but the advice given above is no more than a policy of good management.

On the other hand, a management consultant specializing in the 'turnaround' of troubled companies offers valuable advice on the course to be followed if the health of a company is to be maintained:

Maintain and update corporate strategy
Have an annual health checkup
Emphasize true balance sheet reporting
Set and maintain clear goals
Understand the law[8]

These are survival techniques, so one must assume that failure is the result of ignoring such advice. If the pursuit of such policies fails to bring results, then the advice is: Recognize that the cause is hopeless and plan for bankruptcy!

Our review of the advice available leads to the conclusion that the cause of failure is poor management. It is interesting to see that in the case of one company recently 'pulled back from the brink' (British Leyland) the 'doctor', Michael Edwardes, put the blame for the situation he found wholly on management:

> management over a number of years *lost their will* to manage . . . instead they blamed the unions . . . real blame lay with the management . . . management is not an automatic right, it has to be earned. It is a duty and if it isn't fulfilled it lets everybody down: employees, fellow managers, customer, supplier and shareholder. . . . [9]

There is no beating about the bush here and we entirely agree with Sir Michael. We will revert to this aspect of our subject in the next chapter.

The experts still differ

We have sampled above some of the recent literature on the causes of corporate failure. An excellent summary and analysis of this aspect is to be found in John Argenti's *Corporate Collapse* and it discloses a wide variety of causes.[10] For instance, he quotes one writer who has found four symptoms to be dominant in companies which are in trouble:

Lack of good leadership
An obsolete product
No sense of urgency
No understanding of cash flow.

Another writer, however, noting that managers are seldom aware that their company is on the verge of collapse, only realizing where they are when crisis comes, produces another set of ten commandments, most of them different to those we listed earlier from Ross and Kami:

Ease of obtaining credit
Liquidity problem as a sign of approaching disaster
More bad payers among customers
Obsolete technology
Prestige put above profit
Too few customers
Low growth rate
Employees not well treated
Over-expansion
Excessive borrowing[11]

We think that resemblances between these and other lists are superficial in nature and merely indicate a difference in emphasis. Further, these factors are but elements of the ten cited by Ross and Kami. Some of them are even mutually exclusive: for instance, the last item in the above list follows on from the first.

John Argenti, analysing the findings of his various sources, tries to pick out factors that recur and gives what he calls an 'interim list' of causes which, when put together, might solve the jigsaw puzzle epitomized by business failure. The six major factors so identified are:

Top management
Accounting information
Change
The manipulation of accounts
Rapid expansion
The economic cycle

The manipulation of accounts, referred to above, is not necessarily illegal, but it can be and is often designed to be misleading. A popular term for this type of accounting is 'creative accounting', and we elaborate on the subject in Chapter 20.

There are a number of other factors, including planning, gearing, morale, shortage of capital, bad luck and a host of others. But, once again, surely all these are but aspects and responsibilities of management. Surveying the whole spectrum of reasons given for failure, we come back time and again to various aspects of management. This leads us to the conviction that the nature and quality of the management is the crux of the matter. It is for this reason that we study this specific cause of failure in detail in Chapter 3.

Syndromes of failure

What do we expect to see when a company is on the road to failure? One of the first problems is almost invariably a shortage of cash, with a likely sequence of events thereafter of:

Unpaid suppliers shutting off supplies
Bank calling in loans
Employees leaving (especially the good ones)
Rumours spreading (quite often much exaggerated)
Competitors laughing
Unpleasant telephone calls
Telephone disconnection (unpaid accounts)
Landlord showing the premises to new tenants

The more common syndromes of failure have been rather realistically portrayed in the 'famous last words' of a chief executive as coming in four stages:

1. *Impulsive syndrome – running blind.* This business of ours must be defined in the broadest possible terms if we are to continue to break our past growth

records. We must take risks in order to grow, seize opportunities first, consolidate later.

2. *The stagnant bureaucracy*. Well, our methods and product lines were fine in the past and we'll be damned if we are going to change a successful strategy just because of some temporary fad.

3. *The headless firm*. We pride ourselves on the amount of autonomy that we leave to our divisions and departments. We control the finances, they make all the key strategies.

4. *Swimming upstream – the aftermath*. In order to turn this company around, we have to take sizeable risks. We've got to move quickly to plug up the weaknesses of our operations and go after greener pastures with new blood.[12]

We think that needs no further comment from us.

Another realistic and down-to-earth failure sequence presented by Argenti follows three basic phases that take some five years to mature.[13] It begins with management defects, particularly at the very top of the company – it is a fact that failure begins at the top. Over the next few years management make mistakes. Then, still later, the signs and symptoms of failure appear.

Each of these basic steps in the failure sequence are elaborated upon by Argenti, who highlights certain major mistakes, such as high leverage, over-trading and the big project that goes wrong. We revert to this subject in Chapter 12, when we come to discuss the Argenti system in some detail.

Trajectories of failure

Each failure is unique. A study of the process of failure, however, reveals some broad patterns among the host of failures that occur around the world, and those who have studied the subject have sought such patterns in order to bring some order out of the chaos. We are seeking here to take this analysis a small step further.

We are dealing with the health or sickness of a company, a corporate body. The doctor, seeking to assess the health of his patient, uses certain indicators, such as pulse rate, breathing rate, blood tests, urine sampling, blood pressure, and many others, all used routinely in an annual health check. The doctor finishes up with a complete profile of his patient. He then seeks to associate divergence from the norm with potential disease and its symptoms. Such a diagnosis is the prerequisite for proper treatment and the provision of the appropriate remedies.

We can apply the same approach to the body corporate, but we must first establish the appropriate indicators of the health of the body. We realize immediately that financial indicators must be the most significant, but there are a great many of them. Which are the criteria of health, which indicators of potential failure? We do not know, nor do the experts in this field, and the search for reliable indicators goes on unabated. We will revert to this subject in Part 3, which deals with prediction, but at the moment let us say that we have an indicator available which can be quantified at least to the extent of telling us whether the company we are looking at is 'poor', 'good' or 'excellent'. If the company is worse than 'poor' let us be realistic and speak of failure: if better than excellent, it must be fantastic. In Fig. 2.1 we present the typical curve for a company in no danger of failure, using the nomenclature just outlined. Its status is plotted over time, since it is not only its present position but its present position in relation to its past, that counts. Of course, the precise trajectory will vary from company to company. The nature of the vertical parameter on our graphs has yet to be established, but there are more than one, as we shall see later.

In some cases, after a period on a plateau, a company may enter into a new type of business, and its health may improve or deteriorate. Argenti discerns three basic routes to failure, which we present in Figs 2.2, 2.3 and 2.4. Failure type A (Fig. 2.2) applies to new companies, usually small, which never really get going. Failure type B (Fig. 2.3) is typical of a company which grows rapidly, even fantastically, but falls back just as rapidly. Failure type C (Fig. 2.4) is usually to be found with mature companies, large or small. As a

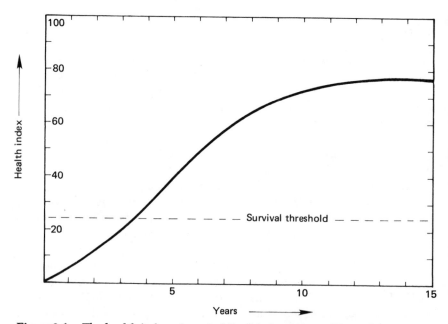

Figure 2.1   The health index. *A typical 'healthy' company. The scale is uniform.*

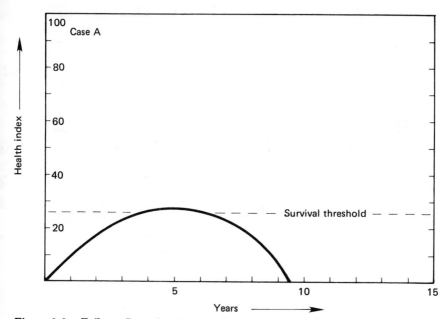

Figure 2.2   Failure Case A. *A typical new company that never gets off the ground.*

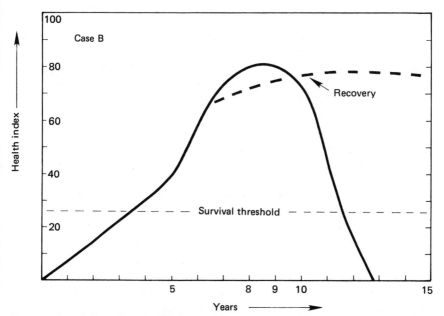

Figure 2.3   Failure Case B. *The average company, initially successful, but running into problems and then failing. The alternative route to recovery is shown.*

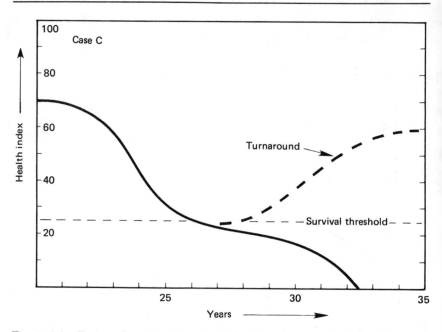

Figure 2.4   Failure Case C. *The situation when a company fails after many successful years in business. The turnaround is indicated.*

result of defects, handled wrongly, the company deteriorates slowly but surely and finally meets its doom. Of course, this is a simplified approach and not all cases of failure will fall into one of these three categories. What we are seeking to do at the moment is to get a broad picture of the problem. This should help in coming to a fuller understanding of the subject when we start to analyse a number of case studies in Part 2.

We have superimposed on the graphs for cases B and C (Figs 2.3 and 2.4) a possible rescue route. With case A (Fig. 2.2) no rescue is possible unless the potential of the situation is recognized and preventive action taken. The rescue of a company is now termed a 'turnaround' and the nature of the turnaround can often be drastic. In our various case studies we shall be referring back to these various trajectories, so we ask you to keep them well in mind.

Summary

The causes of business failure are many and various, presenting us with a most confusing picture, yet we have come to the conclusion that the root cause is almost always to be found in *management*. We are therefore devoting the following chapter to this one factor.

We have also shown a definite pattern leading to business failure. We have for the moment described this pattern in the briefest of terms, but we shall see later how such patterns of company behaviour can be used to discern potential failure and help towards turnaround. But it is the management that is responsible and it will be for that management to take the necessary action, having previously studied the situation and discerned its problems. It is at this point that management consultants should be approached and their expertise applied. It may then be possible for the company to follow one of the turnaround routes indicated on the typical trajectories we have shown.

References

1. Ball, R. 'The fall of the house of Esch', *Fortune*, **108**, 105–6, 12 Dec. 1983.
2. Kharbanda, O. P. and E. A. Stallworthy, *How to Learn from Project Disasters*, Gower, 1983.
3. Ross, J. E. and M. J. Kami, *Corporate Management in Crisis*, Prentice-Hall, 1973.
4. Barmash, A., *Great Business Disasters*, Ballantine, 1973.
5. Smith, R. A., *Corporations in Crisis*, Doubleday, 1966.
6. Smith, B. R., *How to Prosper in Your Own Business – Getting Started and Staying on Course*, Stephen Green Press, 1981.
7. Dyson, K. and S. Wilks (eds), *Industrial Crisis – A Comparative Study of the State and Industry*, Martin Robertson, 1983.
8. Kibel, H. R., *How to Turn Around a Financially Troubled Company*, McGraw-Hill, 1982.
9. Edwardes, M., *Back From the Brink – An Apocalyptic Experience*, Collins, 1983.
10. Argenti, J., *Corporate Collapse – The Causes and Symptoms*, McGraw-Hill, 1976.
11. Cohen, D., 'Confidence comes before a crash', *Business Administration*, Jan. 1973.
12. Miller, D., 'Common syndromes of business failure', *Business Horizons*, Nov. 1977, pp. 43–53.
13. Argenti, J., 'Predicting corporate failure', *Accountants Digest No. 138*, Institute of Chartered Accountants, 1983.

3 Management is the crux

It is our considered view that the root cause of company failure is poor management. As we analyse our case studies we shall seek to demonstrate that particular aspect of management where weakness led to failure. Then, when we come to consider the remedies that may be applied (the panacea) we shall return to the theme of management once again.

The subject of management has attracted an enormous amount of literature from both academic and industrial circles. This is all to the good and a perusal of what has been written should make us wiser. We shall therefore spend some time looking at the literature on the subject, seeking to ascertain those aspects of management that are crucial to success. Successful management will avoid failure – but how?

Back to basics

In view of the volume of information, a simple down-to-earth book on the basics of management is to be welcomed.[1] This book names three foundation blocks for good management:

'Back to basics' management
Interpersonal relations
Effective communication

'Back to basics' management consists of the assimilation of news, information and comment, leading to knowledge. Knowledge, when meditated upon, leads to understanding. Understanding, associated with commitment and discipline, *is* what our authors call 'back to basics' management.

The academician enjoys research and writes on management subjects primarily for the sake of knowledge. Theories galore are developed, but of what use are all these theories unless they can be put into practice? For the academician a theory may be an end in itself, but for those involved in management it is the practice that matters. It is only through practice that managers achieve results and thereby become effective in their business life.

There is, of course, nothing new in the concept of management as such. But while the primary function of a manager is to manage, above all his job involves selecting and developing capable people. The results are achieved not by the manager himself, but by people: a group of people that are often called a 'management team'. It is they who are all-important. If you have any doubts as to the prime importance of people, just listen to Andrew Carnegie, founder of US Steel. He ought to know! 'Take away all my steel mills. Take away all my money. Leave me my people and in five years I will have everything back.'[2]

What are the key characteristics of an effective manager? Let us turn for the answer to an industrial manager who is also active in academic circles, having an MBA in management and a PhD in economics. He is currently a senior institute staff member at IBM Corporation's Information Systems Management Institute. According to him the present complex and competitive business world requires managers with a broad range of skills and a highly developed acuity in *personal* as well as business matters.[3] An effective manager must be able, inter alia, to:

Make financial decisions
Perceive the needs of the marketplace
Implement the latest technological developments
Communicate well with his people
Motivate his people in order to accomplish the company's goals

So, now you know the basic requirements for a good manager. But you may well ask where such paragons are to be found.

The company 'culture'

In our view there is something missing in the above scenario, if we are to have a picture of an effective manager. In the ultimate analysis effective management is not necessarily guaranteed by even the most meticulous attention to the routines of management: matters such as financial planning, personnel policies and cost control. What is of equal importance, especially in relation to the long-term prosperity of a company, is that it have a strong 'culture', compromising the inner values, rites, customs and rituals that become established in a company over time. In this we must not forget what we might call the 'heroes': often the founder of the company. The company 'culture' will strongly influence success at all levels in a company, from the secretariat to the managing director. All companies, large or small, should have a degree of 'culture'. A strong culture makes for a highly successful company. Deal and Kennedy describe company 'culture' in these terms:

> Every business — in fact every organization — has a culture. Sometimes it is fragmented and difficult to read from the outside . . . On the other hand, sometimes the culture of an organization is very strong and cohesive: everyone knows the goals of the organization, and these goals set the pattern for people's activities, opinions and actions. Whether weak or strong, culture has a powerful influence throughout an organization: it affects practically everything — from who gets promoted and what decisions are made, to how employees dress and what sports they play. Because of this impact, culture has a major effect on the success of the business.[4]

So look for, then modify or strengthen as the case may be, the particular 'culture' appropriate to your organization.

In search of excellence

This is the title of a recent book that has sold over 3 million copies in the English language and is probably the best-selling business book of all time.[5] Its main message for business in the US and perhaps elsewhere is very simple: the time is now ripe to break through our long obsession with so-called 'scientific' management systems and return to basics — which is where we began our study of this subject. What is called for is the revival of the basic principles of motivation and organization. This, it is asserted, *will* lead to success. The book has been read widely, even in Japan, whose management style and success is a craze elsewhere in the world. The book may well cause a swing away from current practice, which we term 'over-management'.

Excellence, as this book has now come to be called, found eight common attributes which distinguished outstanding, innovative companies who have been highly successful. These can be briefly stated thus:

1.   A bias for action. The motto is: do it, fix it, try it.
2.   Stay close to the customer. Thereby one learns and is helped to provide goods noted for quality, service and reliability: in short, things that work and last.
3.   Autonomy and entrepreneurship is encouraged, leading to the creation of many leaders and innovators throughout the organization. They even follow the rule: make sure you generate a reasonable number of mistakes.
4.   Productivity through people. Each and every individual in the company is 'seen as a source of ideas, not just acting as a pair of hands'.
5.   Hands-on, value-driven. The basic philosophy of an organization is seen to contribute far more than the resources, structure, innovation and timing.
6.   Stick to the knitting. Barring a few exceptions, such companies stay close to the business they know.
7.   Simple form, lean staff. Such companies have an elegant structure with a lean top: that is, less than 100 people running multi-million dollar enterprises.
8.   Simultaneous loose — tight properties. This describes a subtle combination of centralized and decentralized control, with autonomy pushed down to the shop floor or a product development team.

It is clear that none of the above attributes are startling in themselves. They are straightforward common-sense principles built around a central theme: the theme that *people* are a company's most important asset. All the outstanding companies selected by the authors of this book exhibited a preponderance of these eight attributes. It appears, however, that these attributes are conspicuous by their absence in most large US companies today. Such companies are being throttled by their own staff, structure and systems.

We think that this theme, central to successful management, is well summed up by the acronym KISS — Keep It Simple, Stupid! This acronym has been at the heart of all our writing on management, exemplified, we feel, by a chapter title: Simple *is* beautiful.[6] It is a well-established fact that humans are not good at processing large streams of new data — this is perhaps the only area, apart from speed, where a computer has the edge over the human. Further, it has been established that the most we can hold in our short-term memory, immediately accessible, without forgetting something, is six or seven items of data. Well, here again practice seems well ahead of theory. The companies who excel have not only realized what is needful but have held fast to the KISS principle despite the enormous pressures on them to complicate things. While complication serves to impress, it usually fails to 'deliver the goods'.

Look east, young man!

Japan has emerged from the ashes to reach the top of the industrial league of nations in about three decades, a remarkable achievement by any standard. Experts ascribe this miracle primarily to the Japanese style of management, which has been the subject of a host of books and articles in recent years. Developed and developing countries alike have been exhorted to look to Japan and learn.[7] Having begun as a mere 'imitator', Japan is now seen as the great example for imitation. What a role reversal! Thanks to its productivity, which has steadily increased over the years, together with harmonious management-worker relationships, Japan has come to dominate industry after industry. So impressive has been the progress of Japan in the industrial sphere that the US now seeks to emulate the Japanese style of management. This has its own irony, since most of the so-called Japanese concepts originated in the US. This situation has been most tersely summed up by the co-founder of the Honda Motor Company: 'Japanese and American management is 95 per cent the same and different in all important respects.' What are these differences?

In Japan, men (and women) are the focus of all that is done. The individual is at the centre and family life merges into that of the corporation. Parents are involved at the time of hiring and they are even rewarded for their offspring's achievements. All decisions are by consensus, so important is each individual's role seen to be. No one is left out of anything. This assures commitment, so essential to proper performance, and brings with it a harmonious work team: an approach which guarantees success. Salary is related to seniority, but promotion is on merit. This can lead to what some would consider a paradox: the head of a group receiving a lower salary than some of his team. Director and worker usually wear the same uniform and eat in the same canteen. This ensures a basic work formula: 'us *plus* them', rather than 'us *vs.* them', the attitude that prevails in most of the rest of the world. Excellent human relations are the result which, combined with long hours and complete dedication, have been a major factor in taking Japan where it is today.

Further, Japanese workers and managers are encouraged to continue learning throughout their working career. Specialists broaden their knowledge of allied fields and, with considerable job rotation, can step into another's shoes at short notice. A Japanese worker may well spend some 500 days in training during a 10-year working span. This cross-fertilization encourages creativity and leads to a spate of suggestions for the improvement of quality and productivity. Individuals and groups are recognized and rewarded for such achievements and share the financial gains that follow.

So, what is the lesson for us? No management style, however effective, can be transplanted from one country to another with a very different culture, values and background. But while the Japanese system cannot be directly imitated it can be adapted and its principles used to strengthen current practice. To do this calls for in-depth study of not only the individual situation in any particular country, but also the situation in the individual company, for not only countries but also companies have a culture, as we have seen. One of the most interesting exercises in this field is happening in the UK, where Japanese companies have been setting up factories over the past few years. They have introduced their own management style with a high degree of success, but they have had the advantage of starting with a green field site. They have not, as yet, attempted to reform an existing, long-established company in the UK. A basic element in their approach has been to agree with the unions that one union only should represent *all* those employed at the factory. They have also been successful in agreeing 'no-strike' provisions. The West can learn a lot from the Far East in matters related to productivity and labour turnover. This is typified by Japan, although other countries in that area seem to be learning fast. Both subjects have lately been the cause of considerable concern in most of the industrialized countries of the West and merit very serious attention, but many of the Japanese management practices are specific to Japan and *cannot* be transferred to other countries.

Team-work is what matters

We have just been emphasizing the importance of the individual, but results are achieved by teams rather than by individuals operating on their own. Good managers are not 'doers' but rather the developers and encouragers of 'doers'. This function is all-important and makes the greatest contribution of all to good management and its end result, the success of the company.

How does this come about? A team brings together all the qualities for success: qualities which any one individual could never possess. Belbin has identified eight key roles essential to effectiveness, each of these being associated with a particular personality.[8] We set out this relationship thus:

Leader	Calm, confident, controlled
Office worker	Conservative, dutiful, predictable
Completer	Painstaking, orderly, conscientious, anxious
Monitor	Sober, unemotional, prudent
Designer	Individualistic, orderly, conscientious
Searcher	Extroverted, enthusiastic, curious
Shaper	Highly strung, outgoing, dynamic
Operator	Socially oriented, mild, sensitive

You can, we are sure, identify these roles in your particular company. The 'leader' will be the chairman or chief executive, the searcher the salesman, while a 'monitor' type makes a good inspector. With an optimum mix, a team can achieve far more than the individuals, operating singly, could accomplish: this is called synergy, meaning that the combined effect of the team exceeds the sum of their individual efforts. This comes as a result of their good interpersonal relations – one of the three foundation blocks for good management noted by us at the beginning of this chapter.

Research in this area has established that the outcome of team effort can be forecast if there is sufficient information about the personal characteristics and abilities of the members of the team. The necessary data can be derived from psychometric tests. It not only follows that team performance can be improved by, in effect, 'designing' a team to ensure success, but we could have here a very useful tool for the turnaround of companies on the road to collapse, a theme we take up again in Part Three, where we demonstrate that salvation is possible.

Building the team

Teams *have* to have a leader, whether we think of our team as the company as a whole, or as a group within it. Successful companies will have a multiplicity of teams, each with its own leader: we call them managers whether or not they have that title in the organization to which they belong. But it is a valid point that many of the qualities required in a good manager are mutually exclusive. He is called upon to be highly intelligent – but not too clever. He must be forceful – yet sensitive to people's feelings. He must be dynamic – while exercising patience. A fluent communicator – yet a good listener. What a man! And if you find such a rarity, what do you do when he steps under a bus or a competitor steals him away? Nevertheless, let us assume that we have managers. It is they who have to build a team around them. It is 'build' that is the operative word. Individuals *can* grow in their jobs, assume greater responsibility and thrive, if they are working in a collaborative, team-oriented climate. Bennett puts it thus:

> The task is not to change people. People are perfectly alright the way they are. The task is not to motivate people. People are inherently self-starting. The

task is to remove those things that demotivate them, to get them out of their way. Or, more precisely, to create those kinds of organizational structures that allow workers to get at problems and act in some independent ways so they can develop their skills solving problems related to their own jobs.[9]

Bennett sees the team as a potential resource for problem solving. The key to his approach is to encourage that which is in opposition – be it an individual, a department or a union – to function *as part of the team*. Thus the full potential of the organization is achieved and progress will be made.

The need for effective communication

The last of the three principles we set out at the beginning of this chapter as foundation blocks for good management was effective communication. The manager cannot manage unless he is able to communicate. The team is not a team unless its members can communicate with one another. Peter Drucker, in a foreword to a book on the subject, says that most of us do *not* know:

What to say
When to say it
How to say it
To whom to say it[10]

Need we say more? Yes; we also need to point out that the weakest link in the communications process is the function of listening. We spend nearly half our waking hours listening – though we suggest that most of the time, while we *hear*, we do *not* listen. Listening is a vital skill, yet it is hardly ever taught. Fortunately, the importance of listening is now being realized by more and more business organizations and they are taking steps to deal with the problem. A bank in the UK, the Midland Bank, calls itself 'the listening bank', while the multi-national firm Sperry has built an institutional publicity campaign around the same theme: 'We understand how important it is to listen. When you know how to listen, opportunity has only to knock once.' We will not enlarge further on this theme here, having written about it at length elsewhere.[11]

Yes, get back to basics

Good management is at the heart of any and every successful company, is essential if a company is to avert failure and ultimate collapse. It is as essential as breathing! Unfortunately, the current concept of good management, which concentrates on systems and administration, is false and has brought many, many companies to ruin. While the literature on the subject is vast, we see that only a few simple, basic truths need to be recognized and applied for success to follow. We have seen that results are achieved by well co-ordinated and structured teams, not by individuals, so that a key role in management is to ensure that such teams are there. Yet all this will still be ineffective unless everyone, from the chairman down, can *communicate* with one another. To communicate, they must *listen*! If *you* have been 'listening', you will no longer be surprised that we bring this book to a close with a chapter titled 'Let's listen *now*'.

References

1. Culligan, M. J., S. Deakin, and A. H. Young, *Back to Basics Management— The Lost Craft of Leadership*, Gower, 1983. 161 pp.
2. Brown, R., *The Practical Manager's Guide to Excellence in Management*, Amacom, 1979. (Amacom is the publishing organ of the American Management Association.)
3. Winters, R. J., *It's Different When You Manage*, Lexington Books, 1975.
4. Deal, T. E. and A. Kennedy, *Corporate Cultures – The Rites and Rituals of Corporate Life*, Addison-Wesley, 1975.
5. Peters, T. J. and R. H. Waterman, *In Search of Excellence: Lessons from America's Best-Run Companies*, Harper & Row, 1982.
6. Kharbanda, O. P., E. A. Stallworthy and L. F. Williams, *Project Cost Control in Action*, Gower, 1980.
7. Pascale, R. T. and A. G. Athos, *The Art of Japanese Management – Applications for American Executives*, Simon & Schuster 1982. Kharbanda, O. P., 'Look east young man', *Swagat*, Sept. 1984, pp. 49–51. (*Swagat* is an Indian Airlines magazine.)
8. Belbin, R. M., *Management Teams – Why They Succeed or Fail*, Heinemann, 1981.
9. Bennett, D., *Successful Team Building Through TA*, Amacom, 1975.
10. Parkinson, C. N. and N. Rowe, *Communicate – Parkinson's Formula for Business Survival*, Prentice-Hall, 1977.
11. Stallworthy, E. A. and O. P. Kharbanda, *Total Project Management*, Gower, 1983.

4 Man is management

Having seen that management is the crux of a successful company, having recognized that management is made up of men and women organized into teams, it is but logical to turn to a consideration of those men and women. We have also seen that the Japanese miracle is largely due to the emphasis placed on the individual. There they seem to have taken to heart the following concept:

	for one year	is to plant seed
To plan	for ten years	is to plant trees
	for a lifetime	is to develop a MAN.[1]

Yet in Japan, while the individual is considered to be so important, they identify themselves *completely* with their company. In introducing himself, your visitor does not say, for instance, 'I am an engineer' but 'I am a Matushita man'. This association between the individual and the company goes so deep that one can tell the difference between a Mitsui manager and a Mitsubishi manager, such is the identity of the person with the organization.

In the West, however, attitudes are entirely different. Listen to the plaint of an auto worker:

> You really begin to wonder. What price do they put on me? Look at the price they put on the machine. When that machine breaks down, there's somebody out there to fix it right away. If I break down, I'm pushed over to the other side until another man takes my place. The only thing they have on their mind is to keep that line running.[2]

The man at the top

In an interesting and unusual study corporate leaders during the industrial era in the West have been classified under four groups:[3]

Craftsman
Jungle fighter
Company man
Gamesman

The distinguishing characteristics of these four groups may be summarized as shown in Table 4.1

30

Table 4.1

Type	Basic characteristics	Other characteristics
Craftsman	Drive to build the best, competes only with self.	Only interested in work. His one goal is perfection. Derives great pleasure from building something better and better.
Jungle fighter	Kill or be killed. Dominate or be dominated.	Has a lust for power. Takes pleasure in crushing opponent and has fear of destruction. Only one place for him: the top.
Company man	Climb or fall. Looks for security rather than success.	Has a fear of failure and desires approval by authority. Is fearful and submissive.
Gamesman	Win or lose, still happy. Either triumphs or is humiliated.	Enjoys contest, looks for new options. Has pleasure in controlling the play. Considers work a game. Tense, dynamic.

The 'gamesman' is considered to be the leading character in this study. The type required these days as a corporate executive is seen as a combination of the gamesman and the company man. He has to be a team player. He has to be responsible, yet a worrier, and his career goals must merge with that of the corporation.

This study draws the conclusion that while in the 1960s the gamesman led in the company scene, going all out to win, in the 1970s there was much scepticism about the concept of adventure and seeking for glory. Also, in the US at least, the Watergate affair brought the message that winning is not everything – it is the *only* thing. In business this concept may be equated with profit. The *only* *thing* that matters is to make a profit and the one person who more than anyone else is responsible for this is the man at the top – the chief executive. He can make or break a business and numerous biographies have been written describing such men. We thought that the best way of building up a picture of this key figure was to make a rather random selection from men who have gained notoriety in the past in the business arena. This should help us to get something of the 'feel' and 'flavour' of such people. We should begin to know what we should be looking for in the chief executive – and what to beware of.

Andrew Carnegie

Maccoby's study sees Carnegie as one of the most intelligent and subtle 'jungle fighters' in the corporate world of his day. His father, an unaggressive craftsman, failed in his own small business. His mother is shown as a protective, self-sacrificing tigress whose ambition almost terrorized her son into success. She was jealous, confident and shrewd. At his first dinner meeting with his future partner, Henry Clay Frick, Carnegie proposed a toast to the new Carnegie–Frick partnership and after an embarrassing silence, his mother said: 'a very good thing for Mr Frick, but what do we get out of it?'

One imagines Carnegie as a man continually searching to see what *he* could 'get out of it'. He had a mind open to new ideas, new technology and financial techniques, but only as a means of increasing profit. He had no qualms about seducing, manipulating and even betraying his associates. He was ungrateful to people who had helped him, once he no longer needed them. His twin goals were power and profit. He believed himself to be a good man – don't we all – deeply concerned about the progress and well-being of his workers, yet he had no hesitation in forcibly crushing the labour union movement in order to keep up production at his steel mills. However, it is true that, having gained control of the situation, he did offer shorter hours and other benefits to his workers.

So absorbed had he been in his business that he felt uneasy in retirement. After some thirteen years in retirement he is said to have commented: 'Life outside the business environment is boring: it is the pursuit of wealth that enlivens life.'

Carnegie's partner Frick is also seen as a 'jungle fighter'. In later years they parted company and there was no love lost between them. When Carnegie, busy in his later life with philanthropic activities, desired to meet his partner for the last time, if only to say 'bygones should be bygones', Frick's reply was sharp and pointed: 'Tell Mr Carnegie I'll meet him in hell.'

Harold Geneen

Geneen retired after running ITT for 17 years. Thanks to his intellectual ability and hard work, ITT grew fast under his stewardship and was a favourite in the stock market for many years. However, the group seems to have started crumbling even before Geneen left, perhaps because it did not 'stick to the knitting'. What was an international telephone company doing acquiring Continental Baking and Sheraton Hotels? Did this divert attention, with the result that ITT 'missed the bus' in the innovative years for the telecommunications industry? Let us have a look at the man who led his company for such a long while. What better for that purpose than his own words?

In a 1984 article Geneen candidly admits that during his regime at ITT he kept his board 'pretty much under his thumb' and now felt that it was a bad idea.[4] Geneen goes on to generalize about top companies, expressing the belief that the vast majority of their directors are *not* doing what they are supposed to and *couldn't* even if they wanted to! What are they supposed to do? Look after the interests of their shareholders and employees. What do they actually do?

According to Geneen, collect their salary, sip cold coffee, get treated for lunch and then go home! Does that sound familiar? Isn't that going on everywhere?

Yes, it is and it does. Geneen operated in the United States. If we cross the globe to India to listen to R. K. Talwar, former chairman of the State Bank of India and the Industrial Development Bank of India, we find him saying: 'I have known instances of directors never opening their mouths except to partake of refreshments and never seeing papers except for sitting fee cheques, and yet their "valuable" and "invaluable" services are lauded on suitable occasions.' Geneen elaborates on this theme. The odd director, he says, may ask a question and the answer may lead to more questions; if he persists he is labelled a troublemaker. The chief executive is likely to say that he cannot work with such a man and next time round he is not nominated to the board. Only those who have the knack of 'getting along', having been nominated, stay there. As a result such boards of directors are largely ineffective, especially when the chief executive is chairman as well, as was Geneen. But he is honest enough to admit that such an approach is not fair to the stockholders. Have you ever noticed that even when a company is on the verge of bankruptcy, there is seldom a cut in the chief executive's salary, although of course his bonus could fall.

What is the solution? Well, Geneen suggests that the chairman should be an outside director and report to the shareholders, not to the chief executive. The latter should be appointed by and report to the board. An informed board — better informed than is often the case at present — led by one of them as chairman would raise the quality of board meetings. The board would be in a position to tell management, through their chief executive, how well it expects the company to perform, rather than the other way round. Such a board would truly manage and be reviewing company performance, judging the company not on the basis of what is *has* earned, but on what it *should* have earned. What a difference that would make!

Lee Iacocca

Iacocca represents a rare combination of creative and administrative skills and was the 'whiz kid' of the McNamara team at Ford. Yet he was fired by Henry Ford II because 'I never liked him'. Iacocca was instantly seized upon by Chrysler, then on the verge of bankruptcy. As president of Chrysler he put together an elaborate and realistic rescue plan and got it through the congressional committees. We shall revert to *that* story in Chapter 10, but let us listen for now to Iacocca on managers. Managers who have gone through management schools in the US are proud to put a three-letter suffix after their name: MBA. Iacocca said of them: 'MBAs know everything but understand nothing.'[5] This remark provides a real insight into what has gone wrong with management, fascinated by 'method' rather than seeking to *understand* what is going on.

Armand Hammer

This remarkable man, now approaching 90 years of age, chairman of Occidental Petroleum Corporation, now holds a mere 1 per cent of the stock but operates this US$19 billion multinational as if it were his own private company. When he took over the company some 30 years ago it was a tiny oil producer, but it has been nurtured by Hammer to become the giant it is today. In the words of Harvard Business School professor, Robert Stobaugh: 'He still looks upon it [the company] as *his* baby.' Anyone who questions his authority is abruptly pushed aside or out, and so far he has always got his way. But for how long now? And what comes after him? We have no answers, although *an* answer may well come before this book is finally published.

Hammer has been particularly successful in negotiating a number of major deals, such as a US$20 billion barter deal with the USSR and more recently a similar deal with China. All such negotiations have been conducted by him personally, dealing with the highest authorities in the countries concerned. No doubt such deals are advantageous to both parties, even though they have been criticized by some. The secret of his continuing youth? In his own words: 'I have a way of taking naps for ten minutes, anywhere at all. I just shut my eyes and think I am lying in a forest, listening to a babbling brook.'

Kim Woo Choong

The founder of the giant Daewoo Group, who is still under 50, is described as the hardest worker in South Korea. Take note of what *Fortune* has to say about him: 'dashing around the world, he sleeps in airplane aisles, never takes a vacation, and sometimes worries bankers with the risks he takes. . . .' How interesting. He himself does not worry: he leaves that to his bankers. Let them have sleepless nights, not him. His advice to the 30 000 employees in his industrial empire is simple and straightforward: 'Sacrifice yourself for the next generation.' It looks as though South Korea has taken that particular exhortation to heart as it goes steadily onward and upward to become a leading industrialized nation and a formidable competitor to its main rival and mentor, Japan.

Kim Woo Choong works 7 days a week, 52 weeks a year. We do not doubt he finds relaxation in his work: this is true of all who enjoy their work. Within 17 years of operation his group of companies has moved steadily upward, till it is now sixty-second in *Fortune*'s listing of the 500 largest corporations outside the US. Sales in 1983 totalled more than US$6 *billion*. His bankers may well worry about the risks he takes, but he himself says: 'If you are going to a risky place, you pay more attention to everything, so actually there's no risk.'

One of his greatest challenges came in 1976, via the late President Park. Kim took over a state-owned machinery manufacturing plant that had been consistently in the red for 37 years. He worked, ate and slept (soundly, we are sure) at the factory, now Daewoo Heavy Industries, and within nine months the company was making its first ever profit. Most certainly a job well done. But how?

'Never in my life have I worked so hard,' said the man whose *normal* routine includes a 15-hour working day, 7 days a week! This may well be a one-man empire, but see what that one man has achieved. We would not suggest that such devotion to work is essential to success, but it seems that those with such attributes are unable to let up.

Cathie Black

To show you that this is not exclusively a man's world, we will look at Cathie Black. Now 40 years old, this 'supersaleswoman', as she is called, has recently been appointed publisher of Gannett's national newspaper. Cathie started her business life in 1966 selling advertisements for the magazine *Holiday*. Two years later she was appointed advertising sales representative for *Travel and Leisure* and shortly thereafter took up a challenging appointment with *New York*. Then, at the age of 22 she joined the newly started magazine *Ms*. She went back to work for *New York* in 1977 as associate publisher with the promise of becoming publisher within two years. In 1981 she joined *USA Today* where she now faces, as publisher, the hardest challenge of her life. This new magazine had a startup loss of US$50 million, since it was an entirely new and radical concept in magazine style and content. The losses may well grow to some US$250 million before the turnaround comes. But this is just the sort of situation upon which she thrives. To quote her: 'I like dicey situations . . . I like startups and the new things and turnabouts.' An admiring business associate says of her that she has only one significant facet: 'She's an icicle. She appears on the outside to be a cheerleader, but she's an executive – and she can be a cold person who stands two arms length away.'

With her earlier success at *New York*, which she helped turn around to a highly profitable magazine by the time she left, one would say she cannot fail. The circulation of *USA Today*, which started at around 200 000 a month when launched in October 1982, increased seven-fold in less than two years. Cathie lays much emphasis on increasing both sales and research staff. The comment of those who deal with her is: 'Her orientation is on what she has that meets your needs rather than just selling you what she has'. That certainly sounds like a formula for success, but the media keeps wondering about her, using headlines such as: 'Has Black the Magic?' and 'Can Cathie Black pull *USA Today* out of the red?' Time will tell, but meanwhile one can consider her style of management and seek to learn a few more lessons.

G. D. Birla

Affectionately known as 'Babuji', this grand old man who died at the age of 89 on a visit to London in 1983, was a colossus among Indian industrialists. With his death the golden age of pioneering entrepreneurship in India came to an abrupt end. He died in harness, his physical and mental faculties fully intact. Starting with one jute mill 65 years ago, the Birla Group now has more than 200 companies, assets in excess of US$25 billion and annual sales around US$3.0 billion. It is by far the largest family company in India. It has been a trail-blazer, easily outpacing the other family-controlled group in India, Tata, in both the range and breadth of its operations.

Over 30 of the 250 largest private sector companies in India are Birla companies, and the range includes aluminium smelting, engineering, fertilizer manufacture, jute, paper and rayon manufacture, shipping, sugar mills, railway wagon manufacture: the list goes on and on. It is also truly multinational, with operations in a dozen countries, also in great variety. In Africa alone the group controls or manages assets exceeding US$6.0 billion. The operations are closely knit, yet completely decentralized, being in the hands of individual members of the family. This was meticulously planned by G. D. in his lifetime and largely implemented, the choice of managers being dictated by the need, capacity and capabilities of the members of the family, spanning four generations.

Largely self-educated, G. D. never stopped learning and his extensive reading enabled him to talk knowledgeably and with confidence on any topic, whether scientific, political or industrial. He attained the highest honours in business, social and educational fields, helping to establish a variety of foundations. He even learnt French when over 60. Although the business was largely decentralized he maintained close contact and a degree of control over the entire operation. No matter where he was he used to receive a daily telex summarizing the operating results of all the companies in the Birla fold. By a mere perusal he could point out trouble spots, so intimate and quick was his understanding of the business which he had founded and nourished with loving care for more than half a century.

One of the major companies in the group, Century Spinning and Manufacturing Company, with sales in 1983 of US$270 million and a profit of US$32 million, is regarded as India's bluest 'blue chip' company, a barometer of the Indian economy. The company may seem small by international standards, but in India there are inbuilt penalties for being too large.

This one-man rule proved highly successful over a long period for the Birla Group and may well continue, albeit modernized and diluted, now that G. D. is no longer there. The philosophy may still be preserved, company by company. One-man rule *can* be a success, but it depends so much on the man.

What have we established?

We demonstrated in Chapter 3 that management is the crux of the matter, but we now see that it is the quality of the man (or woman) who leads a company that is all-important. This seems to be completely independent of the quality of the rest of the men and women within the company. An outstanding personality *below* the top cannot bring success: Iacocca had to *go* to the top before his abilities could bring real results. The chief executive more than anybody else will make or break a company. Thus, when assessing potential disaster, always look closely and very, very carefully at the chief executive. Our mini-biographies of a few outstanding characters in the management field were selected quite arbitrarily, so that you might get a feel for the type of personality that runs a successful company. We have left unanswered the question of whether one-man rule – the single dominant personality – is really desirable, despite its apparent success in the few cases we have cited. Let us not forget that these are but a few of the many thousands of separate companies, all striving to succeed. How should *they* be run? In Part Three we begin to look at the factors which can tell us what is happening to a company, where it is going, and how it can be prevented from collapsing, if that is its prospect.

References

1. Kharbanda, O. P., 'Look east, young man', *Swagat*, Sept. 1984. (*Swagat* is an Indian Airlines publication.)
2. Stuart-Kotze, R. and R. Roskin, *Success Guide to Managerial Achievement*, Reston Publishing, 1983.
3. Maccoby, M., *The Gamesman – the New Corporate Leaders*, Simon Schuster, 1976.
4. Geneen, H. S., 'Why directors can't protect the shareholders', *Fortune*, **110**, 22–6, 17 Sept. 1984.
5. Culligan, M. J., S. Deakin and A. H. Young, *Back to Basics Management – The Lost Craft of Leadership*, Gower, 1983.

PART TWO
Back from the brink?

5 Two classics

A catalogue of major industrial crises in the recent past in the developed countries shows that crisis comes not only in what are termed the 'sunset' sectors, such as textiles and shipbuilding, but also in growth industries such as aerospace and computers. Rolls-Royce and ICL (Computers) are examples from these two fields. Indeed it seems that such crises are a continuing and striking feature of advanced industrial societies.[1] To take the four major industrialized nations of the West as examples, we can cite:

France	Vosges (a textile giant); Steel Industry of Lorraine; and the Willet empire.
USA	Chrysler (cars); Douglas Aircraft; International Harvester; Lockheed (aircraft); and Penn Central Transportation Company (operating railroads).
UK	British Leyland (cars); British Steel; ICL; and Rolls-Royce.
West Germany	Heavy steel industries in the Ruhr and Saar areas, notably Arben Saarstaal; and AEG Telefunken.

Some of these, together with others, will be taken up in the following chapters, but here we will be studying two classics among them, Penn Central and Rolls-Royce. Our analysis (or should we call it *post mortem*) is based largely on the research of Argenti and Altman[2,3,4] in particular a refined technique for the prediction of corporate failure published recently by Argenti.[5] Our purpose is to see whether such a prediction technique could have furnished those watching those companies at the time ample warning of impending failure. However, as we shall show later in Part Four, this technique is but a starting point for prediction. If it indicates that a company is in danger then one must go on to use qualitative techniques, also discussed in Part Four, to confirm that the dangerous position that has been indicated is indeed real. That realization should lead inevitably to the conclusion that collapse will occur unless the appropriate corrective steps are taken. That is our basic objective. We are not studying this subject so that prospective investors may be warned of hidden dangers, but rather so that ailing companies can be restored to health.

Penn Central Transportation

The basic problems encountered by Penn Central have arisen in most railroad companies and are the result of the specific nature of their activities. Penn

Central is a public service activity with very low profit margins: so low in fact that there was no capital available to be ploughed back. This led to ageing stocks, decaying track and obsolete operational and management procedures.[6]

The background and history of the Penn Central failure has been recorded in minute detail in a voluminous 100-page report prepared by the US Senate Committee on Commerce in 1973. While the company had its origin in railroad construction some 140 years ago, its history as Penn Central is rather short, since that company resulted from a number of mergers which took place in 1967, barely three years before it went bankrupt. To set the scene for those mergers we should tell you that two of the largest and most successful railroads in the US towards the end of the nineteenth century were the PRR (Pennsylvania Railroad) and the NYC (New York Central Railroad). They both served practically the same highly industrialized area in the north-east of the US and competed fiercely with one another. Their management styles were very different to one another. PRR was professional with the conventional management of honest men, while NYC was typified by the wheeler-dealer Cornelius Vanderbilt and his colourful financial techniques.

However, they both desired to improve their performance by eliminating the cut-throat competition and thought that this could be achieved by merger and acquisition. The depression of the 1930s was marked by reduced profits, creating conditions near to bankruptcy for many of the railroads in the US, but that decade was also marked by a number of innovations, such as the introduction of diesel power units and electrification. There was also a major qualitative change in the transport industry: business was moving away from the railways to the roads, adding to their financial problems. In this context a merger between PRR and NYC was thought to be a way out.

The merger took a long time to merge

This was to be the biggest merger ever in the US and the drama started in 1957. The two leading characters at that time were Perlman of NYC and Symes of PRR. Perlman had acquired a great reputation, having transformed NYC, a company which had gone bankrupt four times and had paid no dividends for nearly 80 years. But he did not like Symes, nor did the executives in the two companies like one another: that came from their very contrasting styles of management, outlined above. The talks were broken off in 1959 and Perlman then looked around for possible mergers with other railroad companies before resuming negotiations with Symes in 1961. There was no doubt that NYC and PRR really needed each other and that a merger would be mutually beneficial. Agreement was finally reached and ratified in 1962, giving birth to Penn Central. That agreement, however, was but a piece of paper. The merger would have created a near monopoly, the combined turnover in 1962 being some US$1.5 billion. This brought forth a host of objections from the trade unions, state agencies, trade associations and other railroad companies. The hearing of these objections, required by law, continued for 18 months but just as it appeared that a decision had been reached and the merger would be implemented, another railroad, New Haven, sought to become part of the proposed Penn Central merger. This delayed matters for nearly five years, since the due processes of democracy had to be fully exercised. Finally the problem of 'sweeping New Haven under the Penn Central rug' was resolved and the merger took effect in 1968, 10 years after the talks first began. This prolonged delay certainly worsened the financial position, which had been none too good to start with: that was why the merger had been proposed in the first place.

Cost savings

Substantial cost savings had been expected as a result of the merger, one estimate placing these at around US$100 million. The actual saving flowing from the merger was about half that, but at the same time there were additional costs that more than nullified those benefits. The inclusion of New Haven cost US$30 million, US$60 million was spent on redundancy and other payments to employees, the resolution of operational problems took some US$30 million and a further US$90 million was spent on alterations to equipment. These last two costs arose from an accelerated programme for the physical merger of the assets and operating facilities of the two companies. As all this took place at a time when there was a severe turndown in the economy, the merger saved nothing: rather it cost perhaps US$150 million.

Creative accounting

As we have just seen, the merger took six years to accomplish and we wished to examine what happened to these two companies during those six years.

A review of the accounts over those years show that they were both pretty sick companies, yet they had to maintain a 'respectable' appearance. This was largely achieved by what in those days was called 'imaginative accounting', but has now achieved a measure of respectability and is described as 'creative accounting' (see Chapter 20). How did they do this? Comparing the policies adopted by the two companies, we can sum it up as follows:

NYC Borrowed large sums to maintain payment of dividends. Used leasing extensively, to give lower gearing.

PRR Leased extensively under the guise of 'profit maximization'.
Cut down expenditure on the tracks, and treated it as revenue rather than as capital.
Capitalized major overhaul expenditure.
Extraordinary income was not separated out, but treated as ordinary income.

Ordinary expenses were described as 'extraordingary expenses'.

Paper profits on property deals were taken in as earnings.

Earnings from subsidiaries where PRR had a holding of 50 per cent or less were taken into profits. Previously only the profits of wholly-owned subsidiaries were so treated.

It is obvious from the above that PRR excelled in 'creativity'. These various financial 'adjustments' to the published accounts most certainly helped to prop up the companies and impressed the outside observer, including those who were lending the money. This makes one aware of the naivete of many financial people in those days and helps one to appreciate the real value of the various systems of analysis of company accounts that have been developed since then. The warning for those in trouble today is: do not imitate them. It is certain that these policies helped to make the collapse when it came that much more violent, since they were designed not to strengthen the companies but to sustain an appearance of health. Sound accounting is an essential prerequisite of a healthy company.

Sudden death

The tragic end – tragic at least for those who had invested in the company – appeared to come suddenly, but the discerning observer could have anticipated it by several years. Following the merger, Penn Central was immediately faced with a severe cash shortage and the losses mounted. The cash position could have been improved and the company might have been saved if, at the time of the merger, fresh equity had been sought, or a debenture issue made, because at that time there was still considerable public optimism and confidence in the future of the company – due, of course, to 'creative accounting'. (But no doubt those running the company were themselves deceived, because that is what happens in the end.)

By 1970 there was no escape, although those most immediately involved, including the government, thought rescue possible. With losses mounting at the rate of US$1 million per day, the closing days went as follows:

27 January	Banks lent Penn Central another US$50 million, but with strings attached.
April–May	Penn Central unable to repay loans maturing during this period and government approached to nationalize its passenger services.
12 May	Loan Prospectus issued, but withdrawn due to lack of confidence in the market.
15 May	Heavy share selling, price falls to US$10. (It had been US$86 some two years earlier.)
8 June	Bevan and Saunders (managing director and financial director) leave the company. Shares rise to US$13.25.

Note the popular belief in the power of the individual. Of course, at this point it made no difference at all.

9 June	Government began rescue operations, contemplating a possible loan of US$200 million.
19 June	Final decision by government: no loan, no guarantees.

And so

21 June	Penn Central file a petition for bankruptcy.

This petition for bankruptcy was filed under section 77, which meant that the Receiver, on appointment, could run the company indefinitely as a going concern.

Why did it happen?

One can always be wise after the event, but we are attempting to learn from somebody else's mistakes. According to the Senate Committee who investigated the downfall of Penn Central, the major reasons for its collapse were:

A hostile environment
Low profits
Faulty management

That last is the only item on which action could have been taken, since no one can alter the environment in which a company has to operate and low profits would be the result of the other two factors.

Where did the management go wrong? It should have used the cash available to improve operations and not to buy property. It should not have paid dividends, pursuing a policy of profit maximization to achieve that. The merger should have been called off, or should have been followed immediately by a massive loan while the climate was right for that. The New Haven merger should *never* have taken place. The directors should have been alive to the market trends and should have co-operated much more closely. Finally, if the government *was* concerned, since Penn Central was a major public utility, Congress should have intervened and tackled the real problems, rather than just 'papering over the cracks'. But that required courage, a rare quality in political circles.

Daughen and Binzen's investigation of the Penn Central collapse places the blame entirely on the three main characters: Bevan and Saunders of NYC and Perlman of PRR.[6] It was said that they just could not work together as a team, blamed each other continually and hardly ever spoke to one another. Of course, they blamed circumstances: never themselves. Saunders, for instance, attributed it all to the decline in freight traffic on the railroads, subject to intense competition from road haulage and air transport, alternative modes of transport that were being massively subsidized directly or indirectly by the government.

Of course, external factors did play a significant role, but good management would have met and countered them. Union problems, rising interest rates, the downturn in the economy were perhaps just the last straw. Altman adds a new dimension, pointing out that since the entire railroad system in the US is government regulated it can adjust prices, close down lines or reduce manning[3] — this in an industry with a rigid cost structure; with labour costs being the predominant operating cost it *must* be vulnerable! Also, since railroads have high fixed costs and high gearing, they are particularly prone to economic depression — hardly an industry in which to invest.

Could collapse have been predicted?

Altman's answer is: yes. Both his Z-score model, which we shall discuss in detail later, and the movement in the share price, were indicators that gave warning of impending disaster. The share price moved as follows:

1968	$68
September 1969	$43
April 1970	$23
19 June 1970	$11

At least a year before collapse, the precipitous drop in the price of the shares on the stock market sounded a warning signal. However, the Z-score indicator, as developed by Altman, gave even earlier warning. The signs were there perhaps four years before collapse, so that had the technique been available and *had it been listened to* a rescue operation could have been mounted and might have succeeded.

Another researcher, Argenti, had an entirely different approach.[2,5] He evaluated the management, rather than the accounts. His prediction model gives us the A-score, and we present our assessment of the A-score for Penn Central according to the Argenti sequence in Table 5.1. The higher the figure, the closer the company is to failure. As you will see from Table 5.1, Penn Central had a score of 55, when a company can only be considered safe if the score is 25 or below. Once above 35, a company is most definitely in danger. Whether or not review of the activities of the management along the lines set out by Argenti, taking action to eliminate or reduce some of the factors that brought the score so high, would have averted disaster, is an open question. But the analysis certainly makes it very clear that it was management that was at fault. Good management is basic to success.

Turnaround achieved!

When we look at Penn Central today we see a prosperous company now concentrating on energy conservation, electronics and telecommunications. Its railroad interests were transferred to Conrail in 1978 and since then the company has

Table 5.1   An assessment of Penn Central. If the overall score is greater than 25, then the company is considered suspect. Over 35 and it is seriously at risk. The symptoms tabled below were evident to experienced outsiders at least 3 years prior to collapse.

			Score
Defects	Passive		2
	Weak Finance Director (Bevan not on the Board)		2
	Chairman and Chief Executive the same (Saunders)		4
	No cash flow plans		3
	No costing system		3
	Poor response to change		15
Score	29	**Pass**	10
Mistakes	Big project (merger gone wrong)		15
Score	15	**Pass**	15
Symptoms	Financial signs (reducing profits, increasing losses)		4
	Creative accounting (profit maximisation)		4
	Non-financial signs (low morale, poor service)		3
Score	11	**Total score**	55

branched out into these new activities. Some six years, 20 acquisitions and several divestitures later, the Penn Central revenue for 1983 was US$2.5 billion, with a profit of US$19.7 million. Its most valuable asset was a tax loss carried forward. During the first nine months of 1984 the sales were US$1.9 billion, an advance of 3 per cent over the previous year, while the profit at that point was US$131 million, an advance of 47 per cent. The stock is being traded in the market at around US$46 a share, some 14 times current earnings, supported by rumours that Penn Central may now 'go private'. What a turnaround!

Rolls-Royce

The name Rolls-Royce was for decades the symbol of all that was best in British quality and workmanship. The company was excellence personified, its reputation unquestioned, yet on 4 February 1971 it collapsed. The headlines bringing the news were received with incredulity and the whole engineering world stood amazed. Yet it was all due to one single project that went sadly wrong.

At that time, Rolls-Royce was developing the RB-211 aero engine. The company's failure contributed to the collapse of the American airframe company Lockheed, whose latest design, the L-1011, later called *Tristar*, was designed around the RB-211.

A strength becomes a weakness

The reputation of Rolls-Royce for high-technology, high-quality aero engines was beyond dispute and it was logical to build upon this strength. The aeroplane industry was of course a key industry in the Second World War, but when that war came to an end in 1945 a workforce of some 50 000 fell within six months to less than 25 000. However, over the next 20 years the company went from strength to strength, building upon its skills, until the workforce exceeded 100 000. In the 1960s the company was a leader in Europe, the RR jet engine powering more than half of all the civil aircraft flying in the Western world.

In 1967 the company launched the development of the RB-211, designed for the wide-bodied airliners then on the drawing board. The arithmetic of the operation was as follows:

	£ million
Development cost	60
Expected sales, 1970–79	800 (3000 engines)
Profit (before loan interest)	260

To put these figures in context one has to be aware that the annual profit of RR in 1967 was £20 million. Another significant factor was that the development cost was funded to the tune of 70 per cent by the British government, whereas their normal backing was never more than 50 per cent.

Trouble soon loomed. The initial engine tests in 1968 were disappointing, development costs rose to £100 million and the manufacturing cost of each engine rose from £150 000 to £190 000, turning a potential profit into a dead loss. But the design problems would not go away, so that by January 1971 the development cost had risen to £203 million and the estimated cost of each engine to £280 000. On 3 February of that year there was great jubilation: test bed results had shown that engine performance was now close to expectations. A few hours later the Receiver was called in! Events moved even faster than the engine!

Jetting to the end

Despite the problems with the RB-211 there were no financial worries in 1969, but projections for 1970/71 began to look alarming and grew worse by the month. Putting it simply, the company ran out of cash to fund its operations. By January 1971 it needed £94 million for that year alone. In addition, there was the burden of its contract with Lockheed. There was a penalty of some £50 million for late delivery, perhaps £300 million if they failed to deliver at all. The situation was impossible, yet the chairman of the company at that time said in June 1970 that the board was 'satisfied' that the company had sufficient working capital and at the AGM in July he talked of the company being 'in good shape' and on the verge of 'reaping the benefits' from the RB-211, despite the fact that the latest estimates showed a major loss situation in relation to that project. In October of the same year Lord Cole took over as chairman and arranged a further loan of £60 million, but the situation was already beyond redemption. Faced with the threat of a major claim for damages from Lockheed, the board conceded failure and called in the Receiver.

The post mortem

The official report puts the blame for the collapse squarely on the directors and particularly the chairman for failing to even hint at the consequences of failure on a major project.[7] It was called, with hindsight, a 'rash commitment'. The cost figures were based on estimates that included an 'unknown' — development costs — yet the Lockheed contract stipulated a fixed price for the engine. Further, the estimated development costs, which eventually escalated some four times, were nearly a third of the company's net worth at the original estimate. The board was composed almost entirely of engineers and the financial information systems were found to be sadly deficient.

Argenti, writing in 1976, sees the company as having taken the wrong strategic decision: to build a big jet and sell it to the Americans.[2] The RB-211 project was too ambitious for a company the size of Rolls-Royce, the contract with Lockheed was too tough and the board lacked the financial expertise to realize what they were getting into.

Everyone knew better than the board once the company had called in the Receiver. The *Financial Times* (6 August 1973) blamed the management for putting all its eggs into one basket, the *Economist* (4 August 1973) doubted whether the company had the technical skills to undertake the development work, while Robert Heller of *The Observer* criticized the management for paying dividends without a profit.

Could collapse have been predicted?

The Altman Z-score model for the prediction of bankruptcy was developed on the basis of data relating to US companies. Can it be applied elsewhere? Argenti translated some of the American accounting terms to their nearest British equivalent[2] and we have plotted his results in Fig. 5.1, indicating not the Altman boundaries between success and failure but those proposed by Argenti for UK conditions: they are somewhat lower. We are not much wiser, but what we do see is that Rolls-Royce were in danger as early as 1966, four years before the collapse, and we suspect that the improvement that followed was largely due to 'creative accounting'. For instance, the R&D costs were being capitalized when they should have been treated as a loss and set against expenditure.

The approach proposed by Argenti is, as we have seen already (Table 5.1)

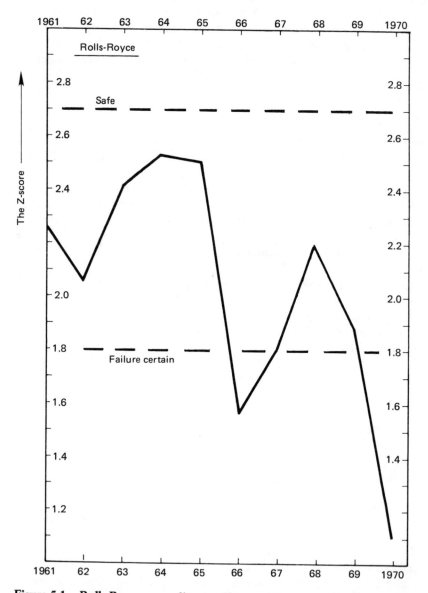

Figure 5.1   Rolls-Royce according to Altman. *Note that according to Altman Rolls-Royce should have gone bankrupt in 1966 and was never safe. Argenti has set the 'failure certain' point lower for the UK conditions as Fig. 11.1.* (Source: *Argenti 1976.)*

an assessment of management. When we make this assessment with respect to Rolls-Royce, the score is 74, a very high figure indicating almost certain failure. Most of the adverse factors reviewed in the Argenti sequence were in evidence long before the RB-211 was launched and we ourselves doubt whether that was really the 'last straw'. We see it more as further evidence of bad management.

A remarkable turnaround

Some fifteen years later we have witnessed Rolls-Royce's remarkable recovery. Hundreds of RB-211 engines have been sold and the engine is now a star product, with applications not only in aircraft but also for marine and industrial purposes worldwide. The name and reputation of the company has been preserved. No wonder we can read a headline such as: 'RR maps out a flight plan to profitability'.

Summary

This chapter, dealing with two well publicized examples of company collapse, sets the scene for our case studies in the following chapters and current prediction techniques, had they been available at the time, would certainly have sounded a warning, but we question whether the end result would have been any different. Now that they *are* available, practice seems to fall far short of theory, as we shall see. What we are looking for is prevention and cure, not prediction as such. Prediction is only of value if, having seen where you may be going wrong, you *do* something about it.

References

1. Dyson, K. and S. Wilks (eds), *Industrial Crisis – A Comparative Study of the State and Industry*, Martin Robertson, 1983.
2. Argenti, J., *Corporate Collapse – The Causes and Symptoms*, McGraw-Hill, 1976.
3. Altman, E. I., *Corporate Bankruptcy in America*, Heath Lexington Books, 1971.
4. Altman, E. I. and A. W. Sametz (eds), *Financial Crisis – Institutions and Markets in a Fragile Environment*, Wiley, 1977.
5. Argenti, J., 'Predicting corporate failure', *Accountants Digest No. 138*, Institute of Chartered Accountants, London, 1983.
6. Daughen, J. R. and P. Binzen, *The Wreck of Penn Central*, Little, Brown, 1971.
7. Department of Trade Official Report '*Rolls-Royce Limited*', HMSO, 1973.

6 Contemporary history

Having considered two classic business failures of the early 1970s, we propose now to look at some more recent — and hence post-oil-crisis — failures. During this period the worldwide recession has been steadily widening and deepening, adding a new dimension to the problems of running a successful business. In a harsh economic climate competition becomes ever fiercer. Our choice of case studies is purely arbitrary, except that we have tried to take a worldwide view. We are going to look at a case in Northern Ireland, a part of the UK with unique economic problems, and then at a US airline. From there we go to South Korea, Thailand and Hong Kong, each very different in terms of business climate.

Our objective in presenting a wide range of case studies is to gain some idea of the causes and common factors in company collapse. The key to a successful cure in medicine is a good diagnosis: a palliative for indigestion will not help a stomach ulcer. We chose that example because the stomach ulcer is the hallmark of the overworked executive.

We selected companies from around the world in order to establish whether the same disease runs through them all, or whether there are some rather special variants. We think you will agree that there seems to be a common theme.

The De Lorean Motor Car Co.

John Z. De Lorean proved his mettle at General Motors and rose like a meteor to the 14th floor, with a mere 15 years of service, at the age of 47. (The norm is 30 years.) This he achieved despite an un-GM lifestyle in such matters as dress and social conduct. He even went so far as to criticize his company in public when he felt it was deserved. In an exposé of GM,[1] De Lorean said that the ill-fated Corsair's unsafe features were well documented and debated within GM before the car was introduced and long before Ralph Nader's book *Unsafe at Any Speed*. De Lorean also describes some of the other sinister business practices and serious management blunders that occurred within GM. He resigned his prestigious job, with a salary in excess of US$500 000 per annum, in April 1973.

We are told that De Lorean left in disgust, in order to set up his own business manufacturing an 'ethical' car: safe, fuel efficient, affordable and long-lasting.[2] Starting with US$20 000 of his own money, he quickly raised US$8.6 million from 345 automobile dealers and a further US$18 million from 134 selected partners to set up the company. The plant was to be built in Puerto Rico but the location was abruptly shifted to Northern Ireland, following promises from the British Government of almost unlimited funding against a potential 2000 jobs. An ultra-modern factory was built in some two and a half years, but the flashy sports car it produced failed to sell and the company headed into bankruptcy. Had the De Lorean who brought the invalid Pontiac Division of GM back to life lost his magic touch?

What are the facts? Sales never topped 150 a week although the factory was capable of producing 400 a week. The car was mechanically faulty and over-priced, offered at US$25000 when GM had a corresponding model selling at US$ 18000. At the same time the car market was in decline and the factory was overstaffed (2500 employees instead of 2000). No corrective steps were taken and finanical distress set in. By early 1982, a year after the first car rolled off the production line, over 4000 cars remained unsold and the factory was in the Receiver's hands. Then many shady financial deals came to light, including the astounding fact that De Lorean, despite his nominal investment, had a controlling interest in the company. He paid himself some US$500000 a year, lived in style, and engaged in many other interests apart from the Belfast factory. According to one financial analyst the company was never really managed and everything moved far too fast. As De Lorean came up with a request for a further funding of some US$70 million from the British government, Members of Parliament there were describing the project as a 'rip-off'. Further refunding was categorically refused. The De Lorean venture failed miserably, despite his having once said: 'I haven't failed at anything of importance . . . I am not capable of addressing failure.' The company filed for bankruptcy in October 1982 and a Grand Jury in the US is investigating allegations by some creditors that about US$17 million in company assets is missing.

What went wrong? The project was risky to start with, but was brought to disaster by De Lorean's mistakes, together with market factors over which he had no control but which should have been anticipated. Sales were brisk to begin with – 3000 in the first six months, when the car came on to the market in the summer of 1981. By December, however, the severe winter and the recession had almost halted sales. The car itself was sleek and racy, with a stainless steel skin, but apart from the 'gull' doors, designed after the 1954 Mercedes Sport Coupé, there was really nothing distinctive or special about the model. It was far too expensive and took too long to get on the market. In addition, while the most optimistic sales estimates were in the region of 12000 a year, plant produc-tion had been pitched at twice that level. So confident were De Lorean and his friends, riding on his outstanding success at GM, that the word 'failure' was not even in their vocabulary. Even the British government was blinded by the lure of 2000 new jobs into outbidding Puerto Rico's financial package and promising US$110 million if the factory was built in Ulster.

A lot has been written, not only in the automotive and financial press but also in the popular press, about the De Lorean collapse and its causes. Some of these we have highlighted above, but we wonder whether at the heart of it all may not have been Barmash's prognosis, to which we referred in Chapter 2: 'greed, human greed, simple and unadulterated'.

Braniff International Corporation

Braniff was a well-known US-based airline. The company took off when the US Congress deregulated the industry in 1978 and expanded at a tremendous rate. Yet only four years later it filed for bankruptcy with a loss of US$ 336 million in the previous three years of operation and a total debt of around US$1 billion. This did not surprise anyone at the time. Indeed, the general comment was one of surprise that the company had lasted as it did. One reason for its failure was put very succinctly by someone who knew the airline industry well.[3] He said: 'Braniff thought quality meant Alexander paint jobs and comely stewardesses. Delta knows it means planes that arrive on time.' Delta should know: it is one of the few airlines in a strong financial position and no scars despite the competition introduced by deregulation.

The actual collapse had its own drama. On 9 May 1982 there was a Braniff party and the photographs that later appeared in the press showed Howard D. Putnam, the chairman, with his wife, both cheerful and apparently without a worry in the world. Yet barely four days later Putnam, then 44, announced that the company was bankrupt and ordered its fleet of 71 jets back home to base at Forth Worth Airport, Dallas. At the press conference Putnam said bluntly: 'The airline is dead.'

There is not doubt that Braniff overexpanded following deregulation in 1978, under the stewardship of one Harding Lawrence. After his departure in December 1980 operations were curtailed considerably, the marketing strategy was revamped and employees were persuaded to take a 10 per cent pay cut. Putnam, who took over late in 1981, opted for an all-coach service with rock-bottom fares, which his competitors then had to match. Traffic soared but cash in hand dwindled. To conserve its cash resources Braniff deferred eight days pay for its workforce (about US$8 million) in March and sold off some of its routes to Eastern the following month. The load factor dived from over 50 per cent in April to around 30 per cent in early May, well below the breakeven point. The cash drain was then some US$1 million per day.

While the collapse was bad for Braniff, it was good for the industry. The cut-rate, cut-throat route to disaster was clear for everyone to see and helped discipline the industry. But the lesson was soon forgotten. What was left of the company was taken over by the Hyatt hotel chain, and a US$1 billion reorganization plan drawn up, with two top TWA officers joining the company as senior vice-presidents. By early 1984 one of the biggest airline startups ever had been drawn up, with a service designed to serve 18 cities with 172 flights a day. To lure the travel agents back into the fold a trust fund was created that would hold the money from the travel agents' ticket sales until each passenger actually flew. Fares were cut and there were attractions such as a 'free trip to Hawaii' – the only problem then being that Hawaii was not on one of their routes. Operations in the first quarter of 1984 resulted in a US$31 million loss and a further round of fare cuts was talked about. But a year later it moved out of the red.

Laker Airways

For this story we come to the UK, but the overtones are similar and by now very familiar. Again we have suicidal fares, designed to increase the load factor but setting up a vicious chain reaction. The case of Laker Airways has been well researched by the professionals: accountants and economists have had a field day. Bankruptcy came to Laker in 1982. The danger signals were there at least three years earlier, but were ignored. The financial gearing was quite high, with a debt/equity ratio of 5:1 in 1981. Yet a further loan of £131 million was sanctioned by the Midland Bank for the purchase of three airbuses. This overstretched an already extended balance sheet. In spite of this, Freddie Laker announced 'Globetrain', a round-the-world 'sky train' (the terms for his London to New York run) at a time when the other airlines were cutting down on their operations to cut down their losses.

A strong case has been made for a greater emphasis on liquidity in assessing a company (called cash flow accounting, or CFA) rather than the conventional preoccupation with profits and asset valuations. A leading exponent of CFA has used the Laker case to demonstrate that in order to stay clear of the bankruptcy courts there should be a sensible balance between cash inflows and outflows.[4] The Laker figures went thus:

	1976	1977	1978	1979	1980
Operating cash flow/total cash flow (%)	100	65	52	30	25
New investment/total cash flow (%)	11	61	82	100	100

By 1979 the new investment was using up *all* the cash, leaving nothing over to service the debt. The position worsened steadily from 1976 onwards, yet during this period profits rose steadily, from about £900 000 in 1976 to £8.1 million in 1980! A few minutes study of the above figures should have restrained – or better, ended – Laker's ambition for geometric growth. Is it any wonder that in February 1982 Laker ceased operations, the bankers withdrew their support and a receiver was appointed? The bankers had only themselves to blame. They should have seen what was coming in 1979 and halted further long-term funding at that point.

Another independent analysis using a very different approach concludes that the failure of Laker Airways could have been predicted as early as 1976. Using

Altman's 1968 MDA score technique[5] Robertson developed Z-score for Laker as follows:[6]

1976	1977	1978	1979	1980
1.54	1.79	1.61	1.27	0.96

A company is in danger once the Z-score falls below 1.8 Laker was already there in 1976 and never got out.

Laker Airways went bankrupt in 1982. Three years later the company is still in the news, with headlines such as 'Laker Airways: Out of court settlement?' Going bankrupt isn't the end of a company: it may well be just the beginning of a lot of work for lawyers. With Laker some very tricky issues with respect to jurisdiction as between the US and the UK are involved, but the most interesting case is the suit for damages taken out by Laker Airways against several British, American and other airlines. Laker claims conspiracy, saying that these airlines joined together to cut their fares below those of Laker, only to raise them once again when the company ceased trading. It is further alleged that the other airlines put pressure on the banks and other interested parties in order to stop a financial rescue operation. If Laker wins, the damages will be tripled automatically under American antitrust laws unless the suit is settled out of court.

The Kwangmyong Group, South Korea

A chain of spectacular bankruptcies in South Korea has exposed a basic weakness in the structure of that country's financial systems, highlighted by the collapse at the end of 1983 of the Kwangmyong Group, a major conglomerate with interests in housing, construction and investment. The bankers, together with some 2000 other creditors, had a stake of some US$100 million in the group, and of this barely half was secured. The company collapsed for what we now see to be a very common reason: expanding too fast with too little capital, by now a familiar story and a repeat of two earlier notorious bankruptcies in South Korea.

Starting with modest lumber operations and apartment construction, the group grew rapidly, creating six subsidiary companies on the basis of loans from the banks and from the market. The firm grew with the property boom in South Korea through the 1970s vying with the country's major contractors and with an annual turnover in excess of US$100 million. This was not enough for the group's flamboyant president, Lee Su Wang, 40, whose philosophy is summed up in the slogan: 'Let's create a legend!' This was for daily repetition by all his employees: He declared 'We must grow in recession time or we will never catch up.' Grow the company did – very rapidly indeed – but it slumped even faster. Money had been borrowed in the market at 20 per cent against a bank rate of 12 per cent, and the interest burden proved too heavy to bear. Government machinery was inadequate to monitor this unhealthy growth and so protect innocent lenders and subcontractors. Lee was reported to enjoy the patronage of high officials in the government and in the banks and this may well have helped him to get the necessary loans.

The group's final insolvency led to the arrest of six top executives, including Lee. In early 1985 the bankruptcies were before the District Court and the hearings on the criminal charges that had been brought against Lee had started. These include that of dishonouring cheques – an offence which carries a jail sentence. Large numbers of small lenders, such as housewives, retired government employees and small merchants, have lost all, and have held protest demonstrations displaying placards with the words: 'Give My Money Back!' Something may be recovered from the wreck. the major lender, Korea First Bank, is expected to take the various construction firms that were being run by the group and the court has awarded those subcontractors and other creditors holding duly guaranteed promissory notes, 80 per cent of the value involved.

Notice the pattern. We have crossed from one side of the world to the other, from a developed to a developing country, from one culture to another vastly different, but the story of collapse is almost identical. Rapid growth, led by a bold entrepreneur, supported by large borrowings. Evidently a recipe for disaster.

Dying for a loan

This is the headline of an article dealing with a spate of business failures in Thailand.[7] However, the Finance Minister there, Sommai Hoontrakul, considers that there is nothing to worry about. His view is that business failures are a natural phenomenon in a free-enterprise economy, where only the fittest *deserve* to survive.

The rate of business failures in Thailand has doubled in a year, from about 50 bankruptcies a month in 1983 to some 100 in 1984, even though new business registrations in that year were somewhat lower (1000 a month) than in 1983. But this is hardly the true picture, since many, many businesses just come and go in Thailand without formal registration or bankruptcy proceedings at the end of their career. Most of the failures have been in the small and medium retail and wholesale business sectors, but many factories in the textile industry have failed, together with pharmaceutical plants and construction companies. To take but one example, at the main textiles trading centre in Thailand, Sampend, near Bangkok, some 20 wholesalers of various sizes closed down in the year, leaving behind them bad debts of some US$43 million.

The main financial channels for borrowing in Thailand are:

	US$ billion	%
Banking system	17.2	30
Finance companies	3.5	5
Other sources	37.0	65

The term 'other sources' includes illegal lending from trust funds, private money lenders and chit fund pools, all lending to small and medium sized firms at considerably above current bank interest rates. The figure, while very large, is, of course, not known very accurately. This type of lending is both indiscriminate and uncontrolled and since it predominates in Thailand, it has led there to an overheated economy and an enormous trade deficit – some US$4 billion in 1983 – which if unchecked will cause havoc in the country's economy. Late in 1983, the Bangkok Bank introduced a policy of tight credits which sent businesses scrambling for cash. Then, early in 1984, the Bank of Thailand ordered the commercial banks to limit their credit expansion in 1984 to 18 per cent. These steps started a chain reaction, bringing a sharp reduction in the funds available, even from the underground money market, and numerous chit funds failed to fulfil their commitments and collapsed. The cash flow problems of a large number of companies increased as did bankruptcies. But the measures had the desired effect: the trade deficit in 1984 fell to about half of what it had been the previous year and inflation was contained, being down to some 4 per cent. In an attempt to soften the blow caused by the limiting of credit expansion to 18 per cent, the government also introduced a system of selective credit control which facilitated the sanctioning of bank funds for loans in priority sectors of the economy.

The reduced business activity following on from the large number of business failures in 1984 may reduce government revenue in 1985 by as much as US$500 million, but Thailand's priorities are clear. In the words of Nukul Prachuabmoh, Governor of the Bank of Thailand:

> If you have to choose between the prospect of letting some small factories go under and the potential situation of Thailand plunging into financial chaos like certain other bankrupt countries such as the Phillipines and then facing the prospect of hundreds of thousands becoming jobless, which would you prefer?

Carrian Holdings, Hong Kong

The case of Carrian Holdings is typical of the intrigue and intricacies of the business system in this unique British colony. Carrian Holdings, a key private company on the fringe of the now defunct Carrian empire, was ordered to be wound up due to the default of another private company, Perak Pioneer. Perak Pioneer owed US$87 million to Carrian Holdings and another US$26 million to other creditors, while its assets were largely shares in defunct companies.

Perak Pioneer, which owned a flat in Butler Towers in Hong Kong (the significance of that fact will emerge later), was partly owned by Chan Chee Kin, the wife of Raymond Sacklyn, the publisher of an investment newsletter called *Target*. The flat was leased to Target Publications and later (1980) sold to some individuals connected with Carrian. Perak acquired more properties and grew, but Carrian began to slip as the result of the failure of a series of transactions in real estate. One of Perak's properties, Butler Towers, mortgaged to the Wing Hang Bank, was sold to Dream Come True Ltd for US$130 million, the bank giving the new owner a 95 per cent mortgage – but Perak's liability to Butler Towers had been extinguished. One wonders who was behind this new company, whose name echoed the fancy names given to many companies in the Carrian Group: Gold Come, Outwit, Extradollar and Smartmoney are typical.

Now the story becomes even more involved. A director of Perak, Helen da Roza, bought a flat in Miami Mansions from the China and South Sea Bank, to which it was mortgaged by Jadial Estates. The flat was the registered address of a director of various Carrian companies such as Extragold and Extradollar, and it had been acquired from Mai Hon Enterprises, which Carrian took over when it went public. Jadial, a wholly-owned subsidiary of Carrian Holdings, was sold a year later (1981) to Carrian's then partner, Eda Investments, now defunct. The Eda Group had as directors the Chung brothers, who were also on the board of Jadial Estates but left in April 1983, giving place to a solicitor, David Pyott. Pyott was also involved with Carrian, since he had been acting for a Malaysian-controlled company, Fleuret Investments, which had offered to buy the Carrian stake in Union Bank and China Underwriters for US$40 million. This transaction was to be the crux of a proposed Carrian debt-rescheduling package. Fleuret's financing for the transaction was to come from BMF, the Carrian Group's largest creditor. The loan was not approved by BMF's supervisory committee in Kuala Lumpur and their representative in Hong Kong, Jalal Ibrahim, turned it down. Jalal was murdered and the BMF chairman Lorrian Osman sanctioned the loan, but the whole deal was still held up by a number of other factors. Perak Pioneer, the Carrian Group and Carrian Holdings all collapsed.

This most complicated story, by its very complication, demonstrates that convoluted financial transactions are no substitute for sound financial policy. The basic cause of disaster was a shortage of funds and that fact had finally to be faced.

Summary

We have discussed in a little detail just a few of the many corporate collapses in the developed world in recent years. The selection has been designed to show that collapse can occur anywhere, in any industry and with any size of company. In each case we have traced the underlying causes of disaster and have seen that every time disaster *could have been averted*. The danger signals were there, but were ignored. When we come to assess *why* these companies failed, we see that it was simple human failings that intervened: pride, jealousy or greed.

References

1. Wright, J. P., *John Z. De Lorean's look inside an automotive giant*, Wright Enterprises, 1979.
2. Morrison, A. M., 'De Lorean's long downhill ride', *Fortune*, **107**, pp. 60–4, 15 Nov. 1982.
3. Peters, T. J. and R. H. Waterman, *In Search of Excellence: Lessons from America's Best-Run Companies*, Harper & Row, 1982.
4. Lee, T., 'Laker Airways – the cash flow truth', *Accountancy*, **93**, 115–16, June 1982.
5. Altman, E. I., *Corporate Bankruptcy in America*, Heath Lexington Books, 1971.
6. Robertson, J., 'Laker Airways – could the collapse have been foreseen?', *Management Accounting*, **62**, 28–31, June 1984.
7. Sricharatchanya, P., 'Dying for a loan', *Far Eastern and Economic Review*, **125**, 49–51, 12 July 1984.

7 The largest democracy is not immune

After looking at a few examples of corporate failure worldwide, we thought it would be helpful to concentrate on one particular country, and chose India, the world's largest democracy. Here, however, we find that company failure is the exception rather than the rule. In a free economy it is broadly true that the survival of the fittest is the order of the day, although governments still intervene from time to time. The unfit collapse and are liquidated or go bankrupt in accordance with the laws of the country concerned. In India, however, the companies that go sick hardly ever die, even when they might well be thought to be terminally ill – if we may pursue our analogy so far. Companies are maintained despite the fact that they are losing money, for the sake of retaining employment. We are not concerned here with the political aspect – the merits or demerits of the policy being pursued – but we do note its results. Company sickness is a peculiarly Indian phenomenon that is now assuming alarming proportions. Almost every day the national newspapers have one or more news items about sick companies – often on the front page.

When is a company 'sick'?

We are concerned principally with industrial companies, either manufacturing or offering a service, since it is these companies that are a major source of employment. When such companies fail to make a profit we are entitled to consider them in trouble. However, it is not unusual for fundamentally healthy companies to incur losses for a year or two, so we should allow some minimum loss period (between, say, one and four years, depending on the nature of the industry) before we start talking of sickness. Perhaps we should make it clear that this use of the word 'sick' is not our own: it is official terminology. Indeed, the Reserve Bank of India has rules about it: a company is termed 'sick' when:

1. It shows a cash loss for the previous year and this situation is likely to continue in the current and next following year and/or
2. there is an imbalance in its financial structure, such as current assets/current liability being less than unity and the debt/equity ratio is rising.[1]

However, this is not a standard definition. Various financial institutions, such as the Industrial Development Bank of India, the Industrial and Credit Corporation of India and the Industrial Financial Corporation, as well as some of the leading banks, each have their own definition of sickness. All such definitions, however, are based upon financial ratios derived from the company's published accounts.

The story in headlines

A random selection of recent headlines on the subject of corporate sickness tells its own tale:

Cause: mismanagement
Flogging a dying horse
High profits: 'Clue' to sickness
It pays to be sick
Kamani Engineering on deathbed
Metal Box up for sale
Putting Titaghur Paper back on its feet
Reviving Rohtas Industries
Shipping Corporation of India in deep waters
Sickness: an All-India phenomenon
Scooters India – Flogging a dying horse
Small scale industries sick units – 50 per cent non-viable
The crunch at Shree Vallabh Glass Works
Stalemate at Binny

Because of the magnitude of the problem in India, as shown in Table 7.1, there has been considerable concern and hence intense activity in this field. This activity

Table 7.1 Public funds locked in sick units, India. This table probably represents only the tip of the iceberg, since advances by other banks and state financial institutions are not included. The data also exclude advances to firms not officially declared 'sick' in accordance with the Reserve Bank of India definition.

As at the end December	Scheduled banks	Financial institutions	TOTAL
1979	16.2	2.8	19.0
1980	18.1	3.3	21.4
1981	20.3	3.9	24.2
1982	25.8	6.0	31.8
1983	29.0	8.0	37.0

(The figure for 1983 is an estimate)

Note: All figures above in billion rupees. The US$ equals approx. 10 rupees.

Source: Centre for Monitoring Indian Economy, Bombay.

has been displayed in three broad fields: the setting up of committees, the holding of several seminars a year on the subject, sponsored by various Chambers of Commerce and other similar institutions, and a steady flow of reports and books. A glance at the *titles* in the Reference section at the end of this chapter will be illuminating.[2]

The literary output on the subject is not confined to India: it is worldwide, as we will see, but most of the activity seems to have been concentrated on the prediction of sickness or collapse. Somewhere along the line we seem to have forgotten something, and the question must be asked: Prediction — but for what purpose? Our purpose has been stated: we see prediction, properly used, as the road to recovery. In order to improve our ability to predict we first review typical case histories, seeking to learn why and how, using here a few case studies from the Indian sector of the world economy.

Binny Limited

This old and well-established firm received a mention in the last of the headlines we quoted earlier: 'Stalemate at Binny'. Binny has two textile mills, at Madras and Bangalore, a garment factory, also at Bangalore, and an engineering works at Madras. The financial progress of the company from 1978 to 1983 is summarized in Table 7.2. We see that sales are rising, but the profit picture is very erratic. Why?

Textiles account for some 80 per cent of the company's turnover and it is true of Binny, as it is true of the textile industry in general in India, that hardly any attention has been paid to modernization. This is undoubtedly the root cause of the present sickness. In 1976 complete modernization of the mills was estimated to cost some US$40 million, but the cash was not there and nothing was done. In 1985, no doubt, it would cost double that. Most of the machinery in use at the mills is between 30 and 40 years old: some even 100 years old,

Table 7.2   **Financial progress of Binny Limited.** A company 'doctor', S. N. Hada, has now been brought in and sales are increasing, while losses are decreasing.

	1978	1979	1980	1981	1982	1983	1984
Sales and other income	743	892	932	622	933	1,062	945
Loss, after interest and depreciation	44	11	35	122	44	10	66

Note: All figures above in million rupees
        US$ = approx 10 rupees
Source: Centre for Monitoring Indian Economy, Bombay

despite the fact that such machinery is normally obsolescent after 15 to 20 years. Old machinery, apart from being far less productive than that now available and in use by the trade, requires considerable maintenance, with the result that nearly one-third of the workforce is engaged in maintenance. There have also been many labour problems, the chief of them being absenteeism, ranging on average between 18 and 20 per cent but at times as high as 40 per cent. There is a productivity bonus scheme but this is masked by a very high 'dearness allow-ance' (in effect, an inflation correction based on published indices) running at some 70 per cent of total wages and paid irrespective of productivity. This has led to gross indiscipline, manifest in many ways but particularly through the high level of absenteeism. As always in a sinking ship, morale is low and there is no feeling of involvement at any level. But, with a workforce of some 8000, the state government does not wish the mills to close, even although the company is incurring a continuing loss – see Table 7.2. The majority of the shares are held by the financial institutions, who nominate eight of the nine directors on the board, yet directors come and go: 30 have come and gone in the past five years.

Can Binny recover? No doubt recovery is still possible, but drastic financial restructuring would be required, together with a massive investment programme for the rehabilitation of the mills. But then many, many jobs would inevitably disappear: nearly all the maintenance workers for a start. The financial institu-tions, with some US\$52 million invested to little purpose in recent years, are anxious to cut their losses. The key institution in this case, the Industrial Develop-ment Bank of India, is against further investment, its view being that the company is no longer viable. But what is 'viable' in such a context?

Coal India

This is a white elephant in the public sector, charged with the operation of the nationalized coal industry. It is the third largest public sector company in India, with a workforce of some 630000 and an annual wage bill of the order of US\$800 million. The balance sheet for the year ending 31 March 1983 presents the following dismal picture:

US\$ (*millions*)

Total share capital	1,200
Reserves	300
Loans	2,100
Accumulated debit balance	900

What is the problem? No, that is the wrong question. The balance sheet shouts the problem aloud. The real question is: Why is the company in this parlous state? Mr M. S. Gujral, who took over as chairman in August 1983, declares:

> There were basically two things wrong: men and machines. I first had to discipline the men because there was an all-pervasive cancer of indiscipline.

Second, I had to make sure that Rs. 2000 Crore [approx. US$2 billion] of expensive equipment was used productively.

The new chairman is determined to wipe out the coalfield Mafia and to improve Coal India's efficiency. He aims to do better than the previous best in every area. Can he? Perhaps, but the going will not be easy. The internal Mafia can be eliminated by legal, legitimate methods, provided the political leadership in the states and at the centre show conviction and have the will to tackle the problem. But will they?

Meanwhile, Gujral is getting on with his task. Several thousand workers have been suspended or charge-sheeted, a substantial portion of the pithead stocks have been moved and wagons are being loaded faster. His previous position as chairman of the Railway Board is a great help here. The man-days lost are down from 1 million in 1982–83 to 200 000 in 1983–84, while lightning strikes have fallen from 10–20 a month down to only one or two. Certainly we have the 'proof of the pudding': production is at last running higher than target, perhaps for the first time ever. But Gujral still has a long way to go: he has to fight rackets that spread all the way from the mine to the consumer, and cope with the frequent wild-cat strikes that are perhaps the biggest weapon of the Mafia.

We may have to wait some five years to learn whether Gujral has succeeded, but the indications are good. He has shown firmness and upholds sound principles of business conduct, although these may have to be supplemented by a 'healing touch'. The political will is the key – the new, young Rajiv Ghandi government has it.

Hindustan Steelworks Construction Limited

This company, the largest in the public sector in the field of construction, with an annual turnover of US$160 million and a workforce of some 25000, is in trouble, but perhaps through no fault of its own. The company was set up in 1964 to cater to the needs of the steel industry. But the company has been crippled by a lack of orders, presumably with the knowledge and approval of the Union Ministry of Steel and Mines, supported by the central and state political leadership. As a result, most of the company's honest and efficient technocrats and administrators have left, thus adding further to its misfortunes. Table 7.3 tells the whole sad story. With accumulated losses of US$64 million to set against its paid-up capital of US$20 million, the company needs a minimum of US$200 million in orders yearly to survive, but is only getting a third of that. Thus nearly half of the workforce is surplus to requirements, but their wage bill of US$15 million a year will still be paid, unless . . .

Just as HSCL was set up to serve the steel plants, so the National Construction Corporation was set up to implement housing projects and the National Power Construction Corporation was set up to serve the power and irrigation sectors of the economy. Yet in practice these three construction companies, themselves public sector companies, are having to fight for orders from that same public sector in the face of cut-throat competition from the private sector. HSCL built up its workforce to some 26000 in the 1970s in order to cater for the increased workload coming from the Bokaro steel plant. Then, under pressure from the unions, that entire workforce was confirmed as permanent staff, even though the current convention with respect to construction workers was that they were hired and fired for each construction project. Later, as the construction workers employed at one construction site refused to be transferred to another, a large number of workers were being paid to be idle. Lack of orders from the steel mills added to this artificial burden.

The problems that confront this company are primarily political in origin but, once trouble has invaded a company, the sickness grows within. The morale of the employees falls at all levels, productivity plummets and all the problems are compounded. The company, and the industry, must be left to fend for itself and not be manipulated politically. Only then can it be brought back to health. Meanwhile turnover is static, but losses are mounting.

Table 7.3   The sad story of HSCL, in figures. The breakeven for sales is 2100 million Rs per year and orders in hand offer no prospect of this being reached. The wind-up of this company is now feared.

Year	1979–80	1980–81	1981–82	1982–83	1983–84
Sales and other income	1303	1561	1589	1620	1570
Loss after interest and depreciation	65	334	119	120	160

Note: All figures in million rupees
        US$ = approx 10 rupees
Source: Centre for Monitoring Indian Economy, Bombay

Metal Box for sale

This is the title of a special report on the downhill journey of this sleeping giant in the packaging field. The company was started in India in 1933, at Calcutta. Initially it had a monopoly in its products in India and earned very high profits. The paid-up capital of Rs900000 (one US$ roughly equals Rs10) in 1933 increased to Rs5 million in the first decade of operation and to Rs30 million in the next, mainly through issues of bonus and rights shares. By 1974 the figure was Rs70 million, but then the British holding was reduced to 60 per cent during the process of 'indianization'. The present equity base is Rs94 million, with a 40 per cent foreign holding: control is in Indian hands. Table 7.4 presents the status of the company today: it has gone into the red. The company is in financial

Table 7.4   Metal Box goes down and down. The management of Metal Box was questioned extensively at an extraordinary general meeting in 1983, but no improvement is in sight.

	1979–80	1980–81	1981–82	1982–83	1983–84
Sales and other income	1347*	1113	1263	1435	1290
Net Profit ( ) = Loss	57	23	10	(22)	(99)
Dividend (%)	14	12	8	–	–

Note: Figures for sales in million rupees
      US$ = approx 10 rupees
* Figures cover 18-month period
Source: Centre for Monitoring Indian Economy, Bombay

distress, largely due to bad management, but an embarassed silence is maintained about this particular crisis. The company did get a headline in the financial press when its ball-bearing factory was up for sale at about Rs250 million. Why was it selling? Was this a 'distress sale', designed to save a sinking ship?

The basic business of the company is in packaging products: tin containers, pilfer-proof metal closures, crown corks, collapsible metal tubes for toothpaste, paper and plastic packaging. Metal Box diversified into the manufacture of packaging machinery and offset printing machines: an attempt at 'vertical integration'. The ball-bearing factory, however, was a venture into an entirely different field, launched with much publicity. This step violated one of the eight tenets for excellence in management that we quoted in Chapter 3. The best companies 'stick to their knitting' or, to put the point conversely, they never acquire a business they don't know how to run.

Metal Box is perhaps the only company in India with such a comprehensive range of containers and packaging products. The new venture was only 5 per cent of its total sales of some US$135 million in 1982, when the slide into the red started, yet we are convinced that it was that 'sore thumb' that was at the root of it all. The packaging market was expanding and Metal Box had a head start over all its competitors, yet it lost ground steadily. Its management was far too slow in adjusting to and acting in relation to the changing situation. The overheads remained high and the sales staff were seen as high-handed and arrogant. Union/management relations deteriorated, while some 15 per cent of both workers and staff were 'allowed to retire', adding the burden of the compensation that had to be paid to these employees. It was this that caused the company to slip into the red in 1976, but it returned to the dividend just two years later.

There is no doubt that the ball-bearing factory project was the last straw. The cost of the project escalated by some 25 per cent, to Rs250 million, there were prolonged teething troubles and the capital utilization was dismal. Above all, the quality of the product was so poor that it was unacceptable in the market. Meanwhile the interest burden resulting from the investment nearly bled the company to death. Expert commentators blame this failure on managing director P. K. Nanda, who piloted the project through, keeping its execution entirely to himself. The plant and machinery are said to be defective; the factory has now been sold to Tata. In addition, the paper and plastics plant at Calcutta, said to be losing some Rs 10 million a year, has been closed down. In fact, Metal Box may well be up for sale, with Tata as a likely buyer. They have a vested interest, as manufacturers of tinplate and a major supplier of this raw material to Metal Box.

Why is Metal Box – in India – where it now is? The main factors are very clear: resistance to change, taking on a major construction project in a new field and poor, yet complacent management. They looked back instead of looking forward. As a consequence there has been an exodus among top management, resulting in a leadership crisis. A new managing director, Kuldip Puri, was appointed in April 1984, but it does not seem that he will be able to pull Metal Box out of trouble. Things may well have gone too far.

Summary

We have now extended our case studies from the developed to a developing country, taking India as a typical example. This is all necessary background material if we are to get sickness in industry into perspective. Our case studies come from both the public and the private sector, from industries as diverse as coal, steel, textiles and packaging. We have seen that while political attitudes may well prevent a sick company from collapsing, all the key management factors we have enumerated still dominate. A good manager at the head may redeem the situation if he is brought in early enough: bad management always brings failure eventually.

References

1. Bidani, S. N. and P. K. Mitra, *Industrial Sickness – Identification and Rehabilitation* (2nd edn), Vision Books, 1983.
2. Sarathi, V., *Company Failure in India*, New Heights Publishers, 1968; Simha, S. L. N., *Sickness of Industrial Units*, Institute for Financial Management and Research, 1977; Lal, S., *How to Protect Industrial Sickness – Symptoms and Rehabilitation*, Navrang, 1979; Gupta, L. C., *Financial Ratios as Forewarning Indicators of Corporate Sickness*, 1979; *Industrial Credit and Investment Corporation of India*, Booklet: 'Problem projects and their rehabilitation', *Industrial Credit and Investment Corporation of India*, 1977; National Council of Applied and Economic Research, *A Study of Industrial Sickness*, Punjab National Bank; Chakraworty, S. K. and P. K. Sen, *Industrial*

Sickness and Revival in India — Essays, Cases and Debates, Indian Institute of Management, 1980; Kaveri, V. S., *How to Diagnose, Prevent and Cure Industrial Sickness,* Sultan Chand, 1983; Padaki, V. and V. Shanbhag, *Industrial Sickness — the Challenge in Indian Textiles,* Ahmedabad Textile Industry Research Association, 1984.

8 The fight for survival

Although we have ranged far and wide across the world, looking at companies in trouble, we also want to diversify in terms of the *causes* of failure. So far these causes have been common to all. The context may be different, and government or bank intervention may cause failure to come later rather than sooner, but some form of mismanagement is always the root of the trouble.

We thought that some European examples would be useful, so we have taken case studies from France, West Germany, Sweden and Switzerland. These are all financially stable countries, yet by no means immune to company failure. Finally in this chapter we shall go to China, to take an example quite out of the common run, although it is likely to be copied.

Combine and survive

This phrase was a banner headline above an article dealing with French construction firms and the way in which they were 'falling into one another's arms' in order to keep in business. Dr Schumacher's well-known saying, 'small is beautiful', is contradicted by the French construction industry. This is due in part to the fact that construction projects themselves are growing ever bigger. This means that construction companies have been forming consortia to cope with major projects for some years now. Such consortia were normally formed only for the duration of the project, and the association ended once the project was completed, but in France the construction companies are joining together and forming ever larger companies on a permanent basis. While this provides a sounder managerial and financial base for coping with the major project, the depressed economy is also a powerful factor.

For instance. following French government approval of the takeover of Colas, a loss-making road builder, by the Société Chimique Routière et d'Entreprise Générale (SCREG), that group is now the largest civil engineering group in France, with an annual turnover exceeding US$3 billion.

Construction activity in France has been running at a low level for some time, with resultant intense competition. The smaller French construction companies were unable to compete with the major construction companies operating across Europe, from home offices in the US or Japan. The only solution, it seems, was to match them in size. So, in 1982, SGE. a part of Compagnie Générale d'Electricité (CGE) took control of Cochery, a road building company, thus becoming the largest French civil engineering group at that time. But the company did not stop there. It went on to merge with the Sainrapt et Brich public works group, a group which itself had been in the making since 1980. Then the French government took a hand. At the end of 1982 it called upon Spie Batignolles and the French Coal Board's construction division to each take a 40 per cent stake in and then plan the restructure of another major construction firm, Coignet.

Thus far the background. We see a general trend towards acquisition, amalgamation and merger. When we look at the acquisition of Colas by SCREG we get a very interesting insight into the takeover mentality. The firm of Colas was not doing well at home and was in serious trouble abroad. It had major contracts in Algeria, Newfoundland and Nigeria which were proving to be lossmakers. The company had also failed in its efforts to diversify as a solution to its problems. Another major – and profitable – private construction firm, Bouygues, had considered rescuing Colas, but abandoned the idea as a potential 'bad bargain'. SCREG thought otherwise. The acquisition of Colas would double its turnover, and this was seen as an essential element of successful competition in the overseas market, particularly Africa and the Middle East. Time alone will tell whether the strategy adopted will prove successful in the long term, but meanwhile the total workload available in the Third World has been diminishing.

The situation is interesting and can afford a lesson. We see companies on the verge of disaster and apparently with little to offer acquired to build up turnover, in the belief that size is an essential factor in the ability to compete for the large projects available worldwide. Thus work is secured that would otherwise be lost. The approach seems logical and demonstrates a factor worth assessment, but only time will tell us whether the strategy is sound in the long term.

An almighty crash

In August 1982 the West German corporation AEG-Telefunken collapsed. The experts said – once it had happened – that the collapse had been 'on the cards' for a decade or more. They also said that the company had brought about its own collapse. AEG-Telefunken, at the time of its collapse the seventh largest corporation in West Germany, was built up on the optimism of the 1950s and 1960s, so that its decision to appeal to the courts (in August 1982) for relief from three-fifths of its then unspecified debts marked the passing of an era. For much of that time the company had around its neck the albatross of its 40 per cent share in Kraftwerk-Union, the nuclear construction consortium. It succeeded in selling its interest to Siemens in 1978, but its owning the company is a classic illustration of failure to 'stay with the knitting'.

AEG is especially interesting because it was operating in an area of high technology that was and still is growing rapidly worldwide. The company seems to have appreciated the potentialities of the situation, but perhaps went too far. It determined, it seems, to be represented in every relevant field, willy-nilly. To achieve that, it invested a great deal of time and money in research and product development. The costs became exorbitant, and a *technological* conglomerate was found to be very hard to manage efficiently.

We begin to see where the trouble lay when we start to compare AEG with Siemens, another West German company in the same business and therefore the obvious analogue. AEG was run by accountants, while Siemens' technologists ruled the roost. The accountants were very skilled at raising extra capital – no less than DM 1000 million in 1979 from the West German banks, for example – but they were much less adept at matching their technical ambitions to the realities of the marketplace. Once in trouble, they applied the usual remedy: they sought to sell off parts of the business and to form joint ventures with other companies, such as Bosch in the field of telecommunications. These efforts at re-formation failed to redeem the situation. Why? The most obvious problem was that AEG was not technically outstanding in any of the fields in which it sought to succeed. A company working in the field of high technology will only succeed through technical excellence. Anything less is but to court failure, however big the company. Sheer size is no help: the end of AEG proves that.

It is interesting to note that in a country famed for its harmonious industrial relations since the Second World War, one of the impediments to the reconstruction of AEG has been the resistance of the labour unions to the threat of redundancy. Here we have another lesson. We see the unions less compliant, less willing to go along with the needs of their employer, once the climate has changed and they are no longer riding happily on an 'economic miracle'. It is interesting to speculate as to the way things might change, even in Japan, that classic in the field of employer/labour co-operation, once the wind of change starts blowing strongly in the Japanese economy.

AEG has to shed at least 40 000 of its 100 000 enployees in West Germany, and perhaps an even greater proportion of its 20 000 or so employees elsewhere in the world. With the unions represented on the board of AEG, as is required by law in West Germany, they are behaving predictably. We do not need to follow the story to the end to know what is in store. The end is inevitable. But, as we mentioned in Chapter 1, when considering the impact of the bankruptcy laws in various countries, it was above all the banks who lost out. Following reorganization, the shares of the company are back in favour, as shown in Fig. 8.1.

The consequences are widespread. Many will lose their jobs, others will lose a large part of their investment in the company, while a host of small companies working as suppliers to AEG will be looking desperately for new business. On the other hand, its competitors will find their markets more buoyant than they were, for the business that AEG is compelled to shed will be picked up by others in due course – and of course, some of those who lose their jobs will find re-employment elsewhere as well. But the legend of West German industrial astuteness has been gravely tarnished.

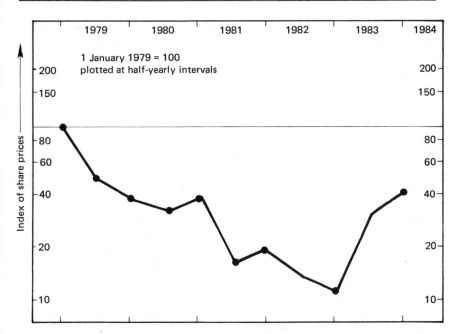

Figure 8.1   The AEG record. *Following a steady fall over some four years, the price of AEG shares rose sharply in the market from the beginning of 1983.* (Source: *Economist*)

The basic question for us is: how was the turnaround accomplished. Dyson and Wilkes attribute it, above all, to a remarkable capacity for self-organization within the West German industry.[1] They further point out the role played by the banks, who insulate the government from such problems, and the strong emphasis on an export-orientated modernization policy. The crisis occurred despite the strong position held by the West German electrical industry in world markets and its ability to maintain that position even after the crisis of 1973. Nevertheless, it was competition on the world market that led to the final crisis. The Japanese and other newly industrialized countries, active in domestic appliances, TV, video and radios, posed a threat which AEG failed to face. It should have switched its production to the high-value and profitable manufacture of data processing equipment. Once again, there was a failure to face up to and adapt to the changing world scene.

The Scandinavian scene

The story has been told of an old family company whose results were worsening by the year. Its equity was running out and the company was up for sale, but there were no buyers.[2] Our informant was with the Norwegian ASV Group, which includes the Nordisk Aluminium Company. The ASV Group acted as management consultants in a bid to rescue the company and a certain L.T. Janzen acted as chairman during the rescue bid. Once again we have a classic situation: a new chief executive taking over.

The company had four products, of which two were long established, while the other two were relatively new. We shall call them A, B. C and D. One problem was that the company was not as yet fully equipped to deal with one of the newer products, D. While the sales of the older products were rather erratic, fluctuating widely from year to year, earnings from the two newer products were much more stable. An analysis of the market situation showed that if the company were to be brought back from the brink, it would be wise to rearrange the priorities and concentrate on the two new products. This would bring the highest return on sales and increase the turnover ratio on the capital employed. However, the preferences had to be switched, because the production of D, though yielding the best return, demanded more capital, which was not immediately available. However, plans were made to create a new facility for the production of D. The strategy for rescue proved highly successful and the results over the next four years were so impressive that loans could be secured, enabling the new plant to be put into operation in the fifth year.

The lessons? We see a plan: a company strategy is developed following assessment of the situation. We have:

A judicial selection of products
Adoption of the route that will bring early profits
Co-ordination of plan, budget and control procedures
Decisive action, if original budget requirements cannot be met.

The control procedures that were followed during the rescue operation were in line with those put forward in an earlier paper by Janzen which raised the question: Why long-range planning?[3] The answer: because it brings substantial long-term benefits. Janzen was able to quantify the benefits that resulted from proper planning and the consequent reorganization, thus:

Factors	*Possible change through planning*
Investment in goods	
rather than sales	−50
Delivery time	−45
Administrative costs	−36
Purchase price	−15
Efficiency	+45
Resulting profit	+100

Thus profits can be doubled. The cost of the exercise? A mere 2 per cent, showing an enormous benefit/cost ratio.

The drastic changes proposed to accomplish the rescue were not easy to implement, but they never are. That is very often why the company is in trouble:

those in charge lack the resolution to take the necessary steps, even when they see what is required, so almost invariably an outsider has to come in to revolutionize the position. He looks a miracle worker, but he is able to be resolute because he is detached. In the present case there was strong resistance to the idea of stopping the manufacture of two long-established products (A and B) and concentrating, at least initially, on only one product (C). It looked very like 'putting all your eggs in one basket'. To convince both management and workers that the proposed strategy would work, the facts and figures had to be set before them. Why convince them? Because while the changes could have been imposed, an enthusiastic and co-operative management and workforce is a great gain. The losses were transformed into profits, as illustrated in Fig. 8.2. A long-established

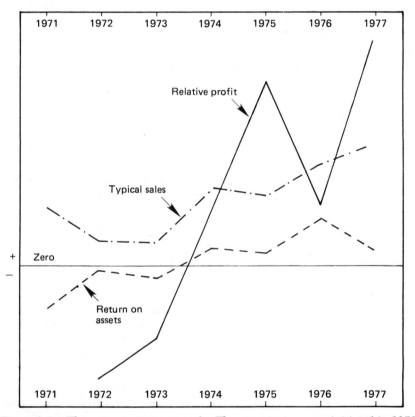

Figure 8.2   The new strategy succeeds. *The new strategy was initiated in 1972. The new plant came on stream in 1976. The impact is clear. The figures are to indicate the trend only, so no scale is given. The drop in return on assets (considered as a percentage) in 1977 comes because the considerable increase in assets had not yet started to yield results. (With thanks to Mr L. T. Janzen, see Ref.2)*

family company, its name a household word in Sweden, has been able to survive, but it is now selling a very different product. Yet the approach taken to achieve this transformation was quite simple and straightforward: no sophisticated tools or techniques were employed. A corporate plan was developed following analysis of the situation. The lesson: a sound corporate plan is essential to success, an aspect of company management that we take up in detail in Chapter 17.

A Swiss watch

Swiss watches are noted for their precision and efficiency and at one time the Swiss watch industry dominated world markets. But the Swiss are also noted for their resistance to change — to change of almost any sort, technological or social. It was their resistance to change that brought the Swiss watch industry to its knees.

What happened? The Japanese and the entrepreneurs in Hong Kong, relative newcomers to the manufacture of watches, took nearly 40 per cent of the world market by introducing relatively cheap battery-operated watches. René Retornaz, the head of the Swiss Watchmakers Federation, said: 'We were just too confident.' What he meant was that, knowing their status, they assumed that they could not be touched. But they could be and they were. For mere survival the industry needed a major injection of both money and morale.

The money, some US$500 million, came from a group of five Swiss banks and the morale from the industry. The industry, working as a team, developed and then produced a new, cheap battery-operated plastic watch built on robot-run assembly lines. The number of separate parts in the watch were reduced from the usual 90 to around 50. The new design, sleek and durable, backed by the Swiss reputation for reliability, gained immediate acceptance on the market, selling at around US$25, against a cost price of around US$10. First introduced to the market early in 1983, nearly a million were sold within nine months. To win popular appeal, the watch was advertised as a classy 'second watch', a fashion accessory rather than a utility. It was made available in a wide variety of dials, styles and colours: a watch to match every dress was the theme. Of course, by implication, the first watch, the utility item, should still be the conventional Swiss watch, guaranteed to work under all conditions, since this new watch was so 'un-Swiss'. It seems, indeed, that in the face of the low-priced watch, very highly priced watches, sold on craftsmanship still have a market.

Before the introduction of the new product the Swiss share of the world market had fallen from some 70 per cent to 20 per cent. The new product has initially provided more of a boost to morale than to market share, but the future is much brighter than it was. Once again we see the need for drastic change to meet changing conditions. The successful company avoids even getting near the brink by seeing change on the way and adjusting to meet it.

Seattle goes to Shanghai

In a transformation of another kind Shanghai Steel Structure Factory bought the steel fabrication plant of the Isaacson Steel Company of Seattle 'lock, stock and barrel'. They bought the entire plant, including all spares, and shipped it from California late in 1983. Everything went, from a numerically-controlled computer-assisted multiple spindle drill to an old-fashioned porcelain commode. Also included in the purchase price was the provision of a team of 11 from the Isaacson Steel Company, to work in Shanghai for three months supervising plant erection and training the Chinese plant operatives. The plant now manufactures steel girders and other heavy construction products. While the training process was time-consuming and had its difficulties, since it was all new to the Chinese workers, nevertheless it was a viable project.

The background to this remarkable achievement, the transfer of a complete factory, lies in the fact that the Seattle plant was proving uneconomic, despite its modern design. Labour costs and hence operating costs were high and there was intense competition from South Korean cheap steel. The company was brought to a state of desperation when they lost an order for the supply of steel for a 76-storey office building in Seattle itself to the South Koreans. This led to the fateful decision to close the plant in June 1983. No US buyer would have been willing to pay an appropriate price for the company on a takeover basis and to sell off the plant piecemeal would have brought very little, but when the Chinese came on the scene, they bought a modern fabricating plant which, although no longer competitive in the US market, was capable of great things in the Chinese market.

This may not be the only purchase of its type. The Chinese delegation that negotiated the purchase of the Seattle plant have indicated interest in acquiring, for instance, the Wisconsin Steel Company's plant, part of the Kaiser facilities. This plant produces slab steel. China has some US$17 billion in foreign exchange reserves, for which it is seeking appropriate use. At present invested in the Eurocurrency money market and bringing in a poor return, it could be much more profitable invested in capital equipment. In a search for suitable opportunities the Shanghai Foreign Trade Corporation has set up offices in far-flung places, such as San Mateo in California and Manhattan in New York. The Chinese market is insatiable, in need of an enormous investment in plant and equipment. What makes the Seattle deal unique is the purchase of an operating entity, rather than buying a new plant, designed and built by some construction contractor. Such an approach gets them into production in the shortest possible time and may well prove a very cheap approach. Both parties gain, since in our example the plant was losing money.

The lesson here for us lies in the realization that there is more than one solution to the problem of a declining market. Here the plant was moved to the market, since nothing could be done about the existing market.

Summary

We have seen that even when it is facing imminent collapse a company can still be the subject of a turnaround. While there are no ready answers, there are some common features to turnaround policy. At the same time, turnaround is not the only answer. The sell-out is another solution – called an acquisition from the other side of the fence. When we move a plant from Seattle to Shanghai acquisition takes on a whole new meaning.

We have seen that a strategy has to be formulated and followed with persistence. Facilities, usually those outside the basic business of the company, can be sold off with effect but at the same time acquisition, even of unprofitable companies, is not out of the question if it is part of a consistent strategy.

References

1. Dyson, K. and S. Wilks (eds), *Industrial Crisis – A Comparative Study of the State and Industry*, Martin Robertson, 1983.
2. Janzen, L. T., 'Company rescue – an example', *Long Range Planning*, **16**, 88–93, December 1983, and personal correspondence.
3. Janzen, L. T., 'Systematic planning and reorganisation', *Long Range Planning*, **4**, 58–62, December 1971.

9 One man can make the difference

Turnaround is a crucial part of any study of corporate failure. Faced with a company in a state of crisis, there are only two serious possibilities: let it die, or set it on the road to recovery. We ignore the road taken so often in India, as discussed in Chapter 7: that of maintaining the company in a state of chronic sickness. 'Kill or cure' is our answer. There is no doubt that in many cases it is best to let nature take its course, but there are times when the effort that is required to bring a company back from the brink is well worth while. The problem lies in deciding when it is indeed a worthwhile effort; each case has to be studied in depth to get the answer to that question.

Turnaround strategy

Let us assume here that we have a company where we feel that the effort is worth while. How does one go about it? The method adopted depends, once again, on the specific case, and the turnaround strategy has to be tailored as appropriate. However, attempts have been made to set up guidelines. One example is to be found in a book most appropriately titled: *How to Turn Around a Financially Troubled Company*.[1] The author is both a teacher and a consultant and speaks from first-hand experience. While protecting the confidentiality of his clients, he has managed to write a manual on turnaround that lays down some general principles and gives practical advice on the road to survival – or revival.

The best way to learn how to approach the problem of turnaround is to consider cases and see how it works out in practice. We shall therefore begin with a look at the work of Sir Michael Edwardes, who shot into the headlines when he took up the task of bringing about the recovery of British Leyland, a government-owned conglomerate operating in many areas of the automotive industry. The British Leyland Group (BL) manufactured a wide range of motor cars (automobiles to the American world), buses, lorries and automotive parts. We are fortunate in having this story straight from the 'horse's mouth', since Sir Michael has written a book describing his five years with BL.[2] We look at his work with British Leyland in detail in Chapter 10, in the section titled 'An apocalyptic experience'.

79

Fresh fields to conquer

Following his experience with British Leyland, Sir Michael Edwardes is now a specialist in turnarounds. After a brief interlude with ICL, whom we shall be looking at later in this chapter, he has gone to Dunlop. That company's bankers, 46 in all, working on a rescue package, had insisted on Sir Michael's appointment as a condition of implementing the financial reconstruction necessary to keep Dunlop alive.[3] The outgoing chairman, Sir Maurice Hodgson, who made it clear that he thought Sir Michael was not the man for the job, has resigned, although he had been asked by the banks to stay until the reconstruction scheme was complete. 'It did not seem to me a sensible thing to do under the circumstances', he said, because 'there might be two of us whose views on the issues would not be coincident.' So he is giving Sir Michael the 'total freedom of action which he wants'.

Sir Michael, in his turn, has made virtually a clean sweep of the Dunlop Holdings board, removing all the executive directors and all the British non-executive directors. Only two non-executive nominees of the Malaysian share-holders, who hold 26 per cent of the Dunlop equity, have survived.

Dunlop in distress

At one time a leader in the world tyre industry, Dunlop has manifestly been in trouble for years. The old board had been trying to sell off various assets in order to improve its debt/equity ratio, as illustrated in Fig. 9.1, under pressure from the bankers. Despite a steady increase in turnover, its losses have been mounting, (Fig. 9.2), with tyre sales representing nearly 60 per cent of that turnover. Indeed, the company's problems have largely stemmed from the tyre division, now sold off. Caught on the hop by Michelin's introduction of the radial car tyre, it never managed to recover its position, despite huge injections of capital. As a result of the attempt to bolster up the tyre division, the highly successful areas, such as the aviation division, have been starved of investment. The outgoing chairman now declares that Dunlop's finances were in any case improving, its net total indebtedness having fallen by £42 million during 1984, to £385 million. In addition, he said, the company was about to complete a major disposal that would practically complete the internal restructuring being demanded by the banks. In other words, 'we've done the job: we don't need Sir Michael'. But the banks quite patently think otherwise, and issued their ultimatum.

The reaction of the various unions involved is very interesting and in marked contrast to the first reaction at British Leyland. They want to talk, but they make no threats. For instance, it is evident that big staff shakeups are coming. The company has a technology division in Birmingham which has now been closed with a loss of of some 250 staff. The operations are being decentralized into seven profit centres, each separately accountable, becoming a limited company. This is the standard routine for improving efficiency, and has been carried

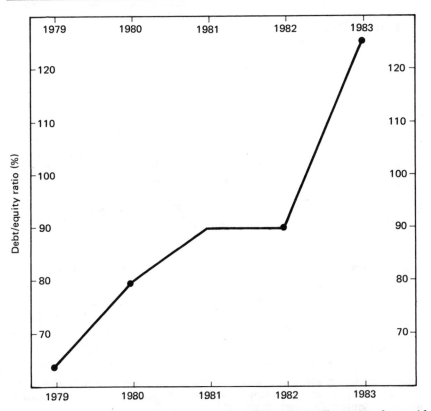

Figure 9.1   The Dunlop debt/equity ratio. *This graph illustrates the rapid growth in the debt/equity ratio for Dunlop.* **(**Source: *Company report)*

out by the various product companies worldwide. The department was set up only some five years ago from Dunlop's old research centre, but the union representatives, when told what was in prospect, only requested 'a consultative meeting with senior managers and directors': 'We are disappointed and more than a little shocked and we want to get some more details from the company before we decide what to do.'[4] This story has reached a surprising conclusion in that Dunlop has finally been taken over by BTR, one of Britain's largest, fastest growing and broad-based conglomerates. The merger deal came as a surprise to the banks, but credit must go to Sir Michael Edwardes, who carried the day by forcing BTR to revise its original offer very substantially in Dunlop's favour.

High technology in trouble

So far we have been looking at companies in long established industries, but the very newest of industries, full of innovation and growing rapidly, especially in

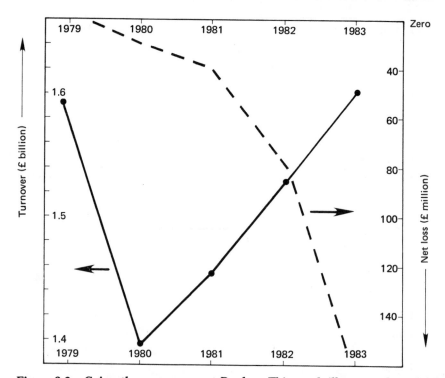

Figure 9.2   Going the wrong way at Dunlop. *This graph illustrates that while turnover was growing quite rapidly, losses were also mounting, a disastrous situation.* (Source: *Company accounts*)

the UK, still has its 'problem children'. In 1979 ICL had 18 per cent of the home market, while its arch rival, IBM, had 24 per cent. IBM, reaching out and marketing aggressively, managed to secure major government orders, beating ICL to a US$12 million contract for computers for the Vehicle Licensing Centre being established at Swansea in South Wales. With this handicap, one could well ask what chance ICL had in the global market. None?

ICL thought otherwise. It borrowed heavily, reaching a debt/equity ratio of 1.3 in 1981, in an effort to expand its product line, but the timing was wrong. Recession set in shortly afterwards and the pre-tax profits plunged to a loss of US$90 million, compared with a profit of US$60 million the year before (see Fig. 9.3). It took a government rescue in the form of a loan of US$450 million to save the company, at least for the time being. Two new executives were appointed in 1982 and the company came back into the black in 1982 with a pre-tax profit of US$40 million, which was nearly doubled in the following year (Fig. 9.3). Are its troubles over? That is doubtful, for Graham Week, an analyst

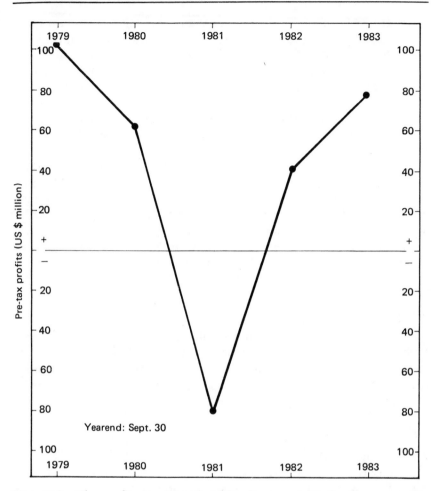

Figure 9.3   The profits turnaround at ICL. *Pre-tax profits for the year ending 30 September, from 1979 to 1983. (*Source: *Company accounts)*

with a London firm of stockbrokers, cautions: 'ICL's future is still uncertain. In this highly competitive industry, it has to run very hard just to stand still.'

How was this dramatic turnaround accomplished? The two new executives were responsible. Sir Christophor Laidlaw, formerly deputy chairman of British Petroleum, took over as chairman, supported by a young (36-year-old) managing director, Robb Wilmot, who had come from the British subsidiary of Texas Instruments. Sir Christophor was able to raise money on the London stock market, thus cutting down the equity/debt ratio to 0.8. Wilmot cut the workforce by about a third, bringing it down to some 23 000, and slashed costs all round. He also broadened ICL's marketing strategy by adding independent dealers to its own retail stores. Developments continue. Mainframe computers constitute some 60 per cent of ICL's total business and a new generation is soon to be launched. The company has also moved firmly into the desk-top computer market with, most recently, an advanced telephone-cum-terminal, the One per Desk, which commentators viewed as one of the industry's most revolutionary products of 1984. What is more, ICL was moving rapidly back into profit, with 1984 profits ahead even of City expectations at £56 million (say US$75 million). But all this has been overshadowed by a takeover.

We said earlier that a frequent followup to a turnaround is a takeover, and this is what happened to ICL. A bid from Standard Telephones and Cables (STC) came out of the blue and succeeded. STC were seeking to expand their international operations and to broaden their product and service range to cover the converging fields of computing and telecommunications. They saw the ICL operation as a logical strategic extension to their activities. STC have some 30 000 employees, and is among the top ten British electronics companies.

The best company

STC is an interesting company. It celebrated its centenary in 1983, but some twelve years ago was itself in real need of a turnaround. Sir Kenneth Corfield took over as chairman and chief executive and transformed its managerial approach. This was first presented to the employees in 1974 and developed in consultation with them over the next four years. Four main priorities were identified:

1. Be efficient and profitable, giving good service to the customers
2. Do business straight and honestly
3. Treat all employees with respect and help them develop and contribute fully
4. Have an open and participative style of management

Yes, we know you've heard it all before, but here it is being put into practice. The company has published a booklet, available to all employees, with the title: *The Best Company Book*, encapsulating all these ideas. The foreword, by Sir Kenneth Corfield, includes the following statement:

> It is almost nine years since we set ourselves the aim of being the Best Company in the United Kingdom. It is for others to judge the extent to which we have succeeded or failed. What is certain, however, is that the Best Company Book is a constant challenge to us to live up to our ideals.
>
> (November 1983 edition)

We cannot quote from the booklet at any length, but it opens with a chapter headed 'Overall Objectives'. This talks of 'profit' as a objective, enabling the company to meet its responsibilities to its shareholders, employees, customers and suppliers, and to the community as a whole. Innovation is another objective. Ideas for new and improved products, new applications of technology and improvements in manufacturing skills and efficiency are to be encouraged. This goes hand in hand with a recognition that full consideration must be given to both problems and opportunities before entering new fields, while accepting that properly quantified risks must sometimes be taken.

Another outstanding feature in STC management practice is that managers from all over STC gather together once a year to learn about the company's achievements and intentions for the future. A photograph of one such occasion, published in the 1983 Annual Report, shows a vast auditorium filled with people, and facing them from the stage some dozen executives. A report, known as the MIM report, is issued of each such meeting. We asked for a copy, so as to get an idea of the scope of such a meeting and the degree of participation from the floor, but were told that such reports are for internal circulation only. Acquisition is a feature in STC policy. In the year preceding their acquisition of ICL (1983) they acquired IAL from British Airways, IDEC, Semiconductors and Telebank Television Rentals from ITT; Celdis Ltd, a distributor of semiconductors, connectors and systems products; Best and May Ltd, an electrical distributor, and the capacitor operations of Union Carbide UK Ltd. Abroad, it exchanged contracts to purchase the tantalum capacitors factory of Standard Electrik Lorenz in Germany and Diode France, an electronic components distributor in the Paris area. It also acquired Celdis SA in France, yet another components distributor. This is called 'vertical integration'. Thus far STC.

Sylvania & Laxman

While turnarounds in the West are usually accompanied by radical surgery, a drastic cut in the workforce and a change of the entire top management, such measures are difficult in the Indian context because of the cultural, socio-economic and legal constraints that exist there.[5] As a result, the turnaround is less costly in human terms, yet it can still lead to long-term strength in the organization. A study of nine such cases leads to two considerations that we do not meet in a Western context, namely:

To convince creditors, bankers, government, union and owners to bear with you during the turnaround period and seek their full co-operation.

To demonstrate the chief executive's fairness, honesty, courage and disciplined hard work.

The story of Sylvania & Laxman is a case in point. Laxman Agarwal, an entrepreneur born with a silver spoon in his mouth, nevertheless decided to chalk out his own destiny. Starting as a distributor and importer he went on to dabble in real estate and was able to accumulate substantial sums for investment in industry.

A lamp manufacturing unit, Osler Lamps, was for sale and he negotiated the deal for Rs2.9 million (there are about 10 rupees to the US dollar). Then Philips entered the scene, doubled the offer and clinched the deal. Agarwal was convinced that this was a good product line – for Philips should know, it was their business – so he negotiated a collaboration with Westinghouse who, however, later withdrew, perhaps under pressure from Philips. Agarwal switched to Sylvania, who in their turn were already collaborating with the renowned General Telephones & Electronics. Meanwhile, Philips set up another facility at Bombay. Sylvania & Laxman commenced production in Delhi in 1967 and shortly thereafter two other firms, Toshiba and Bengal Lamps, also entered the industry. Sylvania & Laxman started production of fluorescent tubes in 1968, GLS lamps in 1969 and mercury vapour lamps in 1970. Their product range was rapidly extended to include the manufacture of components and the company embarked on a major expansion at a cost of Rs35 million. Faced with the recession and severe competition in the marketplace, Sylvania & Laxman lacked the managerial ability to handle the crisis situation. The company went into the red for the first time in 1974–75 and the situation got progressively worse.

Agarwal stepped down, this being a condition laid down by the financial institutions, and two chairmen, Raghu Raj and later Lt. Gen. J. S. Arora, contributed to the financial and managerial aspects, including cost cutting and monetary discipline. A system approach was implemented, including performance budgeting and assessment of variances. Marketing operations were strengthened through 19 sales offices, with some 10 000 distributors covering 60 000 retail outlets throughout the country. Stringent quality control and the testing of each individual bulb was also introduced, with a strengthening of research and development. As a result, the company turned in a profit in 1978–9 and Agarwal is back as the company's chairman and managing director. Plans for further diversification and growth are afoot.[6] The financial story can be shown thus:

	1974–75	1975–76	1978–79	1980–81	1982–83	1983–84
Turnover (Rs million)	59	54	120	212	255	273
Profit (Rs million)	(4.7)	(23.5)	5.7	36.1	31.3	25
Dividend on equity (%)	–	–	–	10	20	22

Turnaround achieved!

NLC's giant strides

NCL is a company in the public sector, Neyveli Lignite Corporation, with an industrial complex built around lignite, or brown coal. The complex comprises a lignite mine, briquetting and carbonization plant, a thermal power station and a urea fertilizer plant. The project dates back to the 1950s but seems to have a faulty background. It is now surmised that the original British consultants had little experience of open-cast mining, which was fundamental to the successful operation of the installation. Any shortfall in quality of the lignite as mined had an immediate chain reaction. Low production of lignite meant poor capacity utilization in all the plant units.

As a result, the company lost money year after year, and by 1976 the cumulative losses totalled some Rs840 million. The situation was serious, but the realization that capacity utilization was the key to the problem was taken to heart and a turnaround started in 1977, when for the first time since commissioning the corporation earned a profit of Rs117 million on a turnover of Rs 790 million. In the year 1981–82 NLC earned a record net profit of Rs379 million on a turnover of Rs1110 million. At this point the company had wiped out the entire cumulative loss and could show a credit balance of Rs30 million. Certainly it had made giant strides and continues to do so.

The turnaround was achieved by modifying the mining techniques so that better quality lignite was mined, the application of preventive maintenance, and the negotiation of a better price for power from their only customer, the Tamil Nadu Electricity Board. Now plans are being laid for expansion, since the lignite fields can sustain production for some 130 years at the proposed increased rate of usage. A recent advertisement by the company, now seeking new talent, places emphasis on its education programme, with the development of the environment and human resources. If their plans mature, NLC a decade hence will be an 'energy centre', based on the mining of 32 million tons of lignite a year. Production per worker has increased by 50 per cent and the current problem is a shortage of managerial talent. We maintain that figures speak louder than words, so let us sum up this dramatic turnaround in Table 9.1.

Table 9.1   The Neyveli Lignite turnaround achieved by G. L. Tandon, chairman and Managing Director.

	1979–80	1980–81	1981–82	1982–83	1983–84
Lignite mined (million tons)	2.9	4.8	5.9	6.4	6.6
Power exported (megawatts)	1768	2454	2686	3073	3027
Urea (thousand tons)	105	135	99	101	124
Thermal power (load factor, %)	45	60	65	73	74
Mining capacity utilization (%)	45	74	90	99	102
Profit, Rs mill.	5	171	379	474	630
Internally generated funds (Rs mill.)	149	305	567	765	855

Source: Centre for Monitoring Indian Economy, Bombay

BSR International

The Indian turnarounds we have just been looking at were both generated from within the companies concerned, so let us look at BSR International, a similar case from the UK. Figure 9.4 presents the company's recent history when its financial position is measured using the PAS-score. This system of company assessment is discussed in detail in Chapter 12, but for the moment all that it is necessary to recognize is that BSR were on a steady downward path for more than three years. The company is active in electronics, audio, household and industrial products and came very, very close to failure, as the graph demonstrates. The turnaround came in 1983. The comment was that there was 'clear evidence of effective, competent, no-nonsense, resolute management'. The board seemed to be in complete control, took the necessary action and then followed a strategic development plan to build on their high technology strength in terms of careful product expansion and volume growth. But rationalization took its toll and more than a quarter of BSR's 1,100 Stourbridge workforce had to be made redundant following downturn in demand for record players and a cut in computer power supply orders. This sounds a warning note and demonstrates the way in which even the most alert and cost-conscious management can over-estimate and overreach itself. While pursuing a course of rationalization and con-solidation, the management was ever ready to take advantage of growing markets

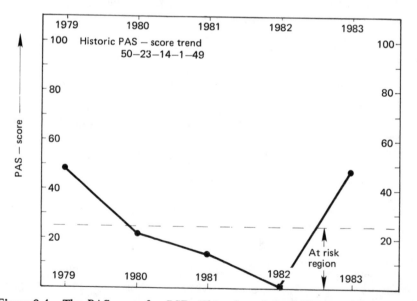

Figure 9.4   The PAS-score for BSR. *This plot of the PAS-score demonstrates the graphic turnaround achieved at BSR following the change in chief executive. (With thanks to Performance Analysis Services Limited, London)*

and so was expanding certain of its manufacturing facilities, particularly in the Far East. The change came when Wyllie, the present executive chairman, took over in October 1982. The transformation within a year was quite remarkable, strengthened by a rights issue of £24.2 million in March 1983 in order to 'strengthen the balance sheet by reducing short-term borrowings'. With rationalization largely completed by the end of 1984, further growth will depend upon the ability of the board to manage growth rather than recovery. We have suggested that a different management style is then required and it will be interesting to see which changes: the style or the management itself.

Summary

Companies in the newest of industries are as much at risk as those operating in long-established markets. Although the management style appropriate to turnaround is not necessarily appropriate once the company is climbing up the road to recovery, nevertheless we have instances where a company at risk has achieved a turnaround and then continued on to established success under the same chief executive.

References

1. Kibel, H. R., *How to Turn Around a Financially Troubled Company*, McGraw-Hill, 1982.
2. Edwardes, M., *Back from the Brink – An Apocalyptic Experience*, Collins, 1983.
3. Becket, M., 'Sir Michael Edwardes clears decks at Dunlop', *Daily Telegraph* (London), 9 Nov. 1984, p.21.
4. Baker, J., 'Edwardes' jobs shock at Dunlop', *Birmingham Post*, 22 Nov. 1984, p.3.
5. Khandwalla, P. N., 'Effective turnaround management', *Business World*, 8–21 Oct. 1984, p. 29.
6. Long, N., 'Sylvania and Laxman – going from a dark past to a bright future', *Directors Digest*, July 1984, pp.26–37.

10 The government `bailout´

Governments cannot stand aloof and watch dispassionately while companies fail. Far too often, too much is at stake. Unemployment is a major concern, and the collapse of one company often leads to the failure of others. Then there is the matter of what is called 'public confidence', of which our study of a bank failure is a classic illustration. The extent to which government assistance, when proffered, is of lasting value, is in doubt. There is always the danger that poor management is being shielded from the consequences of its own shortcomings.

The Chrysler Corporation

This has been one of the most successful of rescue stories. Earnings for 1983 were the highest in the company's history and at that point the long-term debt had been cut by half in a year: from US$2150 million in 1982 to US$1070 million in 1983. Against this background the share price on the market rose to some seven times its 1982 low. Chrysler is back on the road. But let us examine the public records, blazoned largely in the technical journals, and see how it all came about.

Once ranked the fourth largest industrial corporation in the US, Chrysler's crisis erupted towards the end of 1980. After weeks of self-praising advertising, chairman Lee A. Iacocca, of whom we gave a profile in Chapter 4, revealed at a press conference on 4 December of that year that there had been a disastrous slump in sales, that there was no cash in hand and that therefore it was necessary to seek another loan or guarantee from the government in Washington. Congress had authorized a loan of US$1500 million about a year earlier, of which US$800 million had already been drawn. From then on the bad news multiplied from day to day.[1] All the typical signs of imminent failure were there: payment to suppliers was postponed, payment was offered in kind (cars) rather than cash, new assembly lines were postponed and there was a production cut of some 20 per cent. Standard & Poor's rating for Chrysler dropped from 'B' to 'triple C', defined as 'predominantly speculative with respect to capacity to pay interest and repay principal'. Chrysler were most certainly at the brink, yet only three months earlier Iacocca had declared to the press: 'The Chrysler Corporation is now on the leading edge of a dramatic recovery. . . We are on our way back. We are a fighting company that is leading the industry out of its worst depression in 50 years.'

90

What is *your* reaction to that statement, knowing what the actual position of the company *must* have been at that time? There seems to have been no limit to Iacocca's bravado. He talked of Chrysler's leadership: great products were coming from the six most modern plants in the world, he said. He also predicted a fourth quarter (1980) profit of US$250 million as a consequence of this 'historic turnaround'. Well, he was almost right as to the figure, except that it was a loss instead of a profit!

What went wrong? Everything, except the optimism of the ebullient chairman. Chrysler had long been the weakest of the 'big three' car manufacturers in the US and had problems for years prior to their being bailed out by the government in 1979. They had inadequate capital resources and displayed poor judgement in respect of international acquisitions. In addition, they lacked the talent of their rivals in design matters. An expert in the field wrote in mid-1979: 'The company has been known in recent years for neither the prestige nor the advanced styling of its cars – it must sell its "me too" product line at attractive prices in order to retain customers.'

The trouble began around 1974, when the recession in the US brought a steep drop in sales, major cuts in capital expenditure and the loss of key staff, such as designers. In 1978 the loss was US$205 million and the following year it was still worse. Thanks to active lobbying in Washington, Congress authorized US$1500 million as part of a rescue bid. This loan was based on an estimated loss in 1980 of US$493 million. However, in July of that year the estimate had been revised upward to an alarming US$1039 million. By September the figure had crept up to US$1284 million. At the same time sales were slumping below the lowest estimates, the new models coming in late and overpriced. Yet Iacocca's optimism remained high and he prepared a billion-dollar cost-cutting exercise that proved to be completely unrealistic. Of course, 'beggars can't be choosers', so the terms of the rescue plan were accepted despite its inadequate funding – anything was better than the company going bankrupt. The profit projections at the beginning of 1981 were (all figures in US$ x million):

1981: (224) loss.
1982: 349
1984: 1100

How do you change the marketplace and its view of Chrysler cars? Chrysler had been at the brink and with customers fearing complete collapse even the resale value of the cars plummeted. The auto analyst Maryann Keller put it most realistically:

> You can be philosophically in favour of bailing out Chrysler, but when it comes to spending your own money, it is a different matter. Chrysler could sell cars only if they were cheaper or substantially better than the competition. This is a consumer product after all. How would it change your life if Chrysler were not there?

In a free economy such as the US there is no case for a perpetual subsidy to a constantly ailing company, except perhaps in the case of a public utility such as the railroad we discussed in Chapter 5. There have been one-time government loans in the US before – Lockheed was another much-publicized case – and while history was repeated in the case of Chrysler, there was no reason to believe Washington would be disposed to take on the Chrysler burden indefinitely. So, if the company were to change course, it would have to be largely by its own efforts.

Change course it did. A little over a year later the same ebullient Iacocca, against all the odds, could report proudly and truly that for the first time in five years the company had shown a profit for two successive quarters. The first quarter's profit would have been a loss but for the sale of the defence division to General Dynamics, but the second quarter's profit of US$107 million was genuine, with no build-up of stocks. This was in sharp contrast to Ford, whose domestic car operations over the same period were showing heavy losses. Suddenly the situation looked really healthy, with cash assets exceeding US$1000 million, well-timed new models and a market share of 10 per cent, up substantially from the 7 per cent figure for 1980. This is reflected quite clearly in the share price for the company over the years (see Fig. 10.1).

How was it done? Costs were held down, largely by employee participation. Wages were lower than at either Ford or General Motors and the breakeven point

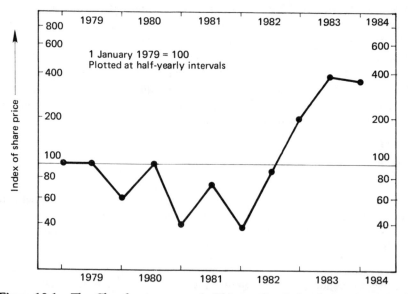

Figure 10.1   The Chrysler turnaround. *This graph of the share price over the years shows the very marked upward movement from the beginning of 1982 onwards. January 1979 is taken as the basis for comparison.* (**Source:** *Economist*)

had been halved: it was down to 1.2 million units. These were great achievements by any standard. The Chrysler union leader, Doug Fraser, is now on the board and the employees own a third of the shares. This turnaround has been most successful and shows very clearly just what determination and the workers' co-operation can achieve. The workers actually took a *cut* in salary to bring *their* company back from the brink. However, while their wages are lower, this is compensated for by a higher pension provision. They have also introduced a 'cost of living' formula for wage adjustment.

An apocalyptic experience

Now we turn to another outstanding chief executive, this time in the UK. We refer to Sir Michael Edwardes, whom we have already met in Chapter 9, and who reached the headlines when he was appointed to turn around British Leyland, a company manufacturing a wide range of automobiles, lorries and buses, wholly owned by the British Government. He was chief executive of British Leyland for five years and wrote a book about his experiences there. The caption at the head of this section is the subtitle to that book. Wondering what Sir Michael meant us to understand from the word 'apocalyptic', we find that it is the Greek word used in the title to the last book in the Bible and is there translated 'revelation'. That book is seen as a record of 'grand and violent' events. That, therefore, is Sir Michael's summing up of his five years with British Leyland. He saw it as a succession of 'grand and violent' events.

He managed to maintain government support throughout, despite much opposition. He managed to prevent what he felt would be a disastrous privatization of the company. He had planned and produced the Mini Metro, a success for both British Leyland and Britain. He had laid the basis for co-operation with Honda of Japan. It is a story of confrontations and breakthroughs: of political manoeuvres, of the ebb and flow of public support. It was a struggle for survival and the book explains the complexity of the problems and the pressures within British Leyland – problems and pressures by no means peculiar to British Leyland, but affecting British industry as a whole. It makes good reading, but what are the lessons for us?

How it all began

British Leyland was formed in 1968 by the merger of a number of manufacturing companies in the automotive industry, following a story of successive takeover and merger going back some 20 years. The industry came under great pressure in the UK following entry into the Common Market. Imports of foreign cars grew over the years following entry, from some 10 per cent to more than 50 per cent of total sales in the UK. The company became a symbol for industrial Britain, with the result that the government was willing to go to any lengths to bail it out.

The problems that confronted Sir Michael when he took over can be briefly listed:

Reorganize the company and restructure the Board
Optimize management involvement
Deal with substantial labour unrest
Improve disastrously poor productivity
Reform relations with the unions
Gain wholehearted government support
Build up a purposeful management team
Decentralize
Upgrade technology and production

Although he pursued these several objectives with zeal and devotion, progress eluded him and he expressed himself as 'frustrated' after some 18 months. His diagnosis of British Leyland's problems at that point in time was brief and candid:

> Management simply lost control of the situation. Models were not, or could not be updated. Quality and production fell to unacceptable levels, and disputes reached four or five times the sort of level that a 'continuous production' industry can stand . . . Britain and the world blamed the unions and turned their back on British Leyland products. But the real blame lay with management, for they failed in their duty to manage.[2]

Sir Michael must have been quite persuasive within government circles, faced with a choice between pumping more and more money to keep British Leyland going, or spending an even greater sum in letting it fail. The policy of the Conservative government of the day, led by Mrs. Margaret Thatcher, was to privatize, a view expressed thus:

> I never want to take on another BL. We shouldn't be in it at all, but now we're in it we have to choose the time and we have to back Michael Edwardes' judgement. He's the manager, I'm not the manager . . .[2]

Despite being so closely involved and desperately committed, Mrs Thatcher never showed the slightest inclination to interfere in British Leyland, not even in relation to issues such as employee relations, which were of prime importance to the government. This is as it should be. You should not have a dog and then bark yourself.

Sir Michael identified the actions required. These involved strong and hard decisions. He provided the much-needed firm management resolve and went *direct* to the employees on key issues. Previously, the management had been weak and vacillating, blaming the unions when the real blame lay with themselves. Sir Michael did not hesitate to give shock treatment when required, in order to lead rather than be led. He became known as 'the man who took on the unions'. Simultaneously he was keeping track of the advancing technology and the latest production techniques and had no hesitation in co-operating with Honda from Japan in order to introduce a new and efficient fuel-saving model on to the market in record time. Assembly lines were streamlined; more than 50 robots were installed.

When Sir Michael took over, British Leyland had ageing models, a declining market share and a very poor world image. It was short of cash, management had failed completely and there were the wrong people in hundreds of jobs. Most of this Sir Michael proceeded to reform from the top downwards. He reduced the size of the board so as to improve communication and achieve consensus, he introduced decentralization and collaboration with Honda. The comments of the reviewers on his efforts were not uniform in their praise. One, while agreeing that British Leyland survived, wondered whether the effort was worth it. Turnaround has been achieved, but the company is not yet in the clear. British Leyland's output, at around half a million cars a year, is highly vulnerable, since it has rivals with much bigger outputs, such as Nissan, Renault, Ford and Volkswagen, who are therefore all in a position to compete on price. In addition, British Leyland must export or die, since the home market is nowhere near large enough to sustain it. The latest blow is the sale of its highly profitable subsidiary, Jaguar Cars, in line with the continuing government objective of privatization.

Massey-Ferguson

Massey-Ferguson, the world's largest tractor maker, has its headquarters in Canada. This group of companies, with factories in several countries, has been in dire trouble, but at long last the corner has been turned. It took a lot of effort and needed a little luck. The rescuers have included four governments and more than 200 banks. There have been two phases to the rescue efforts, the first in 1981 and the second in 1983. The efforts made had to match the size of the loss that was being incurred: almost US$1 billion since 1980. The turnaround has been achieved despite the fact that the market in which Massey-Ferguson operates is weakening all the time. The sales of tractors worldwide are down a third since 1976 and capital spending on diesel engines is also down substantially. This makes the achievement of a turnaround quite remarkable when compared with that achieved by Chrysler, in that the car market, while depressed, has not been so severely depressed as the tractor market. Thus we learn that turnaround can be achieved *even* with a severely depressed market.

Massey-Ferguson shares hit their all-time low at the end of 1981. Since then, however, the price has been rising steadily. By the end of 1982 it was 30 per cent up, by the end of 1983 70 per cent up. In addition, it received permission in February 1984 from the American Securities & Exchange Commission to more than double its publicly traded common shares.

But it has been no easy road. Above all, the company is now far slimmer than it was. The workforce, 68 000 in 1976 worldwide, is now down to some 27 000, while sales are running at less than half the level they were in 1980. Some 15 plants have been sold or closed, including a construction machinery manufacturing company that was sold to IBH, the West German company. The manufacture of snowmobiles and office furniture has also been discontinued. Notice the approach: the move back from diversification to the single product with which the company has a real store of experience and expertise.

Expanding in the right places

The 'single product' or 'back to basics' principle is exemplified by the fact that while there has been much divesting, there has also been acquisition. Massey-Ferguson bought Rolls-Royce's diesel engine's business from Vickers Engineering Group, its first acquisition in ten years: this is vertical integration within the specific framework being set up. The factory was making heavy-duty diesel engines which extended the range of the Perkins engines they were already using. The company is thus given access to several new and sizeable markets in the tractor industry. The third world market is Massey-Ferguson's best hope for the future. It already contributes about a quarter to its total revenue, and is still a real growth area. In an attempt to exploit this position, Massey-Ferguson have devised a new and novel marketing strategy. For instance, in a recent deal the company bartered 22 tractors for copper from Zambia. Figure 10.2 gives the story of the company graphically. While it still has a long way to go, it is most certainly now going in the right direction: for the fiscal year 1984 the company made a profit of US$ 7.2 million. This is small in relation to the size of the business, but it was the first profit since 1979.

It is important to realize that the steps taken towards recovery, although taken under external pressure from governments and banks, are fundamentally the consequence of management decisions that are related to a corporate strategy – a strategy radically different, of course, to the one (if there was one, which we doubt) that was leading to disaster. We would suggest that the company was on course towards disaster because of a lack of corporate strategy: or, at the very least, a lack of flexibility in strategy in the face of drastically changing conditions in the world market for tractors.

A bank goes bust

The salvation of the Continental Illinois Bank in the US has been the largest bank rescue operation ever and at the same time a sort of triumph for bank regulations. It did, however, leave behind the feeling that the official regulatory

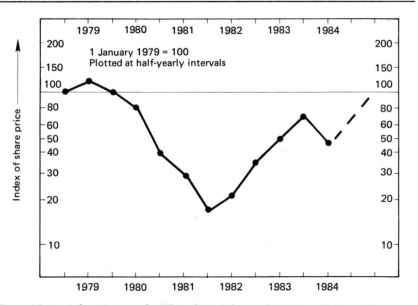

Figure 10.2   A heroic struggle. *This plot of the profitability of Massey-Ferguson over the years demonstrates that a turnaround has been achieved, even if it has not yet been consolidated.* (Source: *Company accounts)*

organization should have taken a tough stand and should also have acted earlier. They were almost too late and the failure of Continental Illinois would have led to a whole string of bank failures.

The main reasons for failure were:

A super-aggressive lending policy, leading to careless loans
The Latin American debt crises
Large loans to several major companies that failed
At the first signs of trouble, a 'run' on the bank
Wild rumours, intensifying the run on the bank

By the term 'run' we mean the rush by depositors to withdraw their money. It was also revealed that one top officer was a heavy drinker, while another was said to be a regular user of cocaine. This may have impaired their efficiency.

Continental Illinois is the eighth largest bank in the US and was a major lender in Latin and North America at a time when oil prices were soaring. But early in 1984 oil prices slumped, while oil exploration costs were soaring. Continental's bad debts mounted as a consequence, reaching some US$4.5 billion. This figure was such that there was no possibility of a bail out by any private bank, and the government had to step in. This it did through the Federal Deposit Insurance Company (FDIC). The rescue package involved FDIC taking over the debt at a cost of US$3.5 billion, leaving Continental with a loss of US$1 billion to write off. A cash infusion was also required. This too came from FDIC in the form of preferred stock. As a result the bank was saved, and it posted a profit in 1985. 'Bail out' indeed!

Various proposals have been made for some reform of the banking system in the US to prevent such a situation ever arising again, but these do not really concern us, except in so far as they highlight areas that require watching. For instance, it is recommended that the bank capital, or equity, should be at least 9 per cent of the total assets instead of the current average of 5.5 per cent. In other words, too much borrowing is a bad thing. Then there is a demand that banks should disclose more details of their business. This is also a factor in company health. If its state is more 'visible', there is more opportunity for others to assess what is happening and sound a warning in due time. While such reforms may not provide a panacea, they would certainly help to minimize a problem that has grown to alarming proportions not only in the US, but elsewhere.

An island rescue

The Construction and Development Corporation of the Philippines (CDCP) is the largest construction company on the islands. It was taken over early in 1983 by the government, who converted its current debt of US$400 million into equity. This rescue, or takeover, has been very candidly described by Jaime Ongpin, president of the Benguet mining group, as 'the most obscene, brazen and disgraceful misallocation of taxpayers' money in the history of the Philippines'.

This particular 'rescue' is one of a series involving substantial funding of deserving industries in the islands. The operation was started at a time of financial crisis, in 1981, and millions upon millions of pesos have been spent – largely, it is alleged, in rescuing companies owned by the President's friends.

CDCP was owned by one Rodolfo Cuenca, who had parted earlier with several of his other companies, such as Galleon Shipping and Luzon Stevedoring. He now holds less than 6 per cent of the CDCP equity. CDCP, with contracts worth more than US$4 billion, over 70 per cent of them in the Middle East, is one of the largest construction companies in South-East Asia. The company is basically sound, but its profits fell from US$15 million to US$2.5 million in 1981 because it was growing and also facing keen competition. It was also losing on some of its contracts – in particular a US$350 million Iraqi highway project. Another weakness came from the fact that it had diversified into fields it knew little about.

The government, its own finances in a sorry state, bought it out. Total foreign borrowings in the Philippines exceed US$17 billion and the significance of that figure is best appreciated when one realizes that loan interest and repayment takes up one fourth of the country's entire foreign earnings. If the government continues with rescue operations in order to save jobs – a good enough motive in itself – the country may well be driven to reschedule its debts. Another alternative is a devaluation of the peso. It is clear that to seek to preserve jobs at any price is mistaken policy. The end result is continuing inefficiency.

Summary

A company facing imminent failure can still be the subject of a turnaround. Some common features to turnaround policy have been exemplified in the various case studies that we have taken. A strategy has to be formulated and followed with persistence. Facilities, usually those outside the basic business of the company, are sold off but at the same time acquisition is not out of the question if it is part of a consistent strategy. When it comes to government intervention, the continuing theme in all the case studies in this chapter, job loss seems to be a major factor in their motivation. But job losses have to be faced if a company is to be run efficiently, since a basic cause of failure is often over-staffing, in itself a sign of poor productivity. We intend to pursue those aspects – corporate strategy and productivity – in detail later.

References

1. Ross, I., 'Chrysler on the brink', *Fortune*, **103**, 38–42, 9 Feb. 1981.
2. Edwardes, M., *Back from the Brink – An Apocalyptic Experience*, Collins, 1983.

PART THREE
Prediction is possible

11 Where it all began

The prediction of business failure is desirable and we believe it to be possible. The real question is: how long before failure comes is it possible to have some indication as to what will happen if the company continues on course? Obviously, the earlier the better, because that gives more time for the company management to take action, either to avert disaster or to lessen its impact. While we assert that the prediction of business failure is possible, we have to qualify that assertion somewhat, since despite the enormous amount of research that has gone into this subject and the vast amount of literature now available, one can still be taken by surprise.

A literature explosion, but . . .

The literature on the forecasting of business failure comes from both academicians and business consultants – dare we describe this as the theoretical, as opposed to the practical approach. Einstein may be said to typify the theoretical approach, writing a formula that was to be proved much later, while Newton typifies the practical approach, observing the falling apple and then enunciating the theory of gravity to explain the phenomenon.

We propose, over the next four chapters, to deal with various aspects of prediction in some detail. While it will remain only a summary of the available data, we hope that you may get some 'feel' for what has been a 'literature explosion' in this field. The bulk of the literature is directed toward the potential investor, with the objective of warning him of danger ahead. In addition, many of the writers on the subject seem to have become obsessed with the technique and all the complex formulae that can be developed and have forgotten the objective – to avert disaster!

A good example of this failure is to be seen in a recent book by Altman, undoubtedly a leading expert in this field.[1] His book carries the sub-title: 'A complete guide to predicting, avoiding and dealing with bankruptcy'. One reviewer points out that this sub-title is an over-statement.[2] He must be considered to be authoritative, since he also reviewed Altman's earlier book on the subject, written in 1971.[3] It is certainly true that while 'avoiding and dealing' with bankruptcy are said to be two-thirds of the subject, they occupy only 10 per cent of the text. Nearly half of the book is devoted either to prediction or to the legal and other aspects of bankruptcy. It is obviously helpful to know how to cope with bankruptcy when it comes, but surely it is far better to avoid it altogether and that is where we propose to place the emphasis.

Prediction — a means, not an end

With this in mind, we have devoted a good third of this book to the means that can be adopted to avoid disaster or alleviate its consequences. We used practical examples in Part Two (Back from the brink) and constructive technical detail in Part Four (Panacea is better) and Part Five (Prevention is best). Prediction is still a crucial aspect, because we *must* be able to ascertain what is happening early enough to be able to do something about it. If a company is on the road to bankruptcy, perhaps because of external circumstances and through no fault of its own, how can it change its course before it goes bankrupt? Or if bankruptcy is inevitable, what should one do ahead of the event to alleviate its tragic consequences. Each case will have its own specific solution, but we believe that a study of cases over a wide range of industries and services, in many different countries, can be very helpful.

Having made the point that prediction is merely a means to an end and not an end in itself, let us examine both the 'why' and the 'how' of the prediction of company failure. Before the experts started to analyse the situation, prediction of business failure was a subjective assessment. It was largely intuition: one could feel, if one had reasonable contact with and knowledge of a company, whether or not it was doing well, or was in danger of collapse. There was no really rational basis for this feeling, and no means available for a quantitative assessment of the position.

Credit-worthiness

The credit rating of a company was perhaps the first indicator to use in assessing the health of a company. Various agencies have been set up over the years specifically for the purpose of providing the data appropriate to an assessment of credit-worthiness. Merchant traders were active in this field, since they had to be aware of the trading status of their customers. Reliance upon word of mouth was inadequate, so in 1826 the first digest of companies defaulting on their suppliers was produced. Subsequently this became known as *Stubbs Gazette*.

Bankers, to whom the credit-worthiness of the potential borrower is crucial, should be experts in the field. We have been in correspondence with the branch manager of a major branch of one of the 'big four' in the London area on this subject and he told us:

> By a regular screening of cheques presented for payment, the first signs can be evidenced by cheques to preferential and other creditors being issued in

round amounts (say £200), in other words, creditors are pressing for payment and the company sends some money as a placatory action.

Another potential danger signal can be gleaned from a sight of bank statements where an account which has previously been in credit or fluctuating from debit to credit, becomes an increasing hardcore borrowing. This is an indication that the company is overtrading in relation to its capital base, or that the company's debtors are delaying payment.

The letter continued with this most pertinent observation:

> Whilst the means of detecting danger as disclosed in the foregoing is by no means exhaustive, one can sum up by saying that *awareness* is the keynote to success and no one is in a better position to arrest a difficult situation than a well prepared Bank Manager with the benefit of a good support team.

Awareness! The emphasis is ours and indeed 'awareness' is the key to success. It is amazing what one can learn about a company, as about almost anything else, by just keeping one's eyes and ears open. Argenti calls this 'banker's nose' and elaborates on the theme thus:

> An experienced banker can often spot the danger signs in the clients. He can 'smell trouble'. In exactly the same way consultants, once they have visited a few dozen companies, acquire a similar ability to smell trouble almost as soon as they walk in the door. An observer anxious about a company would do well to invite the opinion of such experienced professionals. Their methods may not be scientific but at least they are not dependent on the appearance of annual accounts.[4]

We can call this 'qualification' as compared with 'quantification'. We know something is wrong, but we do not know the extent or magnitude of the trouble.

Credit ratings have since become quite scientific, being based not only on published accounts but also on other information, largely gained in the marketplace. This can be an expensive and difficult exercise, but it is well worth while, as we go on to show in Chapter 14, where we turn to our own recommendations. One of the most comprehensive services of this type is that offered by Dun and Bradstreet, in the form of either a printed newsletter or specific reports.

Quantification begins

Quantification in relation to the prediction of business failures started in the 1930s, with the advent and development of accountancy as a distinct and separate profession. Typical of the studies that were made then are those of Smith and Winakor, published in 1935, and of Merwin, published in 1942.[5] These researchers indicated, perhaps for the first time, that the variation in or the trend of financial ratios taken from the company accounts were significantly different for failing companies as compared with those who prospered. This was a very significant finding and it has been the basis of numerous studies. Hickman, some fifteen years later, published a book dealing with such ratios in relation to large companies with problems in meeting their debt obligations.[6] This is one of the first indicators in the case of a failing company and a useful early warning. Such warnings are only useful if they are heeded – heeded, above all, by the management of the company concerned, so that action can be taken.

A classic work

A milestone was reached in establishing a relationship between ratio analysis and company failure with the publication of the work of Beaver between 1966 and 1968.[7] His work has made a major contribution to progress in this field, setting the stage for the many further studies of those who followed him. The crux of Beaver's work lay in his discovery that there were a number of indicators, largely financial ratios, that could enable one to discriminate between a 'failed' company and the rest. The real trick, of course, is to be able to make this distinction early: if possible, up to five years *before* failure actually occurs.

Beaver examined some 30 financial ratios and tested each one for relative efficiency as an early indicator of business failure. Of these, one ratio in particular – cash flow/total debt – was found to be the best, in that it showed the minimum percentage error in prediction for the sample companies studied. It was, however, unfortunate that Beaver, like many others, equated failure with bankruptcy. It is true that failure can well lead to bankruptcy, and bankruptcy is an obvious, unmistakable event. It is also a legal event, occuring on a specific date, but the same is not true of failure. Failure develops over the years and cannot be precisely defined, yet it is more important to discern failure than it is to discern potential bankruptcy, since by detecting the first signs of failure one is in a position to take preventive action. Once bankruptcy occurs, the worst has happened. The patient is terminally sick if not dead and all that is left is a post-mortem. That may well be a valuable exercise, but it serves an entirely different purpose helping to build up a body of knowledge that can be useful in helping other companies avoid failure and eventual bankruptcy.

At about the same time as Beaver published his classic study, a separate attempt to assess the 'cause-and-effect' relationship was being made by Miller.[8] He divided the various ratios into those that were causal and those that measured what was happening. No attempt was made by Miller, however, to relate the ratios to failure and bankruptcy, which is our immediate concern. His study points out the relative importance of the various ratios, but in considering the cause-and-effect syndrome we have a 'chicken and egg' problem. While the connection is clear enough, we are unable to say which is cause and which is effect.

Multivariate analysis

Mutivariate analysis (MVA), sometimes called MDA (multiple discriminant analysis) uses a combination of ratios to discriminate between companies on the road to success and those heading for failure long before total failure, or bankruptcy, occurs. Significantly, Beaver was so pleased with his one ratio that he questioned the utility of using MDA, although other researchers were advocating its use at that time.[9] The various ratios, used either singly or in combination as a tool to forecast failure, indicate the following major aspects of a company's health:

Profitability
Liquidity
Solvency

The use of a single ratio to assess a company's health seems suspect. To return once more to our analogy with the human body, any single measurement, such as temperature, blood pressure or pulse rate is not by itself enough to tell us whether the person is ill: similarly with a company. A firm that is failing to make profits may well seem a candidate for disaster, but if its liquidity is good then it may well be in no danger at all. So it would seem very evident that MDA is the tool to use to assess the position, just as when we go for a checkup we expect the doctor to make a whole range of tests on us. In practice, however, as we shall see, a different rule emerges.

For an in-depth review of MDA and its financial applications we refer you to Altman *et al.*'s *Application of Classification Techniques in Business*.[10] MDA is a statistical technique that assists in the classification of the available data. The selection of the various factors entering into the equation (in our case, ratios) is largely a matter of trial and error and thus an empirical assessment.

Altman's Z-score model

In a classic study, which found fervent adherents all over the world, first published in 1969, and later modified, Altman arrived at a complex discriminant function.[11] We present the modified, 1981, version below:[1]

$$Z = 1.2X_1 + 1.4X_2 + 3.3X_3 + 0.6X_4 + 1.0X_5$$

where Z is the weighted average index, indicating the overall health of a company, and

X_1 = (working capital)/(total assets)

X_2 = (retained earnings since inception)/(total assets)

X_3 = (earnings before taxes and interest)/(total assets)

X_4 = (market value of equity)/(book value of total debt)

X_5 = (sales)/(total assets)

all the above figures being expressed as a percentage.

The above function was arrived at by an analysis of the data for 33 firms who had filed for bankruptcy, matched against another 33 firms, similar in terms of size and the nature of the industry, that had *not* gone bankrupt over the same period (1946–65). The above five ratios appeared to Altman more significant than 22 others that he also tested. The criterion for assessing the potential for bankruptcy – not failure – was:

If Z was less than 1.8, then failure was certain.

If Z was more than 2.7 (originally 3.0) then the company was *almost* certain NOT to fail.

The region between 1.8 and 2.7 was a sort of 'grey area'. You did not know what was going to happen, but obviously companies in the grey area were suspect.

The accuracy of this model in the prediction of bankruptcy was found to be 95 per cent one year prior to bankruptcy and 72 per cent two years prior to bankruptcy. After that the accuracy in prediction fell very rapidly: 48 per cent in the third year prior to bankruptcy. Further detailed analysis has shown that while *all* ratios show deterioration as bankruptcy approaches, the most serious deterioration occurs between the third and second year before bankruptcy.[1] So we immediately have another tool to hand: one should not only measure the absolute value of Z, but also and perhaps even more importantly, one should measure the movement of Z over the years.

What does one do in the case of private companies, for which there is no market value of the equity, as required for X_4? In this case Altman recommends that the book value of the equity be used, but the weighting also needs changing and we get a revised formula, thus:

$$Z = 0.717X_1 + 0.847X_2 + 3.107X_3 + 0.42X_4 + 0.995X_5$$

The cut-off point changes as well. The safe area is now above 2.9, while the grey area is from 1.2 to 2.9. But confirmation of the validity of this latest equation awaits extensive testing by accountants and other practitioners.

In yet another version of the Z-score developed by Altman, the item X_5 is deleted in order to minimize the potential industry effect coming from the use of the industry-sensitive variable, turnover of assets. The equation then becomes:

$$Z = 6.56X_1 + 3.26X_2 + 6.72X_3 + 1.05X_4$$

Here too the book value of the equity is used to arrive at X_4. Once again the cut-off point changes. A company is safe if the Z-score is above 2.6, while the unsafe area is below 1.1. Altman himself warns against indiscriminate use of the Z-score, since experience with it is still rather limited. The companies upon which it was based were of medium size, so it does not necessarily reflect the state of affairs in very large or very small companies. Further, only manufacturing firms were used in the analysis. Will his findings apply in countries other than the US? Or to service companies? Does one need a different formula for each country, or each industry? These are question which we will answer later.

The Z-score and Rolls-Royce

In Chapter 5 we examined the collapse of Rolls-Royce, the world-famed motor car company that operated in the UK. Argenti sought to apply the original equation published by Altman to the case of Rolls-Royce, after it had failed. This was a sort of post-mortem, the objective being to establish the validity of the Z-score for use in a different context. The Z-score for the several years prior to bankruptcy, in the case of Rolls-Royce, are plotted in Fig. 11.1. To make the position quite clear we have also indicated the grey risk area.

The survey covers a period of nine years and throughout that whole period the company was at risk – yet it did not actually collapse until 1970. Argenti's analysis of these results is quite revealing and educative. He points out that Altman does not claim a 100 per cent success rate and Rolls-Royce could well be an exception. Further, the Z-scores for UK companies seem to be in general lower than in the US. For instance, ICI rated only 2.1 and 2.3 for the years 1973–74, while GEC rated 2.3 for both years, yet neither company was in any sort of trouble, nor has been since. On the other hand, British Leyland, a company most certainly in trouble at that time, scored 2.4. A high sales turnover contributes as much as 1.6 to the score, through the factor X_5. Another problem is that the shares of a company quoted on the market can vary widely: which of the many values do you use in the formula?

Argenti, however, raises a more fundamental point when he casts doubt on the use of financial ratios derived from the published accounts. It is well known that in time of trouble companies resort to what is termed 'creative accounting', which we deal with in detail in Chapter 20. They sometimes even go so far as to 'cook the books' in an endeavour to hide the signs of trouble. After all, they are as familiar with the information to be gained by an analysis of the published accounts as you soon will be. There are other factors, such as government subsidy (which played a role with Rolls-Royce), inflation, unrealistic transfer prices and variations in the definition of the accounting terms, all of which could cause wide fluctuations in the value of Z, and so destroy its usefulness. So we ask the question: How reliable *is* the Z-score, based as it is on figures themselves suspect at the crucial point in time?

Are earnings the real key?

In the ultimate analysis, earnings alone may be the best indicator of a company's health. Not, of course, the earnings in any one year, but measured over a period of years and in particular taking note of the trend from year to year. Failure to

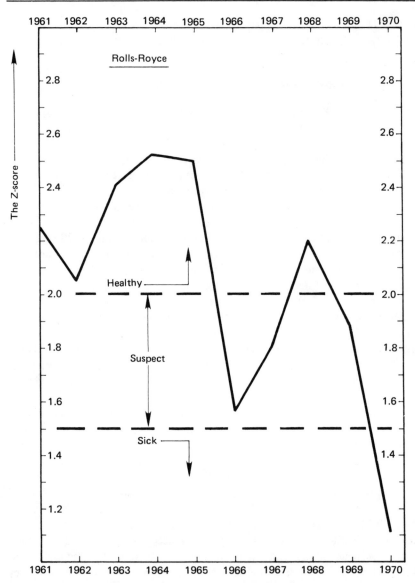

Figure 11.1   Argenti interprets Altman. *Whilst Argenti has used the Z-score formula proposed by Altman, his assessment of the risk area has been adjusted to suit UK conditions.*

maintain satisfactory earnings over a period of years will sap the strength of a company slowly but surely. If you have any doubts, just take note of this:

healthy earnings do more to provide the opportunity for other categories to be healthy than any other factor. Capable men cannot be employed unless the company has the means to do so . . . financial conditions can seldom be kept healthy, and an enterprise certainly cannot properly reward stockowners, pursue research and development, and even provide adequate sales and production techniques, unless it has healthy earnings . . .[12]

So we assert again that earnings can be considered the most important single indicator of a company's health. If earnings reach a plateau and stay there year after year, or start to drop, then there is a chain reaction. The consequent drop in internal funds affects both the working capital and the long-term investment vital for growth. Borrowings, whether they be short-term or long-term, only mask the real drop in earnings in such a case. The effect of reduced earnings over a period of years is cumulative and can soon assume serious proportions. Thus earnings at a plateau is the first sign of trouble ahead.

It is perhaps well to sound a word of warning, just in case you begin to think that there is a simple answer. The earnings of a company have to be assessed *relative* to those of other companies in the same industry and also *relative* to the general economic situation. The relative position of a company in its own industry, *vis-à-vis* that of its competitors, is crucial. Survival lies in maintaining or improving the *relative* position of the company in its industry.

Beaver vs. Altman

Beaver advocated one ratio. Altman developed a factor using a wide range of ratios. We said earlier that the use of only one ratio was dangerous, but it is not quite as simple as that.

Beaver, as we showed earlier, tested 30 different ratios, seeking to predict failure up to five years ahead. His finding was that the 'cash flow/total debt' ratio was the most certain predictor of failure, since it showed the least error when applied to his particular sample of firms. Altman, however, claimed better results for his Z-score, which uses some five different ratios in combination.

Which of the two techniques is the better? Beaver's technique is certainly a lot simpler in use, and if it is at least as reliable as Altman's approach, which is far more complex, why go to all that trouble? Gupta made a systematic comparison of the two systems and found that Beaver's method was definitely more reliable than that of Altman.[13] A comparison of the two yields the following results:

Percentage error in prediction

Years before bankruptcy	Beaver	Altman
1	13	5
2	21	28
3	23	52
4	24	71
5	22	64

The errors in prediction are consistent in the case of Beaver but not so in the case of Altman, who however has a much better accuracy *one year* before bankruptcy. This better accuracy, as measured, was found by Gupta to be largely illusory. In an obscure footnote Altman mentions that the published accounts relating to the last year before bankruptcy appear only 7½ months before bankruptcy actually occurs and this he arbitrarily calls a year. Experience also shows that with companies in trouble the published accounts are often much delayed, and it often happens that the accounts only become available *after* bankruptcy has been declared. To predict bankruptcy at that late stage is of course pointless. We would further comment that the sharp jumps and violent movements in the assessment of the Altman data also make this method suspect.

The wide margin of error only two years ahead of bankruptcy (28 per cent) seems to have been underplayed not only by Altman but by the many researchers who have followed in his footsteps. Such an error is too high for the method to be used with any confidence, since it means that in practice the prediction is going to be wrong at least once every four times it is used. What would be an acceptable margin of error here? We would suggest between 10 and 15 per cent. Three years ahead Altman's approach gives a margin of error, declared by himself, of over 50 per cent. That is ridiculous: one might as well flip a coin!

To be of real value, in terms of using the prediction to initiate action, it *must* be made several years ahead. Then there will be time for countermeasures to be taken. This is not an academic exercise: we are looking to apply this tool to bring benefits *to the company at risk.*

In our next chapter we shall be dealing with various other approaches to the prediction of failure, but since some of them are based on or are related to the Altman model, we think it well to sound this note of warning.

Summary

Prediction of failure and bankruptcy is not only very desirable but also possible – perhaps! The very earliest methods used to assess the credit-worthiness of a company, still in use today, remain a very valuable indicator of trouble ahead, but at that point the assessment is qualitative, rather than quantitative. Having assessed quantitative techniques offered by Beaver and Altman, one using a single financial ratio, the other a weighted combination of such ratios, we come to the conclusion that, odd though it may seem, one ratio is better than a combination of five.

References

1. Altman, E. I., *Corporate Financial Distress. A Complete Guide to Predictions, Avoiding, and Dealing with Bankruptcy,* Wiley, 1983.
2. Wilcox, J. W., Book Review, *Journal of Banking and Finance*, 8, 142–4, March 1984.

3. Altman, E. I., *Corporate Bankruptcy in America*, D. C. Heath, Lexington, Mass., 1971.
4. Argenti, J. and J. Sumner, *Predicting Corporate Failure, Accountants Digest No. 138*, Institute of Chartered Accountants, London, 1983.
5. Smith, R. and A. Winakor, *Changes in Financial Structure of Unsuccessful Corporations*, University of Illinois, Bureau of Business Research, 1935; Merwin, C., *Financing Small Corporations*, National Bureau of Economic Research, New York, 1942.
6. Hickman, W. B., *Corporate Bond Quality and Investor Experience*, Princeton University Press, 1958.
7. Beaver, W. H., 'Financial ratios as predictors of failure', *Empirical Research in Accounting: Selected Studies*, supplement to *Journal of Accounting Research*, Jan. 1967, pp. 71–111. Beaver, W. H., 'Alternative accounting measures as predictors of failure', *Accounting Review*, Jan. 1968, pp. 113–22.
8. Miller, D. E., *The Meaningful Interpretation of Financial Statements*, American Management Association, 1966.
9. Neter, J., 'Discussion of financial ratios as predictors of Failure', *Empirical Research in Accounting: Selected Studies 1966*, supplement to *Journal of Accounting Research*, 4, 1967.
10. Altman, E. I., R. Avery, R. Eisenbeis and J. Sinkey, *Application of Classification Techniques in Business, Banking and Finance*, JAI Press, Greenwich, Conn., 1981.
11. Altman, E. I., 'Financial ratios, discriminant analysis and the prediction of corporate bankruptcy', *J. of Finance*, 23, 589–609, Sept. 1969.
12. Martindell, J., *The Appraisal of Management*, Harper & Row, 1965.
13. Gupta, L. C., *Financing Ratios for Monitoring Corporate Sickness – Towards a More Systematic Approach*, Oxford University Press, 1983.

12 Knowledge grows, but problems grow faster

The whole purpose of prediction, so far as we are concerned, is to be able to take preventive action and so avert disaster. Preventive action demands time, and the more time one has the better. So we seek a method that gives us two, three, perhaps five years' notice. The technique must also bring conviction, if we are to get senior management to take what will be in their view both drastic and undesirable action. They must, first of all, be convinced of its necessity if they are to be made to act.

The prediction of failure using a variety of financial ratios, either singly or in combination, has been a very fertile area for financial analysts. The attraction is that one appears to be dealing with precise numbers drawn from published, public documents. The mind of the accountant is such that a figure is a figure: whereas to the estimator, for instance, a figure can well be but an indication of order of magnitude. It is, however, unfortunately true that many of the figures that the accountant may abstract from the accounts to calculate a financial ratio are worse than unreliable: they are downright misleading.

Nevertheless, a very large number of prediction models have been developed. Some are claimed to be general, applicable to all industries: others are specific to a certain industry or country. Yet others are said to apply, for instance, only to the smaller business, a subject we deal with in Chapter 13.

Bankruptcy models galore

The number of models for the prediction of business failure is far too large for us even to begin to review and assess them all: even a bibliography would be a book in its own right. We therefore propose to discuss only a few and we have based our selection on that made by Altman,[1] having regard to a further evaluation made by Scott.[2]

Let us look first at a model proposed by Deakin.[3] This was put forward in 1972 and modified in 1977, following work done by Libby to which we shall refer in a moment. Deakin analysed 32 failing and non-failing companies, related to the period 1964–70. The misclassification error using his formula, up to three years prior to failure, was less than 5 per cent, a remarkable result. But this was on the basis of specific models developed for each separate model, which was a rather cumbersome approach. The 1977 model was based on a far larger sample,

114

another 31 firms being added to the original 32.[4] In addition, the 'non-failing' sample consisted of 80 firms randomly selected. The terminology changed as well: instead of talking about 'failed' companies, the term 'failing' was used: an improvement from our point of view.

Deakin used 14 ratios. Libby followed this up with a model that only used five of these 14 ratios, those relating to profitability, activity, liquidity, asset balance and the cash position.[5] When his formula was applied to Deakin's 1972 sample, the accuracy was only slightly less than that of Deakin's, yet it was much simpler to use. Bankers found it particularly useful in their work.

Elam, in 1975, was the first to incorporate into a formula and then test the effects of lease data on the accuracy of bankruptcy prediction. Leasing, by this time, was a rapidly growing industry. He took for his sample 48 firms who had gone bankrupt between 1966 and 1972 and matched them with non-failing firms on the basis of comparable industry, sales and lease data. He used the data to test a set of 28 ratios and came to the conclusion that the lease data played no role in bankruptcy prediction. He made no attempt, however, to find the best model appropriate to his data, so his work hardly helps.

Now let us look at the 'gambler's ruin' approach, propounded by Wilcox using a matched sample of 52 bankrupt and 52 non-bankrupt firms.[6] The important variables in his model were the net liquidation value, the average adjusted cash flow and a novel concept of the firm winning or losing a 'bet'. The model is claimed to be of general application, to be used not only across many industries, but also for hospitals and service companies. The accuracy of prediction was impressive, particularly at the extremes of distribution. The model is now being marketed by Advantage Financial Systems (AFS), of Cambridge, Massachusetts.

We go now from the general to the particular. Blum designed a model specifically to aid the antitrust division of the Justice Department in the US in the assessment of the probability of business failure.[7] Business failure is here defined in accordance with the meaning given to it in the courts. Here we have 115 companies who had failed between 1954 and 1968, paired with another 115 who had not failed, the basis for choice being year, industry, sales and number of employees. Blum developed a 12-variable formula emphasizing liquidity, profitability and variability. It was said to be about 95 per cent accurate in the year before failure, 80 per cent accurate two years before failure and 70 per cent accurate for earlier years. Blum's work is theoretically sound and technically competent, but his approach suffers, as indeed do most of the others, from the fact that the choice of variables is in a sense arbitrary. He himself proposed that his model might be further improved if other ratios were tried.

As we have said earlier, this brief sampling review of the wide range of models proposed by a multitude of researchers and investigators is designed to give a 'feel' for what is going on. You will perhaps notice that all the approaches are empirical and subjective. All seem to go for complexity, whereas we share

Gupta's view that a complicated model is not necessarily a better one.[8] We have long advocated the view that 'simple is beautiful'.[9] Beaver's work, to which we gave some space in Chapter 11, certainly fits that description better than most of the models on offer.

Proprietary models

The models briefly referred to above are published in full detail and can be tested by anyone interested in the subject. The ratios, their weighting and the precise definition of the terms being used are all available, often with sample calculations to make it easier. But when we turn to the so-called 'proprietary' models, the position is very different. The formulae are *not* published and their use is restricted to subscribers who have paid for the privilege of an answer. There are quite a number of such information sources on the market, but again for the sake of space we must limit our review. We have therefore taken two, one from each side of the Atlantic.

The Zeta model

The Zeta model is based on the work of Altman and his co-workers.[10] It is an extension of the Z-score model, developed jointly with a private financial company, and is being marketed by Zeta Services Inc. of Mountainside, NJ, in the US. The immediate question this extension of the original idea raises is: What is wrong with the Z-score? In what way is it inadequate?

It appears that there has been a dramatic change in the size and financial profiles of companies in general, including, of course, those that fail. The average asset size of the companies analysed to develop data for the Zeta model was US\$100 million, whereas the assets of the largest company analysed to develop the latest Z-score formula was only US\$25 million. In addition, retailing companies are now included, together with a much broader range of manufacturing companies. The changes that have taken place in financial reporting, reporting standards and current accepted accounting practices have also to be incorporated in the data used for developing the model. Due note is also taken of the footnotes that so often qualify the published accounts of a company. All this research has to be paid for – that is at least one reason why we now have the commercial, rather than the academic approach.

We are told that the test sample upon which Zeta is based was 53 bankrupt firms and 58 non-bankrupt firms, carefully matched for industry and year, and divided almost equally between manufacturers and retailers. It is asserted that the accuracy of prediction one year ahead of bankruptcy is more than 90 per cent, while accuracy of prediction is better than 70 per cent even up to five years ahead of bankruptcy. An independent analysis by Scott of the Zeta models showed that it ranks first among empirical models in terms of accuracy.[2] Further, a simple linear structure for the formula was found to be as accurate as the quadratic form – especially in relation to the long-term accuracy of the prediction. The seven variables found to be the most important are:

Return on total assets, measured by the earnings before interest and taxes.
Stability of earnings, measured over time.
Debt service, a logarithmic relationship between interest coverage, working capital and total debt.
Cumulative profitability, measured by relating retained earnings to total assets.
Liquidity, the current ratio.
Capitalization, which relates the common equity to total capital, both averaged over a five-year term.
Size of firm, its total tangible assets, adjusted for any recent reporting changes.

We are a long, long way from the Z-score model, are we not? We lack the formula, so can make no progress, but thought it valuable to see what factors are considered significant. The model, when developed, was tested against the records of 64 companies that had filed for bankruptcy, and the accuracy of prediction, in terms of years prior to bankruptcy, were:

1st year: 95
2nd year: 90
3rd year: 78   (all figures expressed as percentages)
4th year: 67
5th year: 63

What is most important in relation to the accuracy that has been achieved is not that it is in fact better than with the Z-score, but that we have a continuous progression. The Z-score, as we demonstrated in Chapter 11, was most erratic (5–28–52–71–64) – and we might as well ignore that first figure since, as we saw earlier, it was not really a prediction at all.

The PAS-score

Performance Analysis Services Limited offer the PAS score as part of their advisory service, from their London offices. From the brochures advertising this approach to prediction we learn that it starts from Taffler's Z-score.[11] Taffler's Z-score has four ratios, measuring:

Profitability   (profit before tax)/(average current liabilities)
Working Capital   (current assets)/(total liabilities)
Financial Risk   (current liabilities)/(total assets)
Liquidity   the 'no credit interval'

The last item is the number of days that a company can finance its operations when it generates no revenue.

The ratios given above apply to manufacturing firms, and a different set of ratios have been established for distribution firms. The same arguments used in relation to the Altman data in the United States were used in London in relation to the Taffler data. Conditions in the economy had changed, interest rates had increased, these and other factors had led to the development of the PAS approach to the assessment of the viability of a company. The system has been programmed for a micro-computer and serves as a confidential customer information system. The customer can either approach PAS Ltd with specific requests or purchase the program and derive his own answers by feeding in the relevant data from the published accounts of the company he is interested in. It is claimed that by using PAS a credit manager can 'monitor his credit risk exposure, focus attention on the high risk debtors and highlight opportunities to promote products and services to the healthiest companies.'[12] We are further told that 'the PAS Microcomputer System is designed by users for users and provides the credit manager with an invaluable tool for assessing credit risk . . . to maximise trade, minimise bad debt exposure and optimise credit limits'.

PAS, based on rigorous analysis combined with management experience, seeks to measure the health of a company on an even scale from 0 to 100. The service is being used by some 30 banking and investment institutions, auditors and others. The basic feature of the system is that the score is calculated for recent years and plotted. The trend is the key to the conclusions that are drawn. If the score is below a certain threshold figure, then the firm is 'at risk'. A minimum of data is required and the scores for the past 5 years can be available within some 15 minutes, once the user has had about 4 hours training. The system is supported by several years' experience in the analysis and interpretation of results. The PAS score differs from the usual Z-score in that it is linear. This allows ready assessment of the import of the figures as they are plotted. The company maintains a databank of some 2500 firms, which not only serves to prove the validity of their scoring system but also helps in that a sizeable volume of data is available for monitoring. An interesting feature of the program is that it can detect hidden weaknesses, as when a company overvalues its stocks.

The PAS analysis of the firm Hestair is an interesting example of the system in action. We present the graph as Fig. 12.1. You will see that the company has been in the 'risk' region for five years now, yet it still hangs on. But for how much longer? Well, that will depend on the remedial action its directors take, or fail to take, which then becomes reflected in the PAS score. This is why we have emphasized the pivotal role of management, and especially of the chief executive. We opened that theme in Chapters 3 and 4, and will return to it again when we come to look for a panacea in Part Four. That thought leads us to the Argenti approach to this problem.

The Argenti sequence

If we listen to Argenti, we do not need the financial indicators, except to a very minor extent. What we must have, however, is an intimate knowledge of the

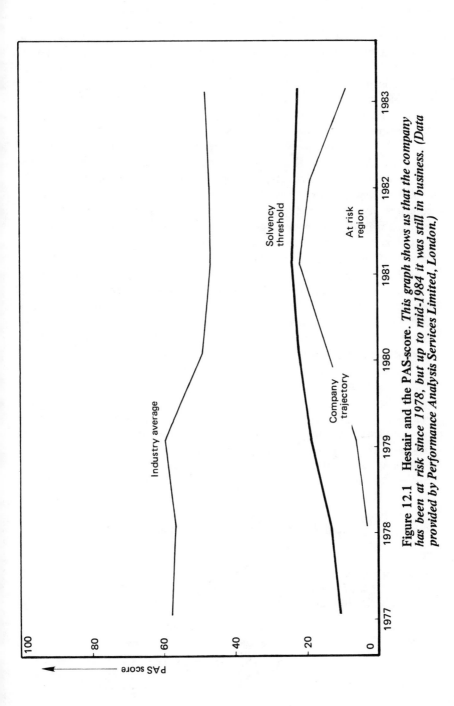

Figure 12.1   Hestair and the PAS-score. *This graph shows us that the company has been at risk since 1978, but up to mid-1984 it was still in business. (Data provided by Performance Analysis Services Limited, London.)*

company and especially its top management. The sequence was first described in 1977.[13] It has now been tested among some thousand accountants, managers and bankers in seven countries, including India, where one of us was associated with the exercise at five seminars on the subject. The misclassification error has been found to be less than 5 per cent.

With Argenti, failure is seen as the culmination of a sequence starting with management defects that bring mistakes, which in turn produce symptoms. These symptoms, and their scores, are presented in Table 12.1. These scores (called the A-score) are all bad marks, so that the ideal company would score zero. There is a probability of failure once the score gets above 25, and a company is at risk once the figure goes above 35. Companies not at risk usually score less than 18, so the 'grey area' with Argenti is between 18 and 35. If a company is in the grey area caution is necessary. We have a warning signal that steps should be taken to reduce the A-score below 18. However, while a pass mark is 25, if the total in the 'Defects' section is more than 10, then there is cause for anxiety even if the total score is still less than 25. It will be seen that this approach assesses the management capability of a company and gives substantial weighting to the chief executive and his board of directors. Management defects lead to mistakes, and thus to failure. A company that had scored 15 for 'Mistakes', but still had a score of less than 10 for 'Defects' might well be at risk, but the lower score for 'Defects' would tend to indicate that the management were competent to deal with the situation.

The various scores presented in Table 12.1 must be used in full or not at all. Intermediate or partial scores have no meaning and should not be used. The philosophy behind the use of the A-score is that if a company is in trouble, then that is due to management defects and the consequent mistakes, which will have been there for a number of years and should be noticed by a careful observer long before the signs of financial distress are seen. The A-score thus attempts to quantify a qualitative judgement. It is therefore highly subjective and the observer needs to visit the company and its factories, meet its directors and get to know them well, in order to make objective assessments. That is not easy and takes time. The A-score is clearly based on these premises. So the

Table 12.1   The Argenti sequence. This table presents the weighting given by Argenti to the various aspects of management performance in order to assess a company's viability. Note that the higher the score, the worse the state of the company.

Defects	in management
8	The chief executive is an autocrat
4	He is also the chairman
2	Passive board — an autocrat will see to that

Table 12.1 continued

	2	Unbalanced board — too many engineers or too many finance types		
	2	Weak finance director		
	1	Poor management depth		
		in accountancy —		
	3	No budgets or budgetary controls (to assess variances, etc.)		
	3	No cash flow plans, or not updated		
	3	No costing system. Cost and contribution of each product unknown		
	15	Poor response to change, old-fashioned product, obsolete factory, old directors, out-of-date marketing		
Total defects	43		**Pass**	10
Mistakes	15	High leverage, firm could get into trouble by stroke of bad luck		
	15	Overtrading. Company expanding faster than its funding. Capital base too small or unbalanced for the size and type of business		
	15	Big project gone wrong. Any obligation which the company cannot meet if something goes wrong		
Total mistakes	45		**Pass**	15
Symptoms	4	Financial signs, such as Z-score. Appears near failure time		
	4	Creative accounting. Chief executive is the first to see signs of failure, and in an attempt to hide it from creditors and the banks, accounts are 'glossed over', by for instance overvaluing stocks, using lower depreciation, etc. Skilled observers can spot these things		
	3	Non-financial signs, such as untidy offices, frozen salaries, chief executive 'ill', high staff turnover, low morale, rumours		
	1	Terminal signs		
Total symptoms	12			
Total possible score	100		**Pass**	25

approach suggested by Argenti is sound enough: the problem lies in its day-to-day application. Perhaps it is better to learn the lesson that has come via the A-score, that the chief executive determines the health of his company. Hence, if a company is failing, then its chief executive is failing and the road to health may lie in replacing him. That is why we have already devoted one full chapter to the characteristics of the 'man at the top' and shall do that again in Part Four. Geneen, whom we studied in Chapter 4, having been both chief executive and chairman, felt on retiring that it is not desirable to combine those two functions. He ought to know!

An explosion in knowledge, but . . .

We hope that our review of the literature on the prediction of business failures has illustrated the possibilities. One would like to think that the problem has been solved: press a few keys at a computer keyboard and we know just where a company is going. Once we know that, preventive measures can be taken if our company is seen to be at risk. We even know *what* preventive measures to take. But the problem is far from being solved. Why?

All the models that we have discussed, except that proposed by Argenti, which is not available to the average person seeking information, use financial data abstracted from the company accounts. This is the picture 'yesterday', whereas what we really want, for successful prediction, is the picture 'tomorrow'. Is tomorrow a projection from yesterday? Far from it. We now know that *all* forecasts are wrong. In another context entirely, project planning, we have declared that it is impossible to forecast the future.[14] Yet forecasts continue to be made: we must have *some* basis on which to build. Another factor is the possibility that the published accounts can be 'doctored' or delayed.

Yet another problem is the fact that company accountants have developed many techniques for hiding the true position. We will deal in detail with 'creative accounting' in Chapter 20. For now, let us just say that we consider it to be destructive accounting. While the outsider is deceived, the internal management is also often deceived as well and the company goes on blindly to its doom.

Summary

We have reviewed more models of the various methods used for the prediction of company failure. All employ the MDA approach, using a number of ratios, to a pattern set by the work of Altman. We prefer and would rather put our trust in the single ratio suggested by Beaver, as in our view all these further models fail to advance the situation. Two proprietary models of this type, the Zeta and PAS, have been briefly described. Argenti proposes a qualitative study of a company in order to discern where it is going, but before that can be done a skilled observer has to spend a lot of time learning to know the company intimately, a procedure that may be resented.

References

1. Altman, E. I., *Corporate Financial Distress. A Complete Guide to Predicting, Avoiding, and Dealing with Bankruptcy*, Wiley, 1983.
2. Scott, J., 'The probability of bankruptcy – a comparison of empirical predictions and theoretical models', *Journal of Banking and Finance*, 5 (3), 317–44, Sept. 1981.
3. Deakin, E. B., 'A discriminate analysis of predictors of business failure', *Journal of Accounting Research*, **10**, 167–79, 1972.
4. Altman, E. I. and T. McGough, 'Evaluations of a company as a going concern', *Journal of Accountancy*, Dec. 1974.
5. Libby, R., 'Accounting ratios and the prediction of failure – some behavioural evidence', *Journal of Accounting Research*, **13**, 150–61, Spring 1975.
6. Wilcox, J. W., 'A prediction of business failure using accounting data', *Empirical Research in Accounting, Selecting Studies*, supplement to *Journal of Accounting Research*, **11**, 163–79, 1973; Wilcox, J. W., 'The gamblers ruin approach to business risk', *Sloan Management Review*, **18**, 33–46, Fall 1976.
7. Blum, M., 'Failing company discriminant analysis', *Journal of Accounting Research*, **12**, 1–25, Spring 1974.
8. Gupta, L. C., *Financing Ratios for Monitoring Corporate Sickness – Towards a More Systematic Approach*, Oxford University Press, 1983.
9. Kharbanda, O. P., E. A. Stallworthy and L. F. Williams, *Project Cost Control in Action*, Gower, 1980. (See Chapter 9: 'Simple is beautiful'.)
10. Altman, E. I. *et al.*, 'ZETA analysis: a new model to identify bankruptcy risk of corporations', *Journal of Banking and Finance*, **1** (1), 29–54, 1977.
11. Taffler, R. J., 'Forecasting company failure in the UK using discriminant analysis and financial ratio data', *Journal of the Royal Statistical Society, Series A (General)*, **145** (3), 342–58, 1982; Taffler, R. J., 'The assessment of company solvency and performance using a statistical model – a comparative UK-based study', *Accounting and Business Research*, Autumn 1983; Taffler, R. J., 'Empirical models for the monitoring of UK corporations', *Journal of Banking and Finance*, **8**, 199–227, 1984.
12. *The PAS Microcomputer System. A Confidential Customer Information System*, Performance Analysis Services Ltd, London.
13. Argenti, J., 'Company failure – long-range prediction is not enough', *Accountancy*, August 1977, pp. 46–52.
14. Stallworthy, E. A. and O. P. Kharbanda, *Total Project Management – From Concept to Completion*, Gower, 1983.

13 Small is not beautiful

In 1973 E. F. Schumacher's book *Small is Beautiful* started a revolution in thinking at a time when 'bigger' was considered to be both cheaper and better.[1] His ideas have since been put into practice in the construction of factories and other similar works. A book has now been written dealing with some applications of the Schumacher concept.[2] It has been demonstrated that the savings resulting from economy of scale in the construction of factory units, which gave such impetus to 'building big', are often lost when the project is considered in relation to the infrastructure.[3] However, our present context is business failure, not factory design and construction, and it is an unwelcome fact that there are many more failures among small firms than amongst the medium-sized and large firms, even when the rate of failure is assessed as a percentage of the total number of businesses of a comparable size. Why should the small firms be so vulnerable? We shall see why later in this chapter, but let us first turn our attention to the means available to us to predict potential failure and collapse in the small company.

Failure prediction

Over the past two chapters we have been reviewing methods for the prediction of business failure, based on MDA techniques. When we come to the small business, however, it seems that these techniques are not immediately applicable.[4] A methodology has been developed in the US and for the purpose of analysis a 'small business' has been taken to be a business that had a loan from the Small Business Administration (SBA). Loss borrowers were considered to be 'failures' and non-loss borrowers 'non-failures'. The sample tested in the course of developing the data consisted of 42 loss borrowers and an equal number of non-loss borrowers for whom three consecutive annual reports were available during the period 1954–69. The sample available for assessment was much bigger – 562 – when only one report was required. Edminster, who carried out the research, analysed 19 financial ratios, including some of those that had been found to be significant in previous prediction studies. His approach focused attention on the testing of four hypotheses as predictors of failure. A seven-variable equation was found to fit the known results:

$$Z = 0.951 - 0.423X_1 - 0.293X_2 - 0.483X_3 + 0.277X_4 - 0.452X_5 - 0.352X_6$$
$$- 0.924X_7$$

With this formula Z is 1.0 for non-failing companies and falls to zero. Using a cut-off point of 0.53, so that when Z was below 0.53 the business was assessed as 'failing' (while with Z above 0.53 it was 'non-failing'), an accuracy of 93 per cent was achieved in relation to the known sample that had been analysed.

In the formula above:

X_1 = Taken as 1.0 if the (annual funds flow)/(current liabilities) is less than 0.05: otherwise it is zero.

X_2 = Taken as 1.0 if the (equity)/(sales) ratio is less than 0.07, otherwise it is zero.

X_3 = Taken as 1.0 if the (net working capital)/(sales)/(corresponding RMA average ratio) is less than 0.02, otherwise it is zero.

X_4 = Taken as 1.0 if the (current liabilities/equity)/(corresponding RMA average ratio) is less than 0.48, otherwise it is zero.

X_5 = Taken as 1.0 if the (inventory/sales)/(corresponding RMA average ratio) shows an upward trend, otherwise it is zero.

X_6 = Taken as 1.0 if the (quick ratio)/(trend in the RMA quick ratio) is downward or level just prior to the loan and less than 0.34, otherwise it is zero.

X_7 = Taken as 1.0 if the (quick ratio)/(RMA quick ratio) shows an upward trend, otherwise it is zero.

Edminster recommended a 'black-grey-white' method of assessment. The term 'white' referred to a non-loss borrower, where the loan application had been accepted, while 'black' referred to a business whose application had been rejected. For businesses in the 'grey' area further investigation would be necessary.

Altman, commenting on this particular prediction model, notes that whereas other models, developed for the larger companies, require just one year's published accounts for an assessment to be made, this particular technique demanded three consecutive yearly statements for an effective analysis.[5] Although the accuracy of the method is quite good, this may be due in part to Edminster's data transformation approach. That is, the initial ratios are converted to either 1.0 or zero. Since the financial ratios for small businesses show a wide scatter, this particular technique does however present us with meaningful data and consistent Z-scores.

Other prediction methods

It appears that Edminster's technique has not gained any acceptability in small business circles, since it is not being used by either the SBA or any of the major lending institutions. What else is available? In the previous chapter we considered two proprietary models, Zeta and the PAS score. The firm offering the PAS score (see p. 117) does offer a 'Smaller Company Service', catering specifically to this sector. Because of the commercial implications, details of the technique being used are not published, but the company claims:

> When granting credit it is implied that risk is measured and accepted. A reliable source of up to date and accurate solvency reports is therefore essential for the credit manager who relies upon external agencies for his risk assessment..
>
> The PAS Smaller Company Service is designed specifically to ensure that the credit manager knows the solvency position of his key customers as given by their latest information available and thereby makes his decision making easier.

The service offered claims to supply a financial analysis of named companies, a summary of the last five years of profit and loss and balance sheet information in a standard format and conventional ratio analysis. A typical PAS Solvency Report presents among other data a Financial Profile as set out in Table 13.1. This shows the company's relative strengths and weaknesses on a scale of 1 to 10. The PAS score is presented on a lineal scale, from 1 to 100, while a negative Z-score indicates a risk of failure.

In the initial development of solvency models the only differences between them are the raw data of insolvent and solvent company accounts. That is what determines the discriminating ratios and their relevant power. Thus PAS has developed a model from privately-owned UK manufacturing companies which has been found to be trustworthy for companies with turnovers of around £1.5 million. This therefore becomes one definition of a small company to whom the PAS score can be properly applied. The important consideration is whether the tax position of the owner has materially influenced the drawing up of the accounts, since tax considerations tend to play a significant role with the smaller business.

Table 13.1   The smaller company service. Here we have an extract from a PAS Solvency Report. Such reports, commissioned by the client, are updated regularly as new accounts become available. (With thanks to Performance Analysis Services Ltd, London, for permission to publish.)

PAS year	1978	1979	1980	1981	1982
Profitability	3	3	2	4	4
Working capital	4	4	5	3	3
Financial risk	2	5	5	5	2
Short-term liquidity	1	2	2	1	1
PAS score	9	25	22	19	10
Z-score	−0.38	1.35	0.06	−0.63	−2.49

What we find remarkable is that the use of the service is limited, in practice, to those seeking to protect themselves from loss. The concept of prediction analysis with a view to prevention is just not there.

No doubt the most effective and perhaps the quickest method of assessing the health of the small business is that proposed by Argenti, which we discussed in the previous chapter. Unfortunately Argenti makes no mention of the small business in his analysis and discussion of results, but there is no reason why the approach should not be completely effective. In so far as it lays emphasis on the chief executive and the vast majority of small businesses are managed by one man, usually the owner, the approach amounts to an assessment of his personal and particularly entrepreneurial qualities. Although certain countries, such as the US and the UK, have specific schemes and programmes designed to encourage and assist the smaller business, wherever we go in the world it is finally the local bank manager who has to face up to this problem of assessment. If he could be encouraged to use the A-score approach, which translates a subjective assessment into a quantitative evaluation, he could well perform a most valuable service not only to his bank, but to his customers.

Why do so many small businesses flop?

This question is part of the title to an article in the journal *Across the Board*, but the title goes on to add 'and some succeed'.[6] Both authors are with the SBA, so once again we are getting the American view, but in view of their position, working for the Agency in Washington, they ought to know the answer. They begin their analysis by describing three disasters in the small business field. The names, the activities and the locations given are fictitious, but the cases are from real life.

Joe Atkins had saved US$25000 and borrowed US$50000 to invest in a ready-to-wear shop for men. The entire amount was spent on the store and its stock, so that on opening day his bank balance was US$2.60. He had not provided for working capital and so was squeezed for cash right from the start. He had to close the shop six months later and file for bankruptcy. Should not the lender have reviewed Joe's unrealistic costings and given him some sound advice?

Mary Williams, a gourmet cook, encouraged by her friends, invested in a city catering operation. An excellent cook but a poor manager, she barely survived for the first eight months. Fortunately she found a willing partner to act as manager and the two together made the operation profitable.

Marion Johnson, a professional 'tinkerer', designed many new products and took out several patents. She decided to go in for manufacturing some of the products she had designed, but failed miserably and declared bankruptcy twice. She emerged sadder but wiser from these experiences and got others to manufacture her products against royalties. This third venture became profitable.

These cases are from the US but we are sure that you will recognise parallels in your own country. An example from the UK illustrates a trap that many small businesses fall into.[7] A small manufacturing company received an order worth £200000, with payment over six months. The company required an overdraft of £15000 to purchase a new machine to carry out the work. However, they were almost bankrupt some three months later because of negative cash flow. They had overlooked one crucial fact: it takes a couple of months to get your money after you have issued the invoice. A simple cash flow analysis showed that they had needed some £80000 (not £15000) extra funding in order to execute the order.

All the above cases illustrate a common weakness: lack of managerial ability. However, there is another type of small business failure that, most surprisingly, comes with success and phenomenal growth. We have the example of Telair (fictitious), who started with an engine-analysing instrument, later a sophisticated electronic transmitter for locating downed aircraft and finally a limited channel radio for aviation use. The company had a successful product and a stable financial position. It then embarked upon an ambitious project with a product in the mainstream of avionics: a new generation of aviation radios using light emitting diodes (LED) in the cockpit. Development costs were enormous and there was a considerable time and cost overrun compared with the original estimates. However, the product was an instant success, so the company expanded fast to cater for the demand. But a competing product and a credit squeeze brought the company down and it had to file for bankruptcy. This business then had a typical Case B failure, as illustrated in Fig. 2.3 (p. 19). A large electronics company acquired the business and made a success of it by the injection of funds and successful marketing.

Let us translate that disaster into something positive by delineating the successful owner of a small business: while he is the most critical driving force in the company, while he *alone* may well determine the direction of the business, he *must* surround himself with good competent people and he *must* stay 'liquid'. If the qualifying factors we have just mentioned are not there, then failure may result. Could the use of the A-score analysis technique identify the successful entrepreneur *before* he sets off on his meteoric course?

Have we a policy failure?

Most countries seek to encourage the formation and growth of the small business through the use of various incentives and fiscal policy. Of course, the definition of the 'small business', in terms of either the capital employed or the number of employees, varies from country to country, but such businesses are contributing an ever-growing proportion of the GNP in a great many countries. While this is generally true in relation to manufacturing industries, it is especially true of the service industries. The contribution of the small-scale sector is about a third in the UK and India, and rising steadily, while in the US it is some 40 per cent and nearly 70 per cent in Japan. These figures are developed by measuring the employment offered and the output of such firms by value. Overall there seems to be a steady decline in the large manufacturing units producing items like cars, trucks and ships, but the small firm, even when working in the same industry, seems to prosper. In the service industries the small business undoubtedly both prospers and predominates.

In Britain the encouragement of the small business is seen as a solution to the serious unemployment problem. The idea has been to build up the self-employed sector through the use of a variety of incentives. For instance, during the period from 1979 to 1983 the Conservative government passed over 760 measures designed to support the small firm. They enjoy generous loan guarantee schemes and by 1983 the government had provided an 80 per cent guarantee on loans to small firms totalling US$500 million (£329 million). Since 1981 the individual has been given tax relief for investment in new or expanding business. Not all such incentives are used for the purpose intended and one letter to the editor of the *Economist* in this context declared:

> Junk all subsidies and tax incentives for small businesses. There is no shortage of money available if you know where to look and if you don't know (or can't find out) then you shouldn't be in business in the first place.

So one wonders whether the various incentives serve the purpose in view. Perhaps the small businesses they are designed to encourage would succeed anyway, and the less efficient, who ultimately fail, just have a 'happy holiday' while the money lasts. We could even pose the question: Don't incentives just increase the number of failures?

When we turn to India, undoubtedly the home of the small business, we see quite clearly that some of the policies have failed. Apart from numerous incentives, including low-interest loans, tax holidays, sales tax and excise tax exemption and a host of others, there are special facilities and attractions offered to those prepared to set up industries in the so-called 'backward areas'. The idea, of course, is to disperse industry and provide employment in areas where it is sadly lacking. Various state and central government bodies offer assistance and in some cases, where for instance high technology is involved, the entrepreneur needs only to put some 10 per cent of his own money into the total cost of a project. Against this background, two types of abuse are of especial interest.

Firstly (and this is what we believe happens elsewhere where incentives are involved) the easy availability of finance attracts the incompetent, encouraging the unemployed to become self-employed and then style themselves 'business-men'. There is virtually no assessment of the capabilities or the credentials of the budding entrepreneur. Although much good advice is on offer, no one is there to see that it is taken. As a result, more than 50 per cent of such new businesses fail and the finance, largely public money, has been spent to no purpose. There is even evidence that many such firms have been set up specifically to 'siphon out' such funds.

Secondly, there has been gross misuse of facilities intended for small-scale industry by the bigger companies. This has been so serious as to warrant a full-length book on the subject.[8] The message of the book can be summed up by saying that those whom the small-scale industry policy was never intended to benefit have exploited it up to the hilt. The authors, fortunately, provide substantial evidence to prove their points. Three aspects of the small-scale industry policy, as formulated by the government, are considered:

The criterion for a small-scale industry unit
The actual constituents of the small industry sector
The product reservation for the small-scale industry units

The criterion for classification as a SSI (small-scale industry) is an investment limit in plant and machinery of Rs2 million (Rs10 is about US$1). This started as Rs750000, and was first revised upwards in 1972 to Rs1 million, even although at that time less than 1 per cent of the SSI units had an investment of more than Rs600000. As late as 1977, more than 90 per cent of the units registered had an investment in plant and machinery of less than Rs100000. So the very high upper limits opened up the system to use by the larger company whom it was never intended to help.

Much more serious was the fact that until recently the ownership aspect of the SSI was not even defined. It was designed to encourage the small entrepreneur, but in the absence of any rules the larger companies capitalized on the system by promoting SSI units. Some 40 examples are listed in the book, where major firms such as Tata, Birla and even multinationals such as GEC and Hindustan Lever had set up small companies to take advantage of the legislation. In an attempt to plug this loophole the government ruled that a SSI unit could not be subsidized or controlled by any other firm, but since there is no legal basis for assessment, the abuse continues unabated and the number of large companies taking advantage of the system was assessed in 1984 at some 900.

Thus the policy to encourage and support the small business has turned into a farce so far as India is concerned. Probably the best solution is to kill the whole idea completely, since it is more than likely, as we said earlier, that those who succeed would succeed in any case, while those who fall by the wayside should never have started anyway.

Government and the small business

Most countries seek to encourage the small business and a wide variety of incentives has been employed over the years. The Economist Intelligence Unit carried out an in-depth comparison of government policy in a number of European countries, to find that the different countries used widely different tools.

West Germany concentrated on capital credit, the UK used taxation relief, while Belgium assisted in relation to business premises. In the USA, on the other hand, the SBA (Small Business Administration), set up in 1953 to cater for the needs of this sector, sought to ensure that the small business had access to the market, adequate financial support and access to government contracts, irrespective of the possible economic advantages of using the big contractors.[9]

Another review of government policy towards the small and medium-sized company in various countries appeared,[10] while a series of five articles in *Management Accounting* provides a very comprehensive survey of what is happening in the UK. It is said that tax incentives, the UK approach, do much to stimulate growth and prosperity of this most important sector of the economy. However, there are a number of areas where a lot can still be done. Life should be made simpler for the small business, a factor that is probably more significant in the US even than it is in the UK. Over-regulation can easily strangle a new business at birth — we cited a fascinating example in another work of ours, under the caption: 'The snail *vs.* the US government'.[11]

Yet, despite all the encouragement and the incentives, the failure rate in the small business sector of the economy in every country is much higher than the average for industry as a whole. We are sure that the reason is the one common to all business failure — bad management. In the small business management has fewer checks and controls: there are fewer people around to provide them. Nevertheless the small business has a vital and continuing role to play. It can be innovative: xerography, insulin, the zipper, the ball-point pen and the jet engine, to name but a few well-known items now seen worldwide, were all contributed by an individual inventor working in a small organization. In addition, productivity appears to be much higher. If we can but encourage the small businessman to look at himself and his company objectively and learn from the mistakes of others like him, using the techniques we are now bringing forward, then we believe this book will have made a significant contribution to the economic well-being not only of the small businessman himself, but of the economy at large.

Summary

Having seen the limits of the application of prediction models to the small business, where the failure rate is much higher than in the rest of the economy, we can only encourage further application in this sector of the economy. We have found one proprietary model, the PAS-score, which has been specifically adapted for the small business, but those who need it most fail to use it. It is the credit manager who benefits, by learning whom to avoid!

The small business sector is seen as vital to prosperity, encouraged to grow and growing in almost every country in the world. The devices used by various governments to encourage such growth vary widely and have sometimes, as in India, largely failed in their objectives, but tax incentives, as offered in the UK, and capital credit, the major inducement in West Germany, are seen to be effective tools.

References

1. Schumacher, E. F., *Small is Beautiful*, Blond & Briggs, 1973. (Also available in paperback.)
2. McRobie, G., *Small is Possible*, Harper & Row, 1981.
3. Kharbanda, O. P. and E. A. Stallworthy, *How to Learn from Project Disasters — True-Life Stories with a Moral for Management*, Gower, 1983.
4. Edminster, R. O., 'An empirical test of financial ratio analysis for small business failure prediction', *Journal of Financial and Quantitative Analysis*, **7**, 1477–93, 1972.
5. Altman, E. I., *Corporate Financial Distress — A Complete Guide to Predicting, Avoiding, and Dealing with Bankruptcy*, Wiley, 1983.
6. Burr, P. L. and R. J. Heckmann, 'Why do so many businesses flop?' *Across the Board*, **16**, 46–8, 1979.
7. Franks, D., 'Growing pains and how to avoid them', *Small Business Digest*, National Westminster Bank PLC, London, October 1984, pp. 5–7.
8. Goyal, S. K., K. S. Chalapati Rao and N. Kumar, *The Small Sector and Big Business*, Indian Institute of Public Administration, 1983.
9. Dyson, K. and S. Wilks (eds), *Industrial Crisis — A Comparative Study of the State and Industry*, Martin Robertson, 1983.
10. Rothwell, R. and W. Zegueld, *Innovation and the Small and Medium Sized Firm*, Francis Pinter, 1983.
11. Stallworthy, E. A. and O. P. Kharbanda, *Total Project Management — From Concept to Completion*, Gower, 1983.

14 We recommend

Our survey of the various methods that can be used to predict the financial future of a company has been of necessity but a sampling from the hundreds of research papers that have been published. Nevertheless we have seen that there are two main tools: the A-score put forward by Argenti, that assesses management capability, and the Z-score, or some similar version of the MDA technique, that makes a quantitative assessment of company status. Before we recommend a specific course of action let us weigh these two basic alternatives in the balance.

Industry type *is* important

It is steadily being realized on both sides of the Atlantic that the type of industry plays a significant role in the validity of the MDA approach. That is, a formula developed from one set of historic data, usually from one range of industries, cannot be applied to other types of industry without modification. It is logical that, in particular, the cut-off point will vary from industry to industry and also from country to country. The intensity of competition, the average size of company, the availability of credit, are all factors which vary markedly from industry to industry. For instance, the Altman Z-score showed a quite marked variation when applied to a range of different industries, as set out in Table 14.1. There is therefore every justification for adapting the model to specific industries, and this is now being done, especially with the proprietary models.

The weakness of the various models when transferred to a different range of business has been commented on quite frequently. For instance Moriarity,

Table 14.1 The Altman Z-score per industry. This table demonstrates that with companies in a normal state of health, there is a marked difference in the Z-score from industry to industry.[1]

	1977	1978	1979	1980	1981
Engineering	3.19	3.18	3.12	3.35	3.16
Hotel and catering	2.57	2.97	3.53	2.86	2.35
Export/import	2.97	3.17	2.68	2.55	2.97
Electricals	3.05	3.08	3.20	3.37	3.50

studying the performance of discount stores, concluded that: 'the Altman model [Z-score, as published in 1968] does not do a very good job of discriminating between bankrupt and non-bankrupt firms'.[2]

Moriarity was surprised at his findings, in view of the high accuracy that had been claimed for this model in previous investigations. In his reply Altman asserts that his 1968 model was *not* appropriate to discount department stores, although we are not aware that he qualified his data in that way when it was first published.[3] But to be fair to Altman, he does state several limitations and qualifications to both his original and modified Z-score models.[4] Certainly the model is said to be effective across a much wider area, but then that is a proprietary model and we cannot check the claims made for it. Altman goes on to assert that the model correctly classifies every failed discount department store and that at least two of the companies categorized by Moriarity in 1977 as still in business actually failed later, thus confirming their dismal fate as predicted by their 1977 score.

Do we go public or private?

The models available in the literature have been the subject of considerable research, but we know little about the proprietary models, since the details and the data are not available to the public, being confined to subscribers to the service. This is rather unfortunate, since the work has been a spin-off from academic research largely paid for from public funds; also we have no way of checking the claims of high accuracy and predictive ability made for such models. The final decision will be made in the marketplace: it is the subscriber who will eventually decide whether the companies offering such services are effective. If we see *them* going bankrupt, we shall know.

The PAS system is recommended because it allows companies to be picked out as potentially at risk on the basis of a downward trajectory, well in advance of their moving into the so-called 'at risk' area.[5] On the other hand DataStream, another UK service, is advertised as the 'most effective screening tool yet devised for the purpose of credit analysis'. Altman is not behind the rest in advancing the claims of the Z model. According to him, it 'appears to be quite accurate for up to five years before failure . . . outperforms alternative bankruptcy classification strategies, ranking first among empirical bankruptcy studies in terms of accuracy'.[4] With all this knowledge available, it is a wonder that investors still lose all in bankrupt companies. Of course, the danger lies in relying on a warning system: that can be quite expensive. Yet if you do not rely upon it, of what use is it? Failure to predict a bankruptcy can cost those involved a lot of money: the reverse is not so bad. A predicted failure that does not occur does no major harm and everyone except perhaps the academician – for he has been proved wrong! – would be happier for it.

Objective *vs.* subjective models

Bankruptcy models based upon a ratio or a combination of ratios (the MDA approach) are objective, in that the score is a finite number. Once the appropriate cut-off point has been decided, there is no judgement involved. The classification is purely mechanical and the answer is either 'yes' or 'no'. This is the case with the Taffler and Altman models and their proprietary derivatives, PAS and Zeta, and the many others on the market. At the other extreme is the purely subjective model, as proposed by Argenti, where the data in the published accounts are considered to be of little value:

> It relies upon the observer actually visiting the suspect company, meeting its directors, seeing its products and forming his own views. In this instance the A-score reflects the opinion of many financial experts that balance sheets alone are not enough. *You need to go there.*[6]

Another subjective model used a point-weighted assessment of management and organizational attitudes.[7] It is a performance system of appraisal and it presumes close access to the management.

Quantification has its limitations

One thing has become very clear. Not everything can be quantified – and this is very true in the field of business management.

After all the attempts at quantification it is refreshing to see an insolvency and rescue expert with a major international firm of auditors and management consultants (Price, Waterhouse) being quite candid:

> it is now possible to 'plug in' a program and obtain a 'Z-Score'. . . . However, remember that the results can only be as reliable as the input data . . . late accounting, creative accounting, can seriously distort the results.[8]

His listing of the danger signs is even more candid. He says that management (does he mean the chief executive?) are preoccupied with a personalized number plate on the Rolls, the founder's statue in reception, the company flagpole, the fountain in the forecourt and the fish tank in the boardroom.

Altman's Z-score has been compared with a 'value line' system, the latter being based on mathematical calculation combined with human judgement.[9] A fairly high correlation was found in the case of these two methods and failure signs were claimed to have been detected as early as 53 months prior to bankruptcy.

Is perhaps a combination of the subjective and the objective approach best? That is where we are driven, when we realize that quantification can only go so far. What is left is personal judgement. The numerical data, whether they come from academic or commercial sources, can only take us so far: from then on we have to rely upon what is called a 'gut feeling', or intuition. Every numerical indicator has its weakness. For instance, one of the deciding factors in the selection of new projects was – perhaps still is, for many – the return on the investment, the famous ROI. But a number of companies are now expressing doubts. Shell went so far as to publish their 'directional policy matrix' for the use of others, declaring that it was the method they adopted to select investment prospects. The method proposed allowed a systematic assessment of qualitative judgements.[10] Union Carbide, another major investor in new plants, has reported that it no longer considers ROI the only criterion. They learnt the hard way, first discovering that whatever the minimum stipulated ROI was before an investment would be made, all the projects studied passed *that* test. Why? Detailed investigation showed that all such calculations are based on a series of assumptions. Those piloting a new project through the company made sure that their assumptions were such that the ROI was always favourable. So now intuition overrules the 'number game'. This seems right to us. Aren't the numbers (such as the 'scores' in bankruptcy production models) really stating the obvious? If it is obvious, it is already too late. Any management worthy of the name should know where it is heading and be able to recognize the danger signs long before the symptoms appear in the company accounts, even with such confusing factors as 'creative accounting'.

Earlier we took as one of our case studies the collapse of AEG. The history of that company would have been entirely different and by no means as sad, we are told, if only there had been some readiness on the part of management to recognize the strengths and abandon the weaknesses in the company. Surely the directorate was aware of what was happening? Didn't their bankers realize what was happening? Or did management deliberately seek to gloss over the problems that were apparent?

The objective *plus* subjective approach

A combination of the objective approach with the subjective seems to us a constructive way to handle the problem, and we expect the future trend in the assessment of bankruptcy prediction to follow this course. Indeed, we have no doubt that it is already being followed, in that those who subscribe to one or other of the many companies offering objective – that is, numerical – data will not rely solely on the figures or the graphs. Even the advertising brochures admit the need for a combination of these two factors: 'The assessment of risk critically depends upon the accurate measurement of a customer's financial health *coupled with a personal judgement* of the ability to make repayment'.[11] The emphasis is ours. The message is clear – the figures alone are *not* enough. Personal judgement has a positive role to play.

We can ask what the experts do? Attempts have been made to find out through surveys of the various agencies involved in lending money, such as banks, financial brokers and economic analysts. In one such survey 98 of the largest banks in the US were asked whether they used a bankruptcy prediction or other numerical scoring model in their evaluation of commercial loans.[12] The conclusion following analysis of the results was that predictive models can help in the review of a commercial loan, but only if the banks are willing to work at the same time with an alternative approach to the making of a decision. In other words and once again, qualify the numbers by using your personal judgement.

Where do we go from here?

Summing up the body of knowledge on the subject of bankruptcy prediction with a view to establishing a logical step-by-step procedure for this purpose, we see quite clearly that no single procedure, method or model is infallible. It therefore must be best to use two or perhaps more methods at the same time and if that approach is to have value, the separate methods chosen must be independent of one another. But what if we use two separate approaches and they give two different answers? This is a very good question and we are afraid that there is only one good answer: wait and see.

It seems that two separate approaches have to be made in relation to the prediction of corporate failure, dependent upon whether one knows the company well or not. Since we are writing, above all, for those who are involved in management, and are concerned with the management of a particular company, then we would expect them to know that company well. They are therefore in a position to begin by using the A-score approach, which we have already described in some detail. One must remember that the lower its *respective* proprietary A-score, the better the health of a company; the 'pass mark' is reckoned to be 25. A score less than 25 (better still less than 18) indicates that a company is not at risk. While the score is still below 35, the company is at risk, and the weighting in the scoring will indicate the road to recovery. This is one most valuable aspect of the A-score approach: it shows you very clearly what is at fault and therefore what needs to be remedied if failure is to be averted. Assessment of the imminence of danger is dependent to some extent upon the size of company with which we are involved. With the smaller company, a score between 20 and 25, while seeming to indicate that the company is not at risk, will nevertheless demand further examination and the application of additional tools. Notice that we are warning, when we say this, that there is no magic associated with that number 25.

The financial tools

There are four tools that we recommend as an extension to the initial A-score appraisal.

The Balance Sheet

We recommend that you 'smell' the balance sheet. We use this unusual word – unusual, that is, in this particular connection – rather than 'read', because what is required is a skill that comes from experience and a sharp eye. Trends are much more important than the absolute figures. The notes and qualifications, usually in fine print, should be perused most carefully. Even the date of issue of the balance sheet has significance: delay in publication is often a prime indicator of trouble ahead.

The Stock Exchange

If the shares of the company are quoted on the Stock Exchange, then the share value and in particular the trend can be an extremely useful indicator of the health of a company. The share value is the public response to a wide range of data and one is amazed at the amount of information that is often available about a company in stock exchange circles, even if it is not all correct. Quite often they seem to have 'tomorrow's information today'. The share value should also be considered in relation to that of others in the same industry. Some experts claim that the share value can indicate potential failure as early as five years ahead, but we doubt this very much.

The credit rating

There are a number of companies, of which Dun and Bradstreet is a long-established example, that on the basis of their intelligence service offer early warning of companies in trouble. We wonder how many companies have the interest and the temerity to inquire about their *own* credit rating? A prompt answer is usually forthcoming. Dun and Bradstreet have their own version of the Z-score, the Dunscore, on offer to their clients. This will be calculated for any company on request and it is compared to the score of other companies in the same industry. It can therefore be a useful barometer of *comparative* health.

Financial ratios

We have discussed the merits of the MDA approach at great length. From the bewildering variety available we suggest you use Beaver's simple, single ratio, cash flow/total debt, since we believe it to be *the* most powerful *single* indicator of a company's health. Get a feel for its significance in your particular country or industry by calculating a number of others as well as the one you are directly interested in. Alternatively, where such things are on offer, one of the firms specializing in the technique can be employed. We have mentioned PAS and Zeta, but there are many others.

To sum up: if you are close to a company and have the information, then there is no doubt that it is best to begin by analysing the situation using the A-score approach. If that leaves you in doubt, then use one or all of the several financial tools we have brought to your attention. If, at the end of all that, you find you have conflicting information before you, then you must use your own judgement or wait on events.

Where ignorance is *not* bliss

Since we believe the A-score to be the best approach, if you do not know the company well enough to apply the A-score technique yourself, then why not ask someone who can? A management consultant can be approached, or you can even do some 'spying' on your own account. It is amazing what you can learn just by keeping your eyes and ears open. Listening to what is being said in the market-place, at industry association meetings and the like, can bring much useful information. The information may well be conflicting at times, but it is usually possible to sift the wheat from the chaff.

There are, of course, firms who are willing to undertake that type of research and submit a detailed confidential report. Ex-employees can often provide a wealth of information — remember that you are seeking to get a 'feel': you are not after explicit information. But be careful if the ex-employee has left under dubious circumstances: he may well bear a grudge.

While one can turn as before to the financial ratios, we would not recommend doing this in isolation. Only if the figures are shouting aloud that failure is imminent are they to be trusted and by that time potential failure is no doubt being signalled quite plainly by the public conduct of the company.

Summary

Here we end our survey of the possibilities in predicting corporate failure. It is now possible to make such predictions with a fair degree of accuracy, even up to five years ahead of final disaster. We have assessed the relative values of the two alternative approaches, the objective and the subjective. We believe the subjective approach to be the more reliable, while recognizing that this demands an intimate, inside knowledge of the company. We have nevertheless suggested a practical approach to this matter of prediction, believing that the real purpose of prediction is to enable something to be done about it. We now go to seek, first, remedies and then — even better — a course that will ensure that a company never gets into trouble.

References
1. Inman, M. L., 'Appraising Altman Z-formula prediction', *Management Accounting*, **60**, 37–9, November 1982.

2. Moriarity, S., 'Financial information through multi-dimensional graphics', *Journal of Accounting Research*, **17**, 205–24, 1979.
3. Altman, E. I., 'Multidimensional graphics and bankruptcy prediction', *Journal of Accounting Research*, **21**, 297–319, 1983.
4. Altman, E. I., *Corporate Financial Distress – A Complete Guide to Prediction, Avoiding and Dealing with Bankruptcy*, Wiley, 1983.
5. Taffler, R. J., 'The assessment of company solvency and performance using a statistical model', *Accounting and Business Research*, **13**, 295–307, Autumn 1983.
6. Argenti, J., 'Predicting Corporate Failure', *Accountants Digest No. 138*, Institute of Chartered Accountants, 1983.
7. Boocock, K. and F. A. Drozd, 'Forecasting corporate collapse', *Chartered Accountants Magazine* (Canada), Nov. 1982, p. 54.
8. Homan, M., 'Insolvency – spotting the danger signals', *Banking World*, Oct. 1984.
9. Altman, E. I. and J. Spivak, 'Predicting bankruptcy – the value line relative financial strength system *vs.* the Zeta bankruptcy classification approach', *Financial Analysts Journal*, Nov./Dec. 1983, pp. 60–7.
10. Kharbanda, O. P. and E. A. Stallworthy, *How to Learn from Project Disasters – True-Life Stories with a Moral for Management*, Gower, 1983. (See in particular Chapter 16, 'Picking Prospects for Better Business'.)
11. *PAS and the Credit Manager – a Logical Partnership*, Performance Analysis Services Ltd, London.
12. Maeever, D. A., 'Predicting business failures', *Journal of Commercial Bank Lending*, **66**, 14–18, Jan. 1984.

PART FOUR

Panacea is better

15 Is there a panacea?

What is a panacea? The *Concise Oxford Dictionary* defines it as 'a universal remedy'. We are told that the word derives from the Greeks, who always had a word for it: this time, *panakeia*, meaning 'all-healing'. But what is a 'remedy'? That in turn is defined as a cure *for* or *against* disease, a healing medicine or treatment. But was is a *cure*? As a noun it is 'things that cure', as a verb it is 'restore to health'. Just to go full circle, we find that a 'cure-all' is described as a 'panacea'! Those who use these words normally think of the human body, but we are thinking of companies in distress, sick and needing to be restored to health. Is there a panacea, a cure-all, a universal remedy, for such companies?

We think that there is and we will assert here and now that the panacea is 'good management'. But that is not as simple as it sounds: it is not a pill but a treatment and, just as a doctor needs to examine and assess the symptoms before he can advise on a course of treatment, so with companies. Indeed, a new breed of managers is evolving whose speciality is to treat sickness and failure in the corporate world. In financial circles they give themselves no titles, but they are termed 'turnaround managers' or 'company doctors'. Typical of the breed is Sir Michael Edwardes, who first gained fame as the chairman of British Leyland, invited in 1977 to take on the awesome task of bringing about its recovery. In October 1982 he finished his five-year term, having averted the disaster.[1] He has now taken over at Dunlop, another ailing company, and first cleared the decks by having all the executive directors removed. One of them had earlier been recruited from the Treasury to attempt a turnaround of Dunlop as chief executive, but very evidently had failed. So we see that even the 'company doctor' is not universally successful.[2]

This new breed of manager is inevitably self-taught, although there is now a growing body of past practice upon which they can draw. To be successful they have to have a broad background of experience, embracing more than one of the four main areas of industrial activity — commerce, engineering, management and finance. Perhaps that was why 'our man from the Treasury' had to be replaced: he lacked the breadth of experience to become effective. The number of companies in distress of one sort or another is growing fast so the demand for 'company doctors' is growing too. Such managers are hard to come by but they do exist and we have already set up for you some basic guidelines to assist in the search or, dare we say, assist you to become one yourself.

What are we looking for?

Before looking at the doctor, let us take a good look at the patient. We have a company in distress, on the road to ruin and we want to bring that company back to a state of health. This turnaround is best illustrated by plotting the health of the company against time, as we have done so far in this book. We present in Fig. 15.1 a typical set of alternatives in that format, following the evidence that a company is in danger. Without a turnaround the company will fail and die, a course indicated by trajectory A. The trajectories B1, B2 and B3 are the various courses that could be the result of turnaround. Not all turnarounds, even when they are achieved, are equally successful.

To add a touch of realism we have taken a real instance as our base case. Scotcros PLC was a company with a turnover of £46 million during the financial year ending 31 March 1983 and at that time employed some 560 people in the UK. It operated in several areas ranging from food packaging and farm supplies to engineering and wines and spirits. The company failed on 8 November 1983. What is quite remarkable about this company is that in its recent history it never made a loss and had in fact a strong stock market performance, increasing its profits from £200 000 to £720 000 for the year ending 31 March 1983. The company actually failed within three months of publishing its 1983 accounts. As you will see from the PAS score in Fig. 15.1, the company had been in steady decline for three years and had been in the 'at risk' region for two years, so no one should have been caught unawares when the Receiver was appointed.[3]

You will notice that we assume that the action is taken when the company is in the 'at risk' region, when it is manifestly under threat and in danger of failure in the immediate future. It is 'sick', to use the term so popular in India. There are a variety of ways of assessing the health of a company, as we have seen, and the key to success is to seek for the early warning signals and then act upon them. The indicator we have chosen to illustrate our case is the PAS score. We speak of the health of a company quite deliberately because that implies that we are concerned with the aggregate of a number of factors and not any single factor. While there is continuous debate as to which particular factors are the most significant, there is no doubt that one must look at the whole, and not any single item, even although one might well use a single indicator, such as the PAS score, as an early warning signal to alert us to the need for action.

Our study of the various approaches to prediction demonstrate clearly that the situation in any one year must never precipitate action: it is the *trend* that is all-important. For instance, an otherwise healthy firm, growing too fast, may have a severe cash flow crisis, although making good profits. The use of two indicators, cash availability and profits, would lead to completely contradictory conclusions. There have been many cases of this sort, where a company became technically insolvent, yet a Receiver was not appointed and good management set the matter right in good time. Again, a loss in a single year is not necessarily

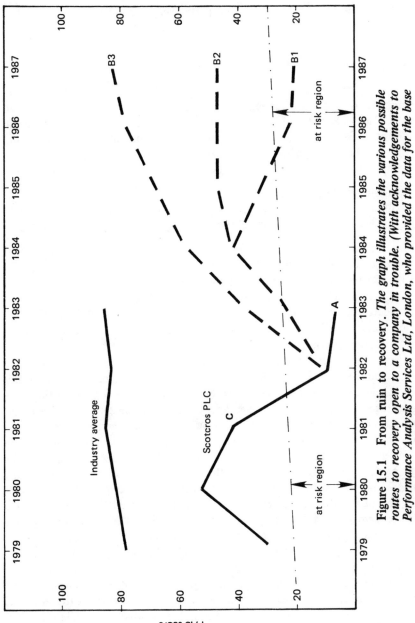

Figure 15.1 From ruin to recovery. The graph illustrates the various possible routes to recovery open to a company in trouble. (With acknowledgements to Performance Analysis Services Ltd, London, who provided the data for the base case, Scotcros PLC.)

an alarm signal. The loss may have occurred, for instance, because of an unusually large write-off of assets in that particular year, and the business as such is still healthy.

A turnaround may not be permanent

Lest you get the impression that once a company has been the subject of a turnaround, all is well, let us disabuse you of that idea forthwith. The turnaround may well be only the beginning of a long, long road to full recovery. To sustain recovery, constant effort and vigilance are essential. Not only may the turnaround effort itself fail, but apparent success may well be shortlived. Various turnaround situations can be seen in practice and these may be summarized as follows:

The turnaround failed in its purpose.
The turnaround was successful, but only in the short term. There was no growth.
The turnaround was successful, and there was sustained growth from then on.

These are the three possibilities presented in Fig. 15.1 as B1, B2 and B3. Is it possible to discern which of the three categories any particular company falls into? Of course not, for if one could then one would never start the turnaround in the first place in relation to those companies where the evil day was only being delayed. Better far to let it die and get the agony over. This allows the residual assets of the company to be redeployed and put to more effective use than would otherwise be the case.

Having seen that a turnaround is not always successful, we ask: what is the success rate in this field? Is it often but a forlorn hope, or can we normally expect success? There are some indicators, although some companies that have been turned around have not necessarily been the subject of a turnaround exercise. After all, when the chief executive discerns that he is running into trouble, he may well take effective action and so transform the situation. He would act at the point marked 'C' in Fig. 15.1. If we take declining earnings as a sign of ill health, then among more than 400 companies reviewed in the UK, some 25 per cent were turned around successfully, as indicated in Table 15.1.[4] It will be noticed that the length of time that the company had been in decline did not seem to affect the ability to effect a turnaround. The companies requiring turnaround were found among some 2100 publicly quoted companies, so we see that about a fifth of all companies in business find themselves in need of a turnaround sooner or later. Of the hundred or so companies where the turnaround was a success, about a quarter were the subject of acquisition, which accelerated the transformation. Such acquisitions usually took place within one to three years of the last reported loss, which may be an indication that the initial turnaround was under threat, but that acquisition saved the day, sustaining the turnaround.

The foregoing all relates to the UK. A similar study in the US showed a very similar relationship. There, also, a quarter of US quoted companies needed turn-

Table 15.1 What is the chance of a successful recovery? This table indicates that roughly one firm in four under threat manages a successful recovery.

No. of years of declining earnings	Firms requiring turnaround	Firms successfully turned around	Success Rate (%)
3	335	81	24
4	84	23	27
5	13	2	15
6	5	1	20
Totals	437	107	24

Source: S. Slatter, *Corporate Recovery*, Penguin, Harmondsworth, 1984, p. 19

around during a 10-year period.[5] Of these a third were successfully turned around, a rather higher success rate than that achieved in the UK. Of course, these assessments are still subjective, in that only one of many criteria available for assessing the health of the companies reviewed is being used to evaluate the situation. In the review of UK companies, declining earnings were the indicator. In the US, the need for turnaround was established by the existence of a loss situation, or a decline in profits of 80 per cent or more in a single year. But we have already said that what happens in any single year is *not* an objective indicator of the health of a company. It can so easily be a 'one off' situation, not calling for turnaround strategy. So to that extent the figures give but a broad indication of the situation. What is very clear is that a substantial number of companies – probably some 30 per cent – run into danger sooner or later.

What of those companies that fell into decline and never recovered? They are those for whom there is no hope: they are not viable on their own. How do we recognize them? Some of their characteristic features are:

Operating in a declining market
Facing severe price competition
Fixed cost is a major component in product price
Single plant or single product companies

The last point is significant, in that in this case there is no possibility of generating cash by divesting the company of some part of its assets.

Some examples of companies that were beyond recovery in the UK are Foden, truck manufacturers; Colston, manufacturing domestic appliances; and Dimplex, makers of heating equipment. They all had one common problem: severe price competition from overseas suppliers with a much lower cost structure. When we look at companies that we might call short-term survivors, in that they lasted for up to 5 years but eventually collapsed, we see final failure for what is essentially the same reason: they were unable to maintain a competitive edge in the market. For instance, Bamfords, suppliers of agricultural equipment, failed some three years after what appeared to have been a successful turnaround, while Inveresk, a paper manufacturer and distributor, after making an initial recovery began to slide down once again, and was eventually sold to Georgia-Pacific, a US paper group who saw the company as a cheap vehicle for penetration of the UK market. They were able to improve efficiency and productivity sufficiently to hold on to an adequate share of the market.

Mere survival or sustained recovery?

Now we are looking at plots B2 and B3 in Fig. 15.1. Mere survival means that the company stays in the danger area: it cannot be said to have fully recovered. A full recovery demands a great deal of time and effort and sometimes the injection of substantial sums of money. If the company operates in an industry with little prospects, or if resources are limited, it can be a difficult decision to make. No one wants to throw good money after bad. Full recovery usually demands a major change in corporate strategy: turning to a new product, for instance, through development or acquisition. Or the company can be acquired by someone else, who sees the opportunity of buying certain assets cheaply and then turning them into something worth while.

It will be appreciated that our classification of turnaround is somewhat arbitrary. For instance, Inveresk, a 'short-term survivor', was transformed and sustained its recovery in the long term because it was acquired by a large American paper group.

A blueprint for a turnaround

Each turnaround is inevitably unique, and the action taken has therefore to be precisely tailored to suit the particular company in trouble. Nevertheless there are certain basic rules which we can set out as a sort of checklist for the turnaround manager. These are:

Diagnosis

This can be very time-consuming but must be the starting point. To return to our human analogy, how can one possibly prescribe a remedy before one is aware of the nature of the disease? The severity of the disease and its nature must be carefully assessed. This demands a historical survey of the company: the decline may be due to a single factor, such as poor marketing, a poor product, poor management or the wrong strategy, but more usually it is a combination of a number of factors. While there may be many causes for the decline, it is important to identify the vital few from the trivial many. This is to follow the so-called Pareto Law, sometimes termed the '20:80 Rule' or the 'A-B-C Analysis'.

This law states that 20 per cent of the causes contribute by 80 per cent to the effect. The prime job of the turnaround manager is to identify that crucial 20 per cent.

Prescription

There is as yet no *Materia Medica* of symptoms that one can peruse to discover the appropriate remedy for an ailing company, although there are some books whose titles sound very promising.[6] The problem is that we may react in the same way as many react to a medical dictionary. Looking through the list of symptoms, one becomes convinced that one is suffering from almost everything listed. The remedy then becomes such a combination of powerful drugs that one is killed rather than cured. Turnaround strategy should be, must be, basically simple and specific. Review and the consequent treatment should be limited to three areas: management, finance and marketing. Change of management, in whole or in part, is always a matter for consideration, since many of the problems will almost inevitably be due to bad management. Financial restructuring may be called for, by a reduction in assets, reduction in costs, or perhaps new investment, either in new facilities or by acquisition. Finally, marketing must always be a subject for detailed analysis and objective assessment. Do the product and the market in which it is being offered match?

Some of these aspects will be taken up in more detail later, since they are of concern not only when seeking turnaround, but also when seeking to prevent the need for turnaround ever arising, an aspect to which we turn in Part Five.

Monitoring

The last phase of our turnaround strategy is monitoring. Having diagnosed the trouble, having established the necessary prescription, the time has come to implement the proposals. During this phase, the turnaround manager must continually ask the question: How are we doing? He should be very willing to change his strategy at any point, on the basis of the experience gained as his plans are being implemented. He also needs to keep an eye on his competitors, and what is learnt there may also bring about a change in strategy. The business environment is not static and the strategy for turnaround must keep pace with changing conditions in the marketplace if it is to be finally successful. The best tool at this point is a plot of the health of the company, using as a barometer one of the formulae discussed earlier. Such formulae are usually applied on a yearly basis, but here we would recommend a quarterly or even monthly appraisal: all the financial data will be immediately available within the company. We have personal experience of a company which adopted this technique, reviewing the situation *once a month*, with the result that it made no cash losses from that point on for the first time in several years. Let us warn yet once more against being misled by single sharp movements in any direction: it is the trend that is all-important.

Help is available

The turnaround manager does not have to go it along. First and foremost, the company will undoubtedly have major loans outstanding, and the creditors should be more than willing to give any assistance they can. After all, it is the best route to the protection of their interests. For this reason most of the major banks now have specialist departments to deal with ailing companies. Typical of these is a unit in the Corporate Financial Division of the Midland Bank where some 50 qualified specialists, including chartered accountants, conduct detailed investigations following discussion with the directors of their troubled client.[7] They seek to agree and have the company implement an agreed strategy for turnaround. The job can be most rewarding to all concerned, but it has been found that the services of outside independent consultants are also needed to supplement the bank's own staff, providing both specific expertise and a fresh, independent approach.

Apart from the fact that in this way the banks can protect their own interests, we believe that they have a specific duty of care, inasmuch as their loans play a significant role in the steps that a company decides to take. The banks see this, for such units are sometimes called intensive care units, once again echoing our medical analogy. We would expect such facilities to remain even when there is a turnaround in the economy, because the problem of company failure will always be with us. One lesson can already be drawn from the experience gained: quick, positive action at an early stage is most effective. Further, if the entire company cannot be saved, then it is best to identify the viable elements and concentrate action there.

Summary

Throughout this part of the book we shall be looking for a panacea — a universal remedy for ailing companies. We have begun by asking the question: Is there such a remedy? Our answer is 'yes', although the necessary body of knowledge is still being built up. We have also seen that while it is possible to turn a company around, and that there are specialists in this field, there is no guarantee of success. Indeed, initial success can later collapse into failure. We see what is necessary: the remedy has to be applied, then closely monitored, the remedy *being changed* if that is seen to be necessary.

References

1. Edwardes, M., *Back from the Brink*, Collins, 1983.

2. Becket, M., 'Sir Michael clears the decks at Dunlop', *Daily Telegraph* (London), 3 Nov. 1984, p.21.
3. Taffler, R. J. and M. Tseung, 'The audit going concern qualification in practice — exploding some myths', *The Accountant's Magazine* (London), July 1984, pp. 263—9.
4. Slatter, S., *Corporate Recovery — Successful Turnaround Strategies and their Implementation*, Penguin Books, 1984.
5. Bibeault, D., *Corporate Turnaround*, McGraw-Hill, 1981.
6. Allsopp, M., *Survival in Business — The Dynamics of Success and Failure*, Business Books, 1977.
7. Wheatley, D. J., 'Intensive care — life saving task for the profession', *Accountancy*, **94**, 86—7, August 1983.

16 Management holds the key

We spent some time in Chapter 3 demonstrating the importance of management, and especially of top management and the chief executive, in maintaining corporate health. Our case studies have also demonstrated that almost invariably good management can minimize and more often than not avert impending disaster. So we make no excuse for returning to this theme once more: we cannot over-emphasize its importance. Of the various prevention techniques presented to us, we see only one, that proposed by Argenti, that evaluates the management role. Altman, on the other hand, in a book with the comprehensive subtitle 'a complete guide to predicting, *avoiding* and *dealing* with bankruptcy' (the emphasis is ours) fails to use the word management: it does not even appear in the index, nor do the related themes 'chief executive', 'long range planning', 'planning' or 'strategic planning'.[1] How is one supposed to avoid or deal with potential bankruptcy without management being involved and some planning being done?

Companies fail and collapse mainly because of bad management: we will go on saying it until the point is fully taken. We now propose, therefore, to discuss some of the characteristics of good management that play a significant role in averting disaster.

Every good company has a culture

A company is a living and dynamic entity, with a life of its own, and therefore has specific characteristics and qualities when viewed as an entity. This we describe as the 'company culture'. We made a brief reference to this in Chapter 3, but believing the company culture to be an integral part of any company's success, we now wish to assess it and its influence in more detail.

In an unusual and interesting article Uttal points out that four of the best-sellers in management books of recent years – *Corporate Culture, In Search of Excellence, The Art of Japanese Management* and *Theory Z* have all emphasized that companies with a record of outstanding financial performance have powerful corporate cultures.[2] The definition of a culture in this context, as it relates to the employees of a company, is:

A system of shared values (tells them what is important)
A system of shared beliefs (tells them how things work).

This system of shared values and beliefs formalizes the company's organizational

152

structure and control systems to produce behavioural norms that prevail throughout the organization. This then becomes 'the way we do things round here'.

What are the dominant values (basic elements in the company culture) in some of the world's best performers? With IBM it is customer service, at Toyota the workers intone a company song every day, while Hewlett-Packard looks for long-term growth and makes every employee an entrepreneur. The recipe for success seems to be: acquire the right culture, or do your very best to modify it if you believe that it is wrong. That may be very difficult, since a developed company culture is very strong, but the effort should be made.

This is simple enough to say, but some experts tell us that it cannot be done. A company either has the right culture, the wrong culture or none at all, and whichever way it happens to be, we are told, there is nothing one can do to change it. One of the books referred to earlier, *In Search of Excellence*, tells us that in most outstanding companies the company culture can be traced back to an influential founder to top manager who lived and preached the value system he set in motion.[3] Constantly hammered home as a basic concept it became the company culture and subsequent managements kept those concepts alive and to the forefront. The culture comes from within and not from without.

That this *is* so is beyond doubt. There have been a number of major companies who have striven to change their culture, without success. Such failures have not deterred consultants setting themselves up to offer such a service and achieve the miracle. Typical of these and perhaps one of the most ambitious is the Management Analysis Center (MAC) of Cambridge, Massachusetts. Their basic premise is that you cannot change strategies without having the appropriate culture. But one of their consultants, Howard Schwartz, warns:

> You can't change culture by working on it directly. You must have some strategic ground to stand on, then build a vision of what a company wants before rubbing their noses in what they are.[2]

Old-time consultants, advising clients on strategic planning, a subject to which we come in the following chapter, do not agree with this concept. It goes right against what they preach and are seeking to sell. Francis N. Bonsignore, a partner in the consultancy firm of Booz, Allen & Hamilton, declares that the company culture is but one aspect among several and goes on: 'to assume that the tail wags the dog is insane . . . '; regarding cultural change, he adds: 'we're making hay of an issue that is topical'.

In an attempt to get a balanced view of the subject let us listen for a moment to those who have no axe to grind. Joanne Martin, an associate professor of organizational behaviour at the Stanford Graduate School of Business Administration states simply: 'Culture may simply exist.' Another academician, Vijay Sathe of Harvard, agrees that it is extremely difficult to alter a culture. Confirmation of this comes from Hewlett-Packard, a company known for its strong culture and excellent track record, believed to be a consequence of its strong culture. Its director of Management Development, William P. Nelson, declares: 'I don't think John Young (*President*) could fundamentally change our values if he wanted to.'[2]

Company culture is something real, strong and all-pervading. It is inherent in the company and comes from within. It is alleged that you cannot change it, nor can it be acquired if it is not already there. You may well say that is not much help, but at least you know what the problem is. If, having reviewed the situation, it is considered that there is nothing to be done with respect to this aspect of the company scene, then you spend neither time nor money on what will be a fruitless effort. No – you tackle the problem in another way. You start all over again and create a new enterprise on the ashes of the old. The best way for this to happen is by the company being taken over: that is a much better course than watching it fail.

Ten commandments for an enterprise

We have already learnt that a strong company culture usually comes from the original founder of the company. In the harsh economic climate of today, however, a new enterprise is usually started by a team rather than just one person. It is rare indeed for a single individual to combine the widely different attributes called for in successful management, so we tend to find an entre- preneurial team that works together and sticks together. There are many ex- amples to be seen among the growth companies, small today but perhaps successful giants tomorrow.

A set of 'ten commandments' has been formulated for such entrepreneurial groups:

1. Limit the total number in the team to those who can consciously agree upon and contribute directly to the objectives in view, which should be precisely stated and planned over time.
2. Define the business in terms of what is to be bought, by whom and why.
3. Concentrate all the resources on achieving two or three specific operating objectives in a given time.
4. Have a written plan, stating who is to do what and by when.
5. Employ key people who have a proven record of success in doing what needs to be done in a manner consistent with the value system of the enterprise (or company culture).
6. Reward individual performance in excess of agreed standards.
7. Expand methodically from a profitable base towards a balanced business.
8. Project, monitor and conserve cash and credit capability.
9. Maintain a detached point of view.
10. Anticipate change by periodically testing the adopted business plan for consistency and reality in relation to the world marketplace.[4]

These 'ten commandments' deal mainly with operating issues, items 1 to 3 being the key startup issues, item 4 the plan and items 5 to 8 day-to-day operating matters, while items 9 and 10 are designed to cloak the entrepreneurial approach with a degree of professionalism. Strict application of these ten points is still not sufficient in itself: one cannot ignore the world in which the enterprise is to be developed. This means that if an enterprise is to succeed and grow, you also need certain basics, such as an identifiable and receptive market, sufficient capital, tenacity of purpose and good timing. That last point is often referred to as good luck!

These then are the qualities and the attributes of any successful enterprise. When we come to an ailing company, therefore, it is these attributes that have to be injected, if the company is to be turned around, its culture transformed − and as we have already said, that can only be done from within! So we are back to the 'company doctor': the entrepreneur who comes *into* the company, takes it over, gathers about him a team of loyal and dedicated managers and proceeds to institute *his* approach and *his* policies. It becomes very evident, as we consider the way in which an enterprise goes forward to success, that half-measures are no good at all. In Chapter 15 we cited the case of Dunlop: a group that first sought to solve their problems by a series of half-measures. But they were making no headway. Then they called in the 'doctor', who became managing director − now he is 'inside' rather than 'outside' − and then he made a clean sweep. So far as management is concerned, he was in effect starting afresh and prepared a comprehensive rescue package involving some 50 banks. The concept of good management seems set to take over. Let us then highlight a few of the attributes of good management − and we won't select a standard prescription. Having said in Chapter 3 that it is basic to the concept of good management to have a co-ordinated and structured team, able both to communicate with and listen to one another, let us see how such principles work out in practice.

Simple form, lean staff

How are we to preserve the team approach as a company grows ever bigger? Growth implies more and yet more people and the mere size of a company generates complexity in its systems and structure. The structure soon changes from a simple, functional 'tree' organigram to a four-dimensional matrix and a logistical mess. For success that complex matrix must disappear − the simple 'tree' *must* reappear. It can be done and it has been done. Not only does a simple structure allow good management as such, but because of its structure such companies are very flexible and able to respond quickly to changing conditions in their working environment. For instance, a US$5 billion company, *Johnson & Johnson*, in effect consists of 150 independent companies each headed by its own chairman. The companies are divided into eight groups, based on either product or geographical similarities. The central staff is small and there are no specialists, located at the centre, travelling to individual companies to watch over their affairs. This is typical of successful conglomerates, as the following examples show:[3]

Schlumberger (US), a diversified oil service company, with US$7 billion annual sales and the largest in its field, has a central corporate staff of 90 to run its world-wide empire.

Emerson Electric (US) has 5400 employees, but less than 100 in its corporation headquarters.

ICI (UK) did have 2000 employees in its central organization some five years ago, but has now trimmed that down to less than 200.

Dana (US), with 35 000 employees, cut its corporate staff from 500 in 1970, down to around 100.

With corporate management, there is no doubt at all that the maxim is: 'less brings more'. A reduction in corporate staff is crucial to the creation of autonomous units within such conglomerates. Central organization still has a role to play, but it is not managerial: it is effectively advisory. This type of organization is sometimes called 'hands off' management, but if that is true and there are indeed 'no hands', then there is no central *management* and as we said, the direction given from the centre is fundamentally political: its function is to establish company policy.

Productivity through people

Productivity is an abstract concept and a very controversial subject indeed. It is hard to find two people who will agree on any aspect of productivity. There is no agreement, even, on what is meant by the word, for each definition that is produced only demonstrates the bias of the definer. Accountant, economist, engineer, trade union official: each has his own definition of productivity, a definition designed to suit his own purposes and objectives, to prove or disprove a particular point of view.

Most certainly, productivity is a great idea. Developing countries should be particularly interested in productivity, yet for most of them it seems a dirty word, next only to profit. This attitude is counter-productive, but it is indeed difficult if not impossible to measure productivity in explicit terms.

For success, productivity must be maintained and improved, but how do we do that when we have no means of measuring what is happening? The best way to deal with that problem is to go to a place where productivity has been improved and is still improving and learn from example. The most obvious place is of course Japan. That country's success shows no signs of abating. From 1975 to 1980 there was a 100 per cent increase in productivity, we are told. Yes, we know it is difficult to measure, but it *did* nearly double. So how do we imitate Japan?

Probably most of all, by increasing morale at work.[5,6] This can be done by increasing pride in the job, by building up the team (or family) concept, and by increasing individual involvement. This demands good communication, which can be achieved by informal meetings, with senior management having an ever-open door. This allows for the personal touch, where interest can be expressed not only in work but in the family and the circumstances at home.

Huddling – the informal way to management success

This is the title of an unusual book dealing entirely with business communications.[7] The *Concise Oxford Dictionary* defines 'huddle' colloquially as a close or secret conference. The book demonstrates that results are produced not by organizations but by people, by a special kind of people – the 'huddlers', who are able to work intimately and informally in small groups. It is one of the most effective means of communication.

A manager therefore needs to be a huddler. Normal communications within an organization are in the form of inter-office memoranda, with copies to all and sundry. If a memo is marked 'Confidential', then it is read by everyone including the messenger, before the message reaches its target – so much for confidentiality. Further, the recipient, already flooded with paper, hardly has time to read it, let alone act on it. The same message conveyed verbally face-to-face will not only remain confidential but will be extremely effective. Clarification, if needed, is sought and given immediately, and in addition instant feedback ensures that there is complete understanding of the message and the resulting action required. We also have, as a bonus, the 'human touch' element, completely lacking in the memorandum.

Huddling, of course, is nothing new. It has always been there in the matter of inter-personal relations. It is effective and achieves results. A few minutes of informal conversation with subordinates, peers and superiors, along the corridors of the office or in the washroom, can be most effective. The practice of this technique, therefore, needs to be encouraged. It is an essential element in good management.

Manage by wandering around

This can be seen as an extension of the huddling concept. It is said to be one of the reasons for the success of some excellent companies in the US.[3] The companies studied by Peters and Waterman, and including such well-known names as Bechtel, Boeing, Caterpillar, IBM, Johnson & Johnson, Proctor & Gamble and 3M, were all found to be action-oriented. The managers in these companies practise what others term 'management by wandering around'. This leads to the formation of small groups and small divisions and the companies tend to form a large number of these. *Ad hoc* groups and task forces are also pulled together at short notice as and when needed to accomplish a particular task. These groups work quickly and informally with the minimum of documentation. They try things out and keep experimenting in order to attain the optimum for any particular operation or situation.

The intensity and effectiveness of such an informal communication system is unbelievable. Though informal, the communication system acts as a remarkably tight control system without the conventional hierarchical control devices. Also, in refreshing contrast to conventional practice, failure is tolerated but they learn from their mistakes: they put the KISS principle, 'keep it simple, stupid', into practice. Their written memoranda are brief and simple, such as the fabled one-page memorandum at Proctor & Gamble.

Peters and Waterman's study also proved that people are not good at processing large amounts of new data and that the utmost we can hold in short memory is a mere six or seven discrete pieces of data. This reinforces the necessity for simple communications. Rene McPherson (another of our company 'doctors') on taking over the Dana Corporation threw out 22 half-inch-thick policy manuals and replaced them with a one-page statement of the company philosophy.

Summary

Having asserted that good management is the key to company success and hence the infallible remedy in relation to sick and ailing companies, we also state that a clean sweep is an essential preliminary if a turnaround is to be achieved. There is a lot of truth and a deal of merit in the old adage: a new broom sweeps clean. We have examined what we consider to be essential elements in good management and find every time that communications are vital. Indeed, good communications are the essence of good management. Good managers have always known this, but today analysts have studied their efforts and codified their work under terms such as 'huddling' and MBWA — manage by walking around. There is much wisdom here for our turnaround manager or the company doctor. A complete revolution in communications technology is under way but, while it is making a most valuable contribution, there is an urgent need to stay with the basics of human nature *vis-à-vis* communication. Please 'keep it simple, stupid'.

References

1. Altman, E. I., *Corporate Financial Distress – A Complete Guide to Predicting, Avoiding and Dealing with Bankruptcy*, Wiley, New York, 1983.
2. Uttal, B., 'The corporate culture vultures', *Fortune*, **108**, 66–72, 17 Oct. 1983.

3. Peters, T. J. and R. H. Waterman, *In Search of Excellence: Lessons from America's Best-Run Companies*, Harper & Row, 1982
4. Brandt, S. C., *Entrepreneuring – the ten commandments for building a growth company*, Addison-Wesley, 1982.
5. Toth, E. R., 'Build morale, increase production', *Chem. Eng.*, **89**, 119–20, 12 July 1982.
6. Kharbanda, O. P., 'Look east, young man!', *Swagat*, Sept. 1984, pp. 49–51. (*Swagat* is the Indian Airlines magazine.)
7. Merrell, V. D., *Huddling – the informal way to management success*, American Management Association, 1979.

17 Corporate planning

The term 'corporate planning' is something like 20 years old now, yet there is still considerable confusion as to its real meaning. The term does *not* refer just to planning relative to products, markets, production, finance or personnel. It is intended to refer to the *corporate whole* and should be quite simple, consisting of two parts:

Corporate objectives
Corporate strategies to achieve those objectives.

The latter is sometimes called strategic planning and tends to be confused with corporate planning, but it is only a part of the whole. Corporate planning is for the long term, and is therefore at times termed long-range planning. There are some hundreds of books now available on the subject, of which those by Hussey and Argenti are typical.[1]

The basics of corporate planning

As we have just said corporate planning should be a simple, straightforward exercise, but that does not mean that it is easy. Why not? Well:

The future is unpredictable
Predictions are subject to large errors
Decisions relating to corporate planning are very subjective

The purpose of corporate planning is to assess the long-term future of a company. The plan as such should be short, simple and straightforward, unlike the short-term plan, which should be based on a large volume of data and incorporate a great number of detailed decisions. The corporate plan calls for very few decisions but these decisions are vital to the future prosperity of the company. Since the long-term future of the company is being assessed, the corporate plan could include acquisition, merger or diversification. It could, however, envisage the very opposite of those things: divestment, splitting off or even closing down.

Now it will be appreciated that a corporate plan is made up of a few simple but significant statements concerning the long-term future of the company. The formulation of those 'declarations of intent' will inevitably take much time and effort and demand extensive discussion at the very top of the management tree.

The plan, when formulated, will be simple enough, but arriving at that plan can be a very complex matter, since it is designed to state the company's objectives, or mission in life. Where does it want to be in 5, 10 or 20 years time? For instance, the corporate plan of a company like IBM may state its market share now and the share desired at a particular point of time in the future. Should it have more products in the same field (computers) or should it diversify? Will it grow even bigger? These are both major and vital decisions that should be taken even if the future is completely uncertain. Why? Because there *must* be an objective, a goal to aim for, since this gives the company purpose. It does not matter if that goal is unambitious — stay as we are, for instance — since even that will probably take a lot of doing.

The formulation of a corporate plan involves the taking of some hard and major decisions and a great many books have been written on the subject, giving much sound advice on how to make and take major decisions of this kind. Such decisions are necessarily qualitative, not quantitative and most managers are trained to handle quantitative data. They are therefore usually ill-equipped to formulate a corporate plan.

There is no doubt that the preparation of the corporate plan should be — must be — a team effort between the top executives of the company. If you have what is termed a 'corporate planner' — another misnomer — then his function must be that of executive secretary or technical adviser. The main components of a corporate plan are:

Objectives, company ethos and targets
Forecasts on the basis of the data for the last five years, corrected for inflation
Appraisals, internal and external. These have to be identified, distilled and ranked
Strategies, with alternatives and their evaluation
Action plans, avoiding excessive detail
Monitoring, not of results but of the team's confidence in the plan it has formulated

The chief executive *must* take the lead in all this. He should form his team, then work systematically through the above sequence, keeping in mind at all times the SWOT analysis (strengths, weaknesses, opportunities and threats) not only in relation to his own company but also in relation to his competitors. When all the various aspects have been reviewed, he should arrive at a consensus and decide. That last point is crucial: he *must* have consensus. If certain members of his team do not agree with the corporate plan, then the whole thing is an exercise in futility. The whole process we have just described can well take the best part of a year, if not longer. A member of the team should be designated as the corporate planner, who listens to and records what is discussed and decided. He should also provide all the necessary documentation.

Such an exercise should, ideally, start with a seminar on the subject of corporate planning, so that the planning team can be exposed to the current state of the art in relation to the subject. Here too the chief executive should take an active part, while the corporate planner provides relevant reading material. It can be a most useful exercise to have an outside consultant on the subject to come and lead a 2–3 day seminar as a sort of 'kick-off' meeting. What will they hear?

Corporate targets

Targets and forecasts are related, but they are *not* the same. A target is what a company *wants*. It is that company's aim, hope, desire, while a forecast is the company's assessment of what may well happen, whether it wants it or not. The corporate plan is a sort of bridge between these two: what the company wants and what it expects to get. Both can be quantified by an indicator, but then we have a problem. There are a multitude of indicators proposed: which shall we choose? Each has its advocates and its opponents, but while many have been proclaimed as the best, there is really no such thing. Argenti, for instance, declares:

> I know of no ratio that is better because it is bigger. A high ROCE (return on capital employed) is not necessarily better than a low one (so long as it exceeds the cost of capital). A big value-added per employee can merely tell us that this company is more vertically integrated than a company with a low one. A high turnover assets ratio can describe a company that is under-capitalized just as well as one that is using its assets efficiently: and horror of horrors, it can even mean that the company is overtrading and will shortly become insolvent. . . . All management ratios are invalid, I believe.[1]

But, to make the best of a bad job, there are three ratios we can commend as having some use:

ROSC Return on Shareholders' Capital, one of the most important ratios except for those companies quoted on the Stock Exchange, where the calculation can be distorted by market fluctuations in share value which bear no relation, necessarily, to a company's performance. While we said in Chapter 4 that the share value *can* be a good indicator of the health of a company, since a great deal of unpublished information finds its way into share market circles, yet at the same time share prices are often manipulated by those operating in the market.

EpS Earnings per Share. This relates quite closely to profits and is understood by everyone. It goes up and down with the profits of the company and is not affected by the share price. In this it has the advantage over ROSC.

Profits This is the most widely used ratio, understood by all, but inflation and the consequences of merger can distort the picture. It fails to reflect the consequences of further share issues and ignores the impact of fiscal taxes, yet it can never be ignored.

These three together make a good combination, when setting up a corporate target in financial terms and assessing where a company is going relative to its targets. The ROSC is an all-embracing ratio, profit is understood by all, while EpS is part of the day-to-day language of the banker and stockbroker. No other ratios, whether used individually or collectively, can match these three in terms of significance. For a company embarking on corporate planning, as every company, large or small, should, this trio reflects its present position quite clearly. Look at them over the years, and you have a clear indication of the way the company is going. Compare your figures with those of your competitors in the same industry and you have a fair indication of your status, although this comparison has to be accepted with reservations, since each company is unique.

The next step is to set targets in terms of these ratios for the future. Specific targets are dangerous: better to express your target in terms of a range, for each of the three indicators we have recommended. While the company remains within the range set up, then everything is satisfactory, although the minimum must always be exceeded. That done, the real action starts: a strategic plan is required to meet the financial targets that have been established.

Alternative strategies

It is no good having just *one* strategy. A list of several possible strategies must be drawn up, developed by what is sometimes called 'brainstorming', or through a survey of informed opinion both inside and outside the company. The longer this list and the wider its range at this stage, the better. Let the imagination wander not only along conventional, logical paths, but also into the unconventional. This should throw up fresh ideas which may later turn out to be both simple and very effective, however bizarre they may seem at the outset. This approach is termed 'lateral thinking', while the refusal to let your mind wander off the path is called 'vertical thinking'.[2] We suggest that you add lateral dimension to your vertical (or logical) thinking.

Having assembled your strategies, they should then be divided into three main categories. Do they relate to company size, the product or the market? Of course, there can be related strategies, concerned with personnel, finance, organization, acquisition, licensing and the like, but the first three are basic. It is there, then, that the attention must be first concentrated. It is now time to come down to specifics, in order to evaluate and select from among the wide range of strategies that have opened up to view. Don't forget that all your strategies should relate to a specific time frame, normally the next ten years. To go beyond that would be a fruitless exercise. The selection process is best carried out in two phases. Start by ruling out those strategies that are clearly inappropriate. Typically, of every 100 strategies thrown up during the brainstorming sessions, some 10 will survive. We mention the numbers to give you some idea of the depth and breadth of good strategic planning. When you are down to say 10 possible strategic plans, the next stage is to re-evaluate them in detail, before deciding which is to be implemented. The screening and final selection has to be achieved through a process of frank and free discussion among the corporate planning team.

Experience has shown that a very valuable 'fall-out' from such discussions is the realization that until the planning process started, almost everyone, including the chief executive, had underestimated the company's strengths and overestimated its weaknesses and the threats to its future. This in itself can be reward enough, since it boosts morale. The process also exposes talents and abilities which may have lain dormant.

In due course a set of viable strategies should emerge, but before they are finally adopted certain basic questions have to be asked all over again. Does the company have sufficient resources to implement the selected strategies? Will it be overstretched? What is the chance of achieving the basic financial targets set earlier? What if the worst happens, and even the minimum target cannot be attained? Will the company still survive?

These are all hard questions to answer, but they must be faced if catastrophe is to be avoided later. Such soul-searching may not always ensure success, but the chances of failure are considerably reduced, since you have assessed the possibilities *before* they were on the doorstep, and so have assessed them calmly, rationally, without fear and with a completely open mind. Once the strategies have been finalized and accepted, then an action plan is drawn up, implemented and then constantly monitored. Commitment to such a plan by all in senior management – remember, consensus is vital – will ensure that the plan will have wholehearted co-operation and support from management. You will remember that in Chapter 3 we drew attention to the fact that consensus is the secret of the success of the Japanese management system.

Mergers and acquisitions

We have mentioned mergers and acquisitions as possible elements in corporate planning and they can well be part of the strategy adopted by a company in order to achieve its corporate objectives. We decided to examine this aspect in more detail, since it is becoming ever more important in the business world of today.

One particular form of acquisition, termed the 'buy-out', is becoming so common in the developed countries of the world that it is a constant feature in the financial news columns. They are not only popular and attractive to both buyer and seller but they have been remarkably successful. The failure rate for buy-outs is estimated at some 10 per cent, compared with the 30 per cent failure rate for new businesses. Small and medium sized operations are usually more successful and perform better if they are independent, but a buy-out by the managers or employees of a company can spell personal disaster if they fail to turn the company around — pending collapse is the usual motivator — since they may well lose their entire savings, together with their job. Let us look at an outstanding example to see what is involved.

A very big buy-out deal related to a motorcar component plant at Clark, New Jersey, in the US, owned by General Motors (GM). The plant was uncompetitive and scheduled for closure, but to preserve jobs locally the unions involved offered to buy the plant for US$53 million. The deal was encouraged by GM, who were prepared to loan the money and buy the entire output of the plant at competitive prices for the next three years, provided that the workforce of some 400 was cut by half. This was most certainly a display of enlightened management, for while GM themselves could never have imposed such a drastic reduction in the workforce, they knew that the new owners could not make a success of the operation unless that most unpleasant decision was taken. The fact that they were prepared to finance the deal clinched it, to the ultimate benefit of all concerned.

In the UK, buy-outs are typically on a much smaller scale. They usually come in the manufacturing sector, with a group of senior managers in a failing factory unit buying it out for around £1 million. The managers involved are usually the majority of the top executives and the bulk of the finance is provided by one of the finance houses. Such buy-outs may well have birth pangs, but these are by no means insurmountable and many have been most successful.[3] It is also interesting to note that finance for such buy-outs is available for the asking, a sure indicator of potential success.[4]

The other side of the coin is the company takeover. These seem to have a strange fascination for financiers, who at times proceed with the utmost secrecy, turning the operation into what is called an 'early morning raid' — and the raider is not always welcome. Nonetheless they threaten to become quite common.[5] Hoardings advertising Dunlop tyres in India have carried the slogan: 'Buy the best — buy Dunlop tyres'. Takeover wizard R. P. Goenka of Calcutta went one better than that: he sought to buy out Dunlop India! Earlier, Goenka had been turned away by Dunlop Holdings, based in the UK, who because of their financial troubles were under pressure from their bankers to sell off some of their assets. But now, while several other financial houses made offers, Goenka outbid them all. It was the 40 per cent stake of the holding company that was on offer, since previous legislation in India had already brought the overseas Dunlop interest down to that figure.

The spate of such transactions seems to have caught governments unawares and there is an urgent need for a clear government policy if the success of such operations is not to be threatened by bureaucratic delay. For example:

Britain's fondness for fudge and compromise produces many bad decisions and unworkable policies: nowhere more unworkable than in its supervision of company mergers. Confusion and controversy have been the hallmarks of the most recent government rulings on mergers, suggesting a need for clearer guidelines for judging mergers, and clearer division of responsibility between those parts of the government involved in merger policy.[6]

Britain is not alone in this desire to supervise and control company mergers. We turn to the US and find that the Sucurities and Exchange Commission there has been conducting open hearings in an attempt to curb the 'wheeling and dealing' that often accompanies such corporate marriages. A Colorado democrat, Timothy Wirth, once declared:

> The tactics and strategies used by both bidders and targets in recent years have raised questions about the adequacy of current laws to ensure the fundamental fairness of the takeover process. In the heat of a contest, important shareholder, employee and community interests may be overlooked.

A merger or takeover is obviously very big business, not only for the two parties directly involved but also for an intermediary, such as the merger and acquisition specialist, an élite group numbering perhaps no more than a dozen. They operate secretly and in a matter of hours they can build up a corporate empire or cause a company to vanish off the scene. To take one example, the US$13 billion merger of Gulf Oil and Standard Oil of California netted Morgan Stanley & Co. a fee of US$16.5 million. Fees ranging between US$2 and US$10 million are relatively common. Of course, such middlemen have to do a lot of work, much of it abortive; the success rate runs at less than 10 per cent.

The merger syndrome began with the objective of rescuing firms in trouble, but no longer. Size used to be a severe limiting factor in a takeover, but no longer. Indeed, we now say that no company, however big, is safe from takeover. We said earlier that sometimes the proposed merger or acquisition was unwelcome, and it is also true that not all mergers end in a happy marriage. Of those consummated between 1974 and 1982 in the US, seven have been major disasters. Overall, it is estimated that of all the mergers that have taken place during the last ten years, one-third have enriched the shareholders of the acquiring company, one-third have been a washout, while the last third cost the investors concerned a great deal of money. So, while your corporate strategy may well involve merger or acquisition, beware! It is no guarantee of success.[7]

Please do plan

Despite many years of experience with corporate planning, controversy continues as to its desirability. A brilliant strategy does not always guarantee success and even the obvious has to be continually restated, namely that unless you can implement plans they have no value whatsoever. Imperial Chemical Industries, the chemicals giant, adopted strategic planning techniques more than ten years ago, but now seem to have reached the conclusion that 'they are of limited benefit in an uncertain world'. It is alleged that they are too rigid, that they are no good in the 1980s. Shell's planners seem to have reached a similar conclusion. They say: 'We have abandoned any idea of forecast planning . . . the risks have become higher and higher . . . the plan is a failure if it is not supported by top management.' Yet a successful British retailing company, Sainsbury, seems to have rediscovered the virtues of corporate planning although its effect has yet to be reflected in their financial results. We wonder whether size and therefore consensus has anything to do with the problems confronting ICI and Shell in this area?

The Argenti system

John Argenti, whom we have quoted extensively (see Chapter 12), has adopted a very positive approach. Since corporate planning is fundamental to a company's success, he offers the Argenti System, described as a 'simple, practical guide to re-shaping your company's strategies'. This system keeps the development of a corporate plan simple, allowing the smaller and medium-sized companies to proceed without hiring consultants (other than Argenti!) or specialist planners. The services of Argenti himself are available in that users of the manuals provided have the freedom to approach him for advice on the planning process. A set of manuals are provided if the 'Argenti System of Corporate Planning' (copyright) is purchased. These show how to form a planning team and then move through a beautifully clear and logical sequence of steps that will produce a strategic plan. The system is widely available, with a number of licensees who distribute the system in their own country, together with the appropriate backup services, including local language translations and independent company appraisals. Companies with up to 30 000 employees have used the system and the comment of a user in a highly sophisticated financial business — health insurance — was:

> Corporate Planning in many businesses is a mess. It is either felt to be too complicated or too sophisticated for an individual company's needs or is delegated to a highly intelligent rising star who has no experience in corporate planning and who typically produces voluminous documentation totally divorced from the practical realities surrounding a business enterprise.
> The Argenti System cuts its way through this maze with all the common sense and practicality of a pair of well sharpened garden shears. It is practical, well structured and easy to use. We are finding it immensely helpful.

Planning pays

Let us conclude this chapter by saying that while no planning is better than bad planning, the objective should obviously be good planning.

Even the smallest of companies can benefit greatly from planning. Even the biggest of companies still have confidence in planning. General Motors, one of the largest in the world, hopes to thrash its major competitors, Ford, Chrysler and American Motors, by meticulous planning and careful strategy. With 60 per cent of the American market and some US$ 13 million in cash available, they propose to expand and diversity – but diversity in the field they know. Their strategy includes a formidable product line-up starting with a high-style front-wheel drive and including new compacts in collaboration with Toyota and Suzuki, leaders in that field.

Summary

We have introduced you to the concept of a corporate plan, with the establishment of realistic financial objectives and imaginative long-term strategies, and insist that even the smallest of companies can benefit from the use of such techniques. An increasingly common strategy is to use the merger or acquisition as a stepping-stone to success, but even that route offers no certainty. Many mergers and acquisitions have brought heavy losses rather than profit. While the future seems ever more uncertain, we still recommend the corporate plan as making a valuable contribution to success.

References

1. Argenti, J., *Practical Corporate Planning*, Allen & Unwin, 1980; Hussey, D. E., *Corporate Planning – Theory and Practice*, (2nd edn.) Pergamon, 1984; Hussay, D. E., (ed.), *The Truth about Corporate Planning – International Research into the Practice of Planning*, Pergamon, 1983.
2. De Bono, E., *The Use of Lateral Thinking*, Penguin, 1971.
3. Upton, R., 'Britain's buy-out boom', *Personnel Management Marketing*, March 1984, pp. 22–5.
4. Coyne, J. and M. Wright, 'Management buyout boom in the UK', *Financial Express*, 11 Oct. 1984.
5. Chander Uday Singh, 'The Goenkas – Corporate Raiders', *India Today*, 15 August 1984, pp. 80–5.
6. Long, T. M. and M. A. Woks, 'Hostile takeovers – wave of the future?', *The Bankers Magazine*, 167, 38–43, Sept./Oct. 1984.
7. Birley, S., 'Success and failure in management buyouts', *Long Range Planning*, 17, 32–40, June 1984.

18 The chief executive

When we set out in Part One the basic concepts involved in a study of corporate failure, we asserted that while management is all-important, and while management must operate as a team, it was also true that the team must have a leader. We then looked at some outstanding examples of the 'man at the top' to illustrate the type of man that succeeds and brings his company to success. The leader is often styled 'the chief executive', and operates as managing director or chairman in many cases. Having looked at the *sort* of man who is successful in this position, we now need to define the qualities and characteristics that are necessary.

What does he do?

What does the chief executive do? How does he occupy his time? Does he sit back and order everybody around? Does he hire and fire? Does he have a 4-hour day or a 16-hour day? A great deal has been written on this subject and we propose to present you with a brief outline. Let us see, first of all, how he sees himself. To take an instance, James F. Beré, chairman of the Borg-Warner Corporation is clear and precise:

> The job [of the top executive] is not to make decisions . . . it is to put good people in place and judge if they are making good decisions. You give them the power. When they come in and say, 'How do I do something', I say: 'That's your problem. . . .'[1]

This is called the principle of delegation, a basic principle in good management. All the textbooks tell us that effective delegation is the key to good management.

Now let us see the chief executive of the 1980s as others see him. We are told that he should be a sort of 'ferryman', a transporter of persons and ideas from one place to another. Thus the chief executive is seen as having the following abilities:

To move easily between the past, present and future of the company
To show his team a clear and convincing route to the company's objective
To set an example to follow. To practise, not just preach
To be a guide, counsellor and mentor to others in the company
To put forward new ideas and get their acceptance

To learn from success and also from failures — his own and others
To foresee technological changes and set strategies accordingly
To achieve himself and also to achieve results through others[2]

The 'ferryman' will constantly ask basic questions concerning his company, such as: Where are we now? How did we get here? Where must we be tomorrow? How do we get there?

We could take any one of those items and enlarge upon its significance. For instance, it is another fundamental principle in good management to 'set an example'. How often is that rule flouted, not only in significant, but also in minor matters? To take one example that is public, at least in the UK, where the salaries of directors have to be published. Perusing the public accounts, what do we see? We see the chief executive voting himself a salary increase while freezing salaries lower down the scale on the grounds that the company cannot afford it. We see the chairman of Dunlop, Sir Campbell Fraser — and you know the state Dunlop was in at the time (Chapter 10) — increasing his salary by 20 per cent when the company was patently in financial distress. We see Lord Pennock, chairman of BICC, getting a 20 per cent increase (£15 000) when his company had just made a loss of £3 million. We see the top executives at Bowater getting a generous 30 per cent rise in the face of a 34 per cent drop in pre-tax profits. Even a company such as ICI, well known for its good management policies, gave its top directors a rise of 6 per cent when pre-tax profits were down by 76 per cent.[3] No wonder Sir Michael Edwardes said in 1984: 'Today I am more pessimistic about UK managers than I was two years ago.'[4]

In speaking of setting an example, good timekeeping throughout a company is a very important factor in relation to its efficiency. Yet in how many companies do we find that managers are the last to arrive, first to leave and take long midday breaks, often euphemistically styled 'business lunches'?

The new broom

We have seen that most of the factors that get companies into trouble have their roots in poor management: management that cannot cope with the numerous problems besetting them from within and from without. Management, poor or good, starts at the top, with the chief executive. This means, therefore, that where there is poor management, the only way to change the situation is by changing the chief executive. That may well lead to many other changes, but change must *start* at the top. This is the basic, major and most significant step in any turnaround.

A change at the top has an immediate and salutary effect on all those involved: the bankers, the investors and the employees at all levels. The positive, 'we are going to do something' attitude so essential to the accomplishment of a turnaround is immediately established. Apart from the symbolic importance of such a change, the new chief executive is expected to develop new strategies, change direction – alter things, hopefully for the better. Everyone remembers the old adage: a new broom sweeps clean.

There is great debate about the proper qualifications for the chief executive in a turnaround situation. Obviously, the best choice, as always, is someone who has done it before. The turnaround situation demands a different set of skills to those called for in a well-run, healthy company. Let us illustrate by example once again.

Knight's next move

This is one eye-catching headline in an article on the career and views of Sir Michael Edwardes.[4] In 1951 he joined the Chloride Group as a trainee manager and was later given the job of reorganizing its Central African operations. On his return to the UK he became chief executive, in 1972, and chairman two years later. In six years he transformed Chloride, whose pre-tax profits rose under his direction from £3.5 million to more than £26 million. In 1975 he received the *Guardian* 'Young Businessman of the Year' award.

Three years later he was persuaded to move to British Leyland, to take on a job that many said couldn't be done. He proved them wrong in a five-year slog which, he says, taught him more than 30 years with Chloride: 'My biggest contribution to BL was in the first three years. The fourth year was a year of consolidation. In the fifth I had begun to phase myself out.'

That is the point we wish to seize on: turnaround calls for a specific management style. The chief executive who accomplishes the turnaround should later go elsewhere, taking his 'style' with him – a style that *demands* a turnaround situation. The continuing career of Sir Michael Edwardes makes the point for us. After a brief spell with Mercury, he joind ICL, but before he had time to implement reforms that were causing consternation amongst ICL's staider managers, STC's Sir Kenneth Corfield put in his successful bid for that company (see Chapter 10). Now the abrasive Sir Michael, nicknamed Little Moe by BL workers, has been appointed executive chairman at Dunlop after a bitter boardroom battle. (See pages 80–81).

Of course, Sir Michael is not alone. He came from a company that employed sound management techniques, and such companies produce competent turnaround managers. GEC in the UK, for instance, has produced notable examples, such as Dr Adolf Frankel at Staveley Industries and Brian Gould at Redman Heenan International. From a study of such people in action we can see the attributes called for in a successful turnaround manager: he needs considerable leadership and motivational skills, he needs the ability and the courage to make rapid decisions from the minimum of data, he must be able to work long hours under stress and have the flexibility to change course if required.

A turnaround demands rapid change and possibly unpopular decisions. The new chief executive has therefore to be a tough, no-nonsense manager, probably disliked at first, but respected once he produces results. The qualities necessary to cope with a turnaround are not those called for in the normal situation and could even become a liability once turnaround has been achieved.

Whether or not top management as a whole should change as well as the chief executive is an open question. There is no consensus and both approaches – change the man at the top and change the board – have been followed with success. At BL the management was not subject to drastic change, but Sir Michael's achievement there was that he drew startling good performances out of people who until then had been doing most things wrong. Coming to Dunlop, however, he made a wholesale clearout of the main board. It is interesting to note the reaction of the Dunlop workforce to that drastic action. Dunlop have a major factory in Coventry and the last time he wielded power in Coventry two factories closed. Yet a union leader there seems to have few doubts about the new chairman. He doesn't see that clearout as an ugly portent. His comment is:

> It was necessary to prune the company from the top and he did it. I don't think he will chop jobs here. We have so much work and we have a good set-up, with successful local management and no industrial relations problems. I think Edwardes is the man to invest in and capitalize on that set-up.[5]

Across the Atlantic

Turnaround 'pros' are by no means confined to the UK. Q. T. Wiles, now in his fifties and trained as an organic chemist, joined Goodall-Electric Manufacturing Company after a spell as salesman and turned it from a one-man show into a formal structured corporation. Following its acquisition Wiles stayed with it and ended up as chief executive, running 18 semiconductor companies with total sales exceeding US$400 million. For the next 10 years he worked closely with a San Francisco banking firm, Hambrecht & Quist, one of whose activities was that of premier underwriter to high-tech companies. When some of the companies with which they were involved got into trouble, the bank assigned Wiles as a sort of 'Red Adair' (the legendary expert in dousing oilwell fires) to extinguish the red ink in the annual accounts. Wiles proved so effective that he was appointed chairman of the banking firm following the death of one of the co-founders, George Quist. Wiles now has the unofficial title of 'turnaround pro' – and no wonder. He is now the working chairman of five corporations, draws more than US$1 million a year in salary and owns some US$20 million in stock options. Yet he has no management training, nor did he take a management degree! Do you want to know what makes a 'turnaround pro'? According to Wiles, most of his time is spent 'making sure people know what their jobs are'.

How does he manage five separate corporations? That is simple enough, it appears. Wiles keeps five 'bibles' handy and has developed an 'exceptional ability to compartmentalize things in his mind'. He has learnt to use his time effectively through a better organization of his life style. Different coloured folders are used for each of the five companies he heads. They are mostly in 'Silicon Valley' in California, a location full of venture capital, bright ideas and . . . trouble.

Wiles, it appears, is not easy to work for. He doesn't 'pick on' people but just drives them hard. If they can't keep up, they fall by the wayside. Those who manage his companies have to be prepared for rapid change, turmoil and disruption. Yet, for a man heading five companies, he is easily accessible to his colleagues and senior executives. He doesn't refuse to take telephone calls and even in the middle of a meeting is willing to go aside and 'talk it over', even reaching agreement on the phone – a reflection of his ability to compartmentalize the various aspects of his work in his mind.

An example of the turnaround technique

Let us look at just one of his many turnarounds. Granger Associates, a telecommunications company, turned to Wiles when in a hopeless condition. In 1980 the company owed its bankers US$10 million, had a negative net worth and had made a loss during that year of US$4.4 million. This was simple but shocking arithmetic. Wiles began as their consultant but soon saw that if effective action was to be taken he had to become chairman. There followed some quick decisions. He cut the payroll by 40 per cent and divided the company into five autonomous subsidiaries. He defined the problems with which he was confronted in the simplest of terms and sought simple solutions. In the very first year after he took over there was a profit of US$9.3 million on sales of US$71 million.

How is it achieved? Putting it simply, he makes the broad decisions and then leaves the implementation of those decisions entirely to his executives. He will not tolerate any change in the decision taken before it has been given a fair chance.

One-man rule

The two outstanding examples we have been reviewing make it very clear that the man in the chair in a turnaround situation is essentially and necessarily, at least in the initial stages, an example of 'one-man rule'. But there is no reason to believe that it should stay that way. While it is true that many large and successful companies have been built up by one man, that is no proof that the ideal way to run a company is autocratically. Where such companies are successful, the secret is ascribed to the vision and leadership of the one man who is 'all in all' but equally, when there is trouble, takes all the blame.

When we were discussing the analysis of situations leading to potential failure in Chapter 12 we saw that autocratic, one-man rule was considered to be a significant factor in the qualitative assessment, contributing much to potential failure.

The negative factor increases if he is not only chief executive but chairman as well. This is because the pattern in such cases is almost invariably the same: early success, soon followed by failure. There are exceptions, but it is the exceptions that prove the rule, as we can clearly see: when a company is small, as is always the case in the beginning, it is advantageous and cheaper to have all the decision-making at one place. The decisions come quickly and are promptly implemented. There are no committees to deliberate on the facts and figures, but there are not many facts and figures to deliberate upon. But as a business grows, it has growing pains, to go back once again to our human analogy: competitors enter the field, new products or new manufacturing techniques assume growing importance. The autocrat at the helm is normally too set in his ways to listen, to change, to react quickly and effectively to the changing circumstances. The company gets sicker and he has to be replaced. A turnaround is at the door. So we make the point that one-man rule, although vital in a turnaround, is only effective over the short term.

Holding the reins

One can ride a horse with a 'slack rein' or a 'tight rein' and the choice is made according to the situation one is in. When searching for the ideal chief executive, we see that while the absolute autocrat will fail, there has to be a degree of rigid control, combined however with a degree of autonomy. Some of the legendary figures in the management field, such as Tom Watson of IBM, Bill Hewlett and Dave Packard, founders of Hewlett-Packard, Levi Strauss (jeans) and Robert W. Johnson of Johnson & Johnson, all believed strongly and sincerely in autonomy at all levels, giving the individual room to perform. But at the same time they were *all* strict disciplinarians. While they gave their managers plenty of rope, they realized that some might hang themselves. So there was freedom within a rigid framework – a framework set by the basic company policy and culture, which must *never* be violated. For instance, to take IBM once again, that company's commitment to customer service must *never* be compromised.

If this sounds a paradox, then all life is a paradox. In the classroom we see that for good teaching we *must* have a code of conduct and a sense of discipline in respect of attendance, punctuality, regular homework and the like. Yet, at the same time, the teacher will get the best out of the students if there is feedback, an easy interchange of ideas, with praise for work well done. Similarly, in a well-run company, autonomy is the product of discipline. The discipline the shared values, provide a safe, protective framework within which individual innovation can blossom and bear fruit. The stable, clearly defined parameters give people confidence and they are prepared to experiment within the known framework. Children are just the same. They *like* a disciplined and ordered structure to their lives: it gives them security. They feel safe. When they go out to play, there is always that firm, supportive atmosphere of home to come back to. With a company it is just the same and we leave you to fill out the analogy and get it working in practice.

Summary

We have taken a brief look at the qualities necessary in the chief executive, only to find that the chief executive in a successful company needs to be different to the chief executive who assumes command in a turnaround situation who should leave once his task is complete. He has to be an absolute autocrat, whereas successful companies are run on a continuing basis with a subtle blend of autocracy and individual autonomy. There has to be a firm disciplinary framework of company policy and culture, within which innovation and experiment can operate safely.

References

1. Beré, J. F., 'Turnover at the top — why executives are losing their jobs so quickly', *Business Week*, 19 Dec. 1983, pp. 56—62.
2. Marlow, H., *Success — Individual, Corporate and National — Profile for the Eighties and Beyond*, Institute of Personnel Management (US), 1984.
3. Smart, V., 'A loss can be good for the boss', *Sunday Observer* (UK), 5 June 1983, p.24.
4. Spooner, P., 'UK squanders its management talent', *Chief Executive* (UK), Nov. 1984, pp. 10—15.
5. Walters, P., 'Workforce fate in lap of Little Moe', *Evening Telegraph*, Coventry, UK, 20 Nov. 1984, p.6.

PART FIVE

Prevention is best

19 From case to case

We come now to an aspect of corporate collapse which has been sadly neglected: its *prevention*. As we have pointed out earlier, all the emphasis in the literature on the subject has been on prediction. The prime purpose of prediction seems to be to guide and assist those considering investment, not those running the company. Even when the concepts of cure (finding a panacea), or prevention (avoiding its ever happening) are introduced, we do not get far. The neglect of these two aspects is well illustrated in what has become a standard work in the field, Altman's *Corporate Financial Distress: a Complete Guide to Predicting, Avoiding and Dealing with Bankruptcy.*[1] Despite the title, not one of his 12 chapters includes the words 'avoiding' or 'prevention', nor are they to be found in his subject index. Most of the book is devoted to the techniques of prediction, with a little on the legal and investment implications of bankruptcy. In this it follows the general trend of the published literature. Argenti, however, while making no such claim in his title, does in fact devote a few pages to the matter of prevention.[2] We do have a whole book devoted to corporate recovery, but even that book begins:

> Corporate recovery is about the management of firms in crisis, firms that will become insolvent unless appropriate management actions are taken to effect a turnaround in their financial performance.[3]

The book starts with crisis, and deals with turnaround strategies: that is, it tells us how to act once the crisis has arrived: the concept of warding off crisis is not there. Yet surely that is by far the better course.

Perhaps this concept of prevention has not been examined because the relevant knowledge rests with only a few individuals who have had to learn from bitter experience, having been personally involved in a business failure or an attempt to turnaround a collapsing company. They might well have resolved never to have such a thing happen again, and to develop their own technique of prevention in company management.

Such knowledge is extremely valuable, so perhaps those with the appropriate knowledge are keeping it to themselves. Such knowledge is also worth a great deal of money as demonstrated by the careers of men like Q. T. Wiles, whom we discussed in Chapter 18. By the same token this ought to be a most lucrative field for consultants but since, as we have seen, reform has to come from within, perhaps the consultant who develops the necessary techniques turns into a chief executive, since he has to join the company to achieve the results. Present efforts to assess the management approach to prevention, on the premise that 'prevention is better than cure', are only a beginning. We would encourage those in the business to share their knowledge with the up and coming generation of managers, to the benefit of us all.

Early warning signals

A disaster such as corporate failure can be prevented if the right action is taken. Our approach to the problem is based on the premise that company failure is a direct consequence of poor management. Of course, there can be external factors outside the control of company management, but we nevertheless maintain that management is the crux, and that sound management holds the key to the prevention of corporate failure.

We have said it before: failure hardly ever comes suddenly. It develops steadily and there are stages in that development to be clearly discerned. Slatter has drawn attention to this and has also set out the corresponding response when the management is poor.[4] We analyse these stages thus:

Stage reached	*Management response*
Hidden crisis	Early warning signals ignored
Denial of crisis	No action, crisis explained away
Organization begins to disintegrate	Some action, too little and too late
Collapse	Too late – the damage has been done

A constant characteristic of poor management is its inability to make constructive decisions. When crisis comes, the decision-making process deteriorates further. A poor management is therefore incapable of effecting a turnaround, a process that demands a series of constructive and often unpleasant decisions. In such a situation it becomes imperative to change the management – above all, to change the chief executive. Good management would take effective action during stages 1 and 2 above, with the result that stages 3 and 4 should not occur if the early warning signals have been acted upon.

From time to time we have elaborated on the likenesses one can draw between the company and the human body. There are striking similarities: both birth and death are inevitably associated with any and every company. Every company dies eventually: the only question open to debate is its life-span. The average life-span among humans is 70 years and it has been that way for some 3000 years. With corporations, the range is perhaps 2 to 200 years. The lower limit can be likened to infant mortality: the company never really gets off the ground. Companies with a history of more than 100 years are rare. Age changes them, just as it does us, and looking at such companies today, we would find them unrecognizable. Accepting that death is inevitable, the objective must be to maintain a company in being as long as possible – but with a proper quality of life. A company that is perpetually sick – and we have seen that we can find many instances of that in India – is of no use to anybody. But, as with us, accidents can happen and they can be fatal: there can always be a catastrophe, an earthquake. We know that the earthquake is inescapable, yet even there the resultant damage can be mitigated if the appropriate steps have been taken beforehand.

Sound management will not only maintain a company in good health, but it will also mitigate against the sudden shock, if it comes. In another context entirely we once devoted an entire chapter to this most important aspect of company management.[5] We said then, and we feel that it is relevant in this context as well:

> 'No sudden shocks, please!' . . . how much better it would be if we could know in good time what was going to happen, rather than just *watch* it happen. It is quite obvious that the most meaningful of all the information that can become available is the *trend* – where we are going. Management never likes to suddenly learn . . . much, much better to know ahead of time. Data that contributes to early assessment is therefore very valuable indeed, since it can provide an 'early warning system' to management.

Which trends shall we watch?

We have already seen that there are a variety of trend indicators, some of which are claimed to give warning of impending disaster from three to five years ahead. We believe that all the various indicators are suspect to some degree, all have some limitations, but . . . 'half a loaf is better than no bread'. We would therefore recommend that the senior executive should initiate a regular assessment of company status using the academic or commercial assessments available to him. He should never –- just never – think that he is, as it were, above that. We all have our blind spots, and an impartial appraisal, such as is offered in such systems, is a check-up that may well pay off. For instance, it is routine these days for senior management to have an annual health checkup. The sensible executive does not say, 'I'm fit – I don't need a checkup'. No, he meekly submits and awaits the verdict with interest.

Assessment in isolation is never really meaningful, so we would further recommend that in addition to watching the trend in relation to his own company, that trend should be set against the industry average. This helps one to gain an objective picture, and one of the great merits of the PAS-score is that this objective assessment is already included as part of the package. The two key points to watch are:

Any adverse trend in the indicator (or score) as measured from year to year
That trend in relation to the industry trend

If the company trend is not only adverse, but worsening in relation to the general industry trend, then there is cause for concern. The actual failure may well still be years away, but the threat is there and management strategy is in need of review. The most immediate step is to start reviewing the status via the indicator once a quarter, say, instead of once a year, but this should be associated with management review. This is where the Argenti A-score approach can help. It offers an analytical assessment of the management style, but we doubt whether the senior executive can carry out such an assessment on his own. Self-criticism is most difficult. Perhaps this is where the management consultant should be called in, to offer an impartial outsider's assessment. In any event, the achievement of a turnaround will be a slow and painful process – but at least early action brings with it the promise of ultimate success.

Who should do what?

If company failure is to be averted then each of the various agencies involved will have to play their part. So far, we have looked at the chief executive and laid on him the responsibility for holding a watching brief. Certain tools are available to him and he should use them. But there are in fact four separate areas where action can and should be initiated: two within the company and two without. We will consider the role of those outside the company first, since they, despite all we have said about the need for sensitivity inside the company, are more likely to 'smell' trouble and realize that it is time to act.

The most important outsider, in our view, is the company's bank. The bank is the best placed of all those associated with the company to detect the first signs of trouble, and against that background should initiate or encourage action that will stop the slide downhill before it gets too fast to be stopped. However, while it appears that banks do watch, in an attempt to protect their *own* interests, and some even use one or other of the commercial indicators available to assist in this watching role, their reaction is generally passive. However, faced with mounting losses due to company failure, banks do seem to be moving to a position where they are prepared to give and want to give constructive advice. In Chapter 11 we quoted the observations of a bank manager who saw that he was indeed able to detect, comment upon and arrest that downward movement among his clients. To quote him once again:

> As it is a feature of banking practice to review the accounts of companies on a regular basis, it is our practice to call for audited accounts which we process on a tabulated card, year by year. The value of this exercise cannot be over-estimated for it is relatively easy to establish patterns within the accounts and if there is an abnormal change in the pattern then this can disclose a problem area.[6]

Once disclosed, what then? The bank should go further than self-protection: it should adopt a positive role towards its client and seek with him a solution to the problem. The use being made by the banks of prediction models is limited and one can only hope for a change in attitudes. There may be an impetus towards change as the banks realize the adverse effect of company collapse on their own business. We expect the banks, once they apply their minds to the problem, to develop their own models for the monitoring of their clients.

The role of government

The second outside influence of major significance is government, both with respect to its policies and also the direct action it may take. Many governments display a readiness to bail out ailing companies, but this policy may well be counter-productive, in that it sustains inefficient management. The objective is usually to preserve employment, but that very objective may prevent the management taking the corrective action it should. The scale of such intervention varies from country to country. We have presented specific examples of outstanding interest in this field from the US and the UK and we have also seen that the policy is taken to an extreme in Japan and India.

There is a positive role for government in the prevention of company collapse, and this is provided by regulatory bodies such as the Securities Exchange Commission (SEC) in the US. Their functions include the monitoring of the business sector and the analysis of published annual accounts so that examples of creative accounting may be detected. If such scrutiny of published accounts is done well, it can be a restraining influence, and will cause any problems to be displayed somewhat earlier – and that is all to the good. Others who have an interest are then alerted and may intervene to ensure that the appropriate preventive action is taken in due time.

The role of the auditor

Apart from the external auditor, many companies have an internal auditor who monitors the preparation of the company accounts. Where creative accounting is the order of the day, it is obvious that the internal auditor is not effective, but there is nothing to stop the external auditor intervening. It is his duty to at least qualify the published accounts with footnotes that highlight any discrepancy or unusual accounting practice that is being newly adopted, even although the practice may be perfectly legal. Unfortunately, such qualifications are rare indeed and by the time the auditor introduces a footnote all the world knows that something is sadly wrong.

In the UK there is a qualification that can be made to the accounts by the auditor that is designed specifically to assess the status of a company. It is called the 'going concern qualification'.[7] Between 1977 and 1983, with quoted companies, only some 25 per cent were qualified on a going concern basis and of those some 70 per cent had obvious problems – so there it was no news.

However, the curious thing is that most of those companies so qualified and under threat did *not* fail. On the other hand, three-quarters of quoted companies failing over the same period were not qualified on a going concern basis before bankruptcy. This illustrates, we feel, that where the auditor, and hence the directors of the company, were alive to the situation, something positive must have been done to avert disaster.

This raised the next question: were the auditors of all those other companies failing in their job? Not necessarily. We have to remember that the auditor is not in business to forecast bankruptcies and we should not expect him to be as efficient and as reliable as those using techniques, such as the PAS-score, that have been specifically developed for the purpose. When preparing the accounts of a company, there is behind it all the basic assumption that the company is going to continue, which makes it difficult for the auditor to make an unbiased assessment of the likelihood of his client's ceasing to be a going concern. Exhortations to the auditors to 'consider whether there are reasonable grounds for accepting that the financial statements, on which he is reporting, should have been prepared on a going concern basis', together with lists of obvious symptoms, are not in themselves much help to the auditor seeking to make a very difficult probability assessment. There is no doubt that the application of reliable Z-score and associated techniques to management and draft accounts during audit via a microcomputer would undoubtedly help overcome the statistical risk assessment problems faced by the auditor and could also aid audit planning. They give an unbiased assessment of the situation, which is what is wanted. The slowness in applying such techniques leads one to the belief that, in essence, people 'don't want to know'. A human failing, but not of much help to failing companies.

However, when it comes to prevention, the published accounts really play only a minor role, since they present the historic picture only. They tell us what was going on six months ago, whereas what we really wish to know is the state of the company today.

Management must act

When we come to consider the potential for preventive action *within* the company, we must look first to the management of the company. The management will be the first to know of trouble and is also the best placed to do something about it. Signs of trouble will not escape the attention of even the poorest management: the problem with poor management is that it ignores the warning signs and is likely to go to extreme lengths to hide the true state of affairs, since it knows well enough where the fault lies. Perhaps it is here that the neutral comment on the situation provided by a commercial company analysis could play a useful role, in the manner we recommended in Chapter 14 (p. 134). Financial analysis is part of the 'objective approach' and should be used by those inside the company as well as those outside.

In this context we are reminded once again of Dunlop (see Chapter 9). Dunlop was in distress – it was, in fact, in danger of collapse for some three years, as is demonstrated by the PAS-score for the company (see Fig. 19.1). Table 19.1 presents the PAS profile and you will note the 'going concern qualification'.[7] There is no doubt that the Dunlop accounts as presented over the years were, according to the PAS-score, continuously below the solvency threshold.

So far Dunlop, as an example and a warning. Yet even with good, efficient management it is still possible for a company to get into trouble, for reasons beyond their control. New and severe competition can develop either at home or from abroad, recession can cut markets, but such things should but test the steel of a good management team. They should be competent to get on top of such situations. What they will not do is to hide their troubles, for they realize that this would be self-defeating. An enlightened management will always frankly admit its problems – and even its mistakes – for without such frankness no effective solution can be found. A frank admission of the problems, associated with a blueprint for the prevention of failure, will always bring both sympathy and practical support from various quarters, including government and the banks. Here lies the best solution for all those involved. Corporate failure is a disaster that spreads its disturbing influence far and wide.

The role of the company board

The board of directors of a company, *if* properly constituted and *if* it is discharging its functions properly, can play a positive, constructive role in the

Table 19.1 Assessing the Dunlop accounts. This extract from the company profile for Dunlop, with profitability, working capital and financial risk assessment on a scale from 1 to 10, shows a movement from bad to worse. (With thanks to Performance Analysis Services Limited, London, for permission to publish.)

Year end	Profitability	Working capital	Financial risk	PAS-score	Z-score	Debt/equity
31.12.83	3	1	1	3	−4.62	1.42:1
31.12.82	2	2	3	11	−2.34	1:03:1
31.12.81	3	1	2	10	−2.23	1.09:1

With £200 million equity and £100 million long-term loan:

Year end	Profitability	Working capital	Financial risk	PAS-score	Z-score	Debt/equity
31.12.83	4	4	5	37	1.81	

Remarks

Risk Rating = 5
Going concern qualification

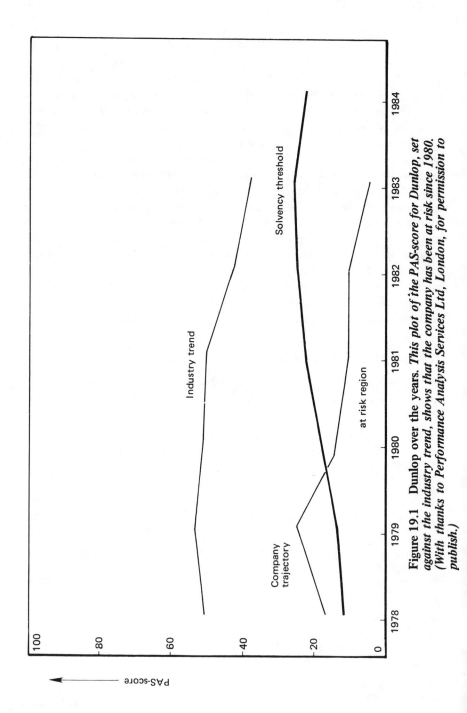

Figure 19.1 Dunlop over the years. *This plot of the PAS-score for Dunlop, set against the industry trend, shows that the company has been at risk since 1980. (With thanks to Performance Analysis Services Ltd, London, for permission to publish.)*

prevention of company failure. We qualified our statement with two 'ifs: let us look at what often happens in practice.

Our first 'if' relates to the constitution of the board. In Chapter 4 we noted that Harold Geneen, in retirement, after being in charge of affairs at ITT for more than 17 years, commented that he had kept his board pretty much 'under his thumb', but now felt it was a bad idea. He also noted that if there was a troublemaker among the directors, he was unlikely to be renominated. The implication here is that most company boards are a group of 'yes men', just going along with the management decisions.

Our second 'if' related to the board members' proper performance of their functions as directors, yes men or no. Here we have the caustic comment from Talwar, also quoted in Chapter 4, that most directors were happy to collect their fees, sip their coffee and enjoy their lunch. It was said that 'the only time they open their mouths is to partake of refreshment'. But what *is* their function? It is to look after the interests of the shareholders and their employees.

Geneen said that the chairman of the board should be an outsider, account-able to the shareholders and not to the chief executive. By the same token, the chief executive should never be chairman as well (as in fact he was). A properly constituted board should be able to tell the management through its chief executive how well it expects the company to perform. It just should not be the other way round, with management telling the board what they are doing and propose to do, as is almost invariably the case at present. Once the board assumes its proper role, providing basic direction, it will become really effective. By comparing what is happening with what was expected to happen, and seeking the reasons, the board will be placing its finger on trouble in store. Seeing danger ahead, it should call for a corporate strategy designed to correct the situation: thus it prods management into action. We will say it again: prevention is better – far better – than cure. Prevention is cheaper and easier than cure. Taking the cure may or may not be effective; it can so easily be a case of sending good money after bad.

Summary

We have said that prevention is better than any cure; but to be effective, preventive steps have to be taken early: hence the need for early warning signals, which are best given by one or other of the prediction models we examined in earlier chapters. While these models have been designed for the outsider, there is no reason at all why the chief executive and his management should not use the same tools, provided always that they are humble enough to take heed when a warning is sounded. The outsider, whether that be the bank, the government, or the auditor, can well be an influence for good, if he will only take an interest and act at the first sign of trouble.

What is the action to be taken to prevent trouble coming? Stated very simply it is this: discover and unearth trouble *before* it turns into a crisis. This can be done by taking notice of and acting upon the early warning signals elaborated upon earlier in this chapter. Geneen's prerequisite for this is a diligent and honest management![8]

References

1. Altman, E. I., *Corporate Financial Distress. A Complete Guide to Predicting, Avoiding and Dealing with Bankruptcy*, Wiley, 1983.
2. Argenti, J., *Corporate Collapse – The Causes and Symptoms*, McGraw-Hill, 1976.
3. Slatter, S., *Corporate Recovery – Successful Turnaround Strategies and their Implementation*, Penguin, 1984.
4. Slatter, S., 'The impact of crisis on managerial behaviour', *Business Horizons*, 7, 65–8, May/June 1984.
5. Kharbanda, O. P., E. A. Stallworthy and L. F. Williams, *Project Cost Control in Action*, Gower, 1980.
6. Private letter from a bank manager at one of the major branches of the big four in the UK, dated 15 November 1984.
7. Taffler, R. J. and M. Tseung, 'The audit going concern qualification in practice – exploding some myths', *The Accountant's Magazine*, July 1984, pp. 263–69.
8. Lubar, R., Review of H. Geneen and A. Moscow, *Managing*, Doubleday, 1984, published in *Fortune*, **110**, 29 Oct. 1984.

20 Figures matter, but...

Of course the figures in a profit and loss account or a balance sheet are important, but they should always be treated with reserve. They may not be right and we should not be deceived by their preciseness. Figures can lie — and they often do. Perhaps we should remind ourselves of a few words from the wise:

'The facts are wrong' (Einstein)
'Get your facts first and then you distort them as you please' (Mark Twain)
'What is it that you want me to prove?' (A statistician)

Let us never forget the common human tendency to take facts and figures out of context in order to prove what one wants to prove. We are not concerned here with the moral issues involved in such actions, but we simply warn you that such misuse of figures is very prevalent.

The Annual Report

In most countries there is a legal obligation on a public company to publish its Annual Report within a certain specified time from the end of the accounting period. The statements made in that report give us the state of a company's health in facts and figures. We are shown what has happened during the past year and it is usually accompanied by the Chairman's Statement, or something similar, summing up past achievements and looking forward to the future prospects for the company. It will include the balance sheet and a profit and loss account, these being the two key documents. The first indicates present status, the second how the company got there during the year. The balance sheet is a most valuable document, but it has some severe limitations inherent not only in the form of presentation of the data, but also in its interpretation. Reading and understanding a balance sheet is an art and several books have been written on that subject alone. What are these limitations? There are four major subjects dealt with in a balance sheet that are open to misuse and mis-interpretation. These are:

Value of assets

This figure equals the initial installed costs of the assets, minus both the installation cost and the accumulated depreciation.[1] This can be grossly misleading,

189

since it represents neither the cash that would be realized if those assets were to be sold, nor their replacement cost if they were to be destroyed. Either of these latter figures has much more relevance when assessing the health of a company than the book value of the assets as normally calculated. To correct this anomaly, the appropriate rules have been framed in certain countries, such as the US, where the Securities Exchange Commission (SEC) introduced a requirement in 1976 to the effect that companies with sales exceeding US$100 million a year *must* provide an estimate of the replacement cost of their assets in the annual accounts.

Intangible assets

Intangible assets never appear in the accounts of a company despite their critical importance, because they are not 'owned'. Such assets include the inherent know-how in management and the employees and the staff themselves. These are 'leased' or 'hired', not owned, so they cannot be included as an asset in the accounts of a company. Their importance will depend to some extent on the nature of the business in which the company is involved. A company such as IBM, with a highly trained technical and sales staff, has a tremendous investment in such people and suffers loss when they go elsewhere and have to be replaced – but they cannot quantify them and count them as an asset in the balance sheet. Of course, quantification is not easy, but it is such a significant factor that attempts are being made to assess it and to put it in the scales.

Year-end picture

The balance sheet is a snapshot, as it were: a picture of the company at one moment in time: at the year end. But snapshot is not really the right word: it is more a studio portrait. It is in effect a static picture of the company on a single day at the end of the financial year, presented after a lot of preparation. You all know what happens when we are going for a studio portrait. We dress up for the occasion and the photographer does his best to arrange us to advantage, often providing a very artificial background. It is much the same with a balance sheet. Need we say more?

Income

A major constituent of the year-end accounts is the income in the year. Now, while the presentation in the balance sheet is static, income is dynamic. It is something that is going on day by day throughout the year, its constituents can change as time passes and it can go up and down. Assets sold contribute to income – but *when* were they sold – at the beginning or the end of the year? That could be crucial, but the information is not revealed in the balance sheet.

Creative accounting

We have just likened the balance sheet to a studio portrait. While there is every reason to set out a balance sheet so that it is readable and presentable, the 'cosmetic effect' does not always stop there. There is such a thing as creative accounting, known variously as:

Accounting irregularities
Cooked books
'Fudge' figures
Sugar coating
False profits

These terms tell you just what creative accounting is without another word from us. The practice is fairly widespread and has been the subject of a lot of comment in both the economic and the general press. Some countries have regulatory bodies, one of whose objectives is to monitor company accounts, catch and punish offenders, but of course they can never detect *all* the irregularities that occur. The hope is that by detecting and severely punishing a few, the many will be deterred from adopting illegal accounting practices.

But the desire to 'look good' is so strong that top management, when under pressure, tends to drive its subordinates into a position where they are striving to attain unrealistic goals. When they fail, creative accounting is resorted to with the help of accountants and even the auditors, both internal and external. Very quickly you have a considerable group who are party to a crime, for a crime it is. But those engaged in it are too close to see it that way: all they see is an array of figures.

That they indeed do not see it — or at least pretend not to — is shown by a survey of going concern qualification statistics for 86 quoted, independent industrial and distribution companies in the UK, who were placed in receivership, voluntary liquidation or wound up between 1977 and 1983.[2] It was found that 73 per cent of these companies which had failed were *not* qualified, whereas most companies so qualified did *not* fail. This is a result of the studio portrait syndrome we referred to above.

Some typical examples

It may help to give a few illustrations from the public domain. In 1982 Stauffer Chemicals overstated their earnings by some 25 per cent by prematurely taking up some sales in the balance sheet. When faced with this charge, the company agreed to revise the figures downward, rather than contest the case and become involved in a dispute that would cost it much management time and money. In 1980 the financial position of AM International Inc. had deteriorated considerably, yet the company showed a profit of US$10 million. Scrutiny showed up a 'special accounting adjustment' of some US$200 million. Once that had been deleted, the company showed an enormous loss. On the other hand, through the use of false invoices and the capitalization of assets, the Barden Corporation helped to inflate the earnings of its US Surgical Corporation. Correcting for this reduced the 1981 pre-tax profits from US$13 million to a mere US$200 000. Here too, as in most such cases, the issue was settled without the company admitting its error, in that it said that it would not argue the case, 'to avoid an exorbitant diversion of management time'.

Naturally enough, the publicizing of such incidents has an immediate effect on the stock value of the company concerned. For instance, in the case of the Financial Corporation of America, SEC demanded that the company restate its figures. This resulted in the company declaring a second quarter loss in that year of US$103 million instead of the originally stated US$31 million profit. Within a week its stock value dropped by 25 per cent.

Another euphemism for what we are talking about is 'diddling'. We would call it cheating or swindling. Yet there are 'experts' who earn a living by showing companies all the 'legal loopholes' of which they can take advantage and they are encouraged to do it to the maximum possible extent:[3] witness a book review with the title 'How to diddle' although the book itself had a more prosaic title: *Buy Low, Sell High, Collect Early and Pay Late – The Manager's Guide to Financial Survival.*[4] So far we have been considering the efforts made to present the company in a favourable light before the public, an improved picture. But when the same company deals with the tax collector, the objective should be to present a very different picture, according to the author we have just referred to. You should adopt an attitude of morbid pessimism with respect to your ability to collect your receivables, even to the extent of writing off bad debts before you think you should. Such an attitude may well discredit your customers, but it helps win the tax battle. Then, if and when bad debts *are* paid, they are reported as new income, which has the effect of deferring tax on that income. The same result can be achieved by delaying the submission of invoices at the year end, thus pushing income into the following year. Of course, such procedures cannot be adopted if the company is casting around for means to improve its picture. Tax paid is related to the published accounts, after all.

The few cases we have quoted from the public record of companies who have been called to account by the SEC have been selected completely arbitrarily, to illustrate the point we wish to make, which is that *it happens.* But why does it happen? Why are more and more companies resorting to creative accounting? A poor picture of the company, as portrayed in its balance sheet, is a reflection upon its management, and if that management is weak it will take the easy course in the short term, and seek to cover up. While there are regulatory bodies to detect and deal with such situations, they can never hope to do more than uncover the tip of the iceberg. In fact, they should not have to act at all: there is another agency charged with the duty of seeing that a company's accounts are properly presented, each and every time, and who is supposed to scrutinize the accounts in detail to ensure that this is so, something a governmental regulatory body could never hope to do. This agency is the company's auditors, both internal and external. Who are they and what are they supposed to do?

Auditor, audit thyself!

What is an audit? It is, according to the *Concise Oxford Dictionary*, 'an official examination of accounts'. The fact that it is 'official' implies that there are rules laid down and that an auditor has a public duty. Yet so many companies on the point of collapse have presented accounts that displayed a very satisfactory position in the US (and we are sure that it is the same worldwide) that it has become a public scandal, prompting congressional probes. One sub-committee, for instance, is focusing its attention on Ernst & Whinney, one of the 'big eight' US accounting firms, for giving an 'unqualified' opinion (that is the best rating) in January 1983 with respect to the United American Bank of Knoxville. Within three weeks the bank was declared insolvent, setting off a chain of bank failures that became perhaps the largest commercial banking collapse in American history.

In fact, as we illustrate in Fig. 20.1, SEC has been much less active in relation to accountants since 1977. It took the Commission over five years to censure another of the 'big eight', Touche Ross, for improperly allowing Litton Industries Inc. to postpone losses resulting from cost overruns on naval contracts from 1972 to 1977. In another case, against Fox & Co., the twelfth largest accounting firm in the States, SEC did move fast, accusing them of violating auditing procedures in failing to detect fraud at Saxon Industries, Flight Transportation and Alpex Computer. At precisely the same time, another major international accounting company, Price, Waterhouse & Company, had given Fox & Co. a clean bill of health, saying that its 'appropriately comprehensive system of quality control was being complied with'. This review, however, did not relate to any specific audit. There is a relevant professional body in the US, the American Institute of Certified Public Accountants, but it has yet to expel a single member, even when it has been criticized by other members. One possible cause for the willingness of the auditor to 'overlook' irregularities may well be his anxiety not to lose an account.

Thus we see that we must assess the auditor as well as the company. Certainly a change from one auditor to another — perhaps because the first one is insisting on keeping to the rules — can well be an indication of financial distress.

The changing balance sheet

We suggested in Chapter 14 that those wishing to assess the health of a company should use one or other of the many indicators that are now available. However,

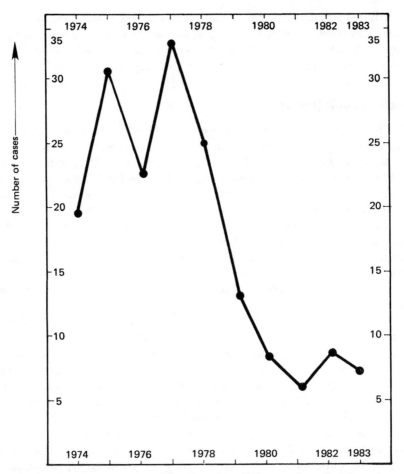

Figure 20.1   Policing by the SEC. *This plot of the number of actions pursued by the Securities and Exchange Commission (SEC) over the years shows a marked falling off since 1977. (Source: Securities & Exchange Commission, American Institute of Certified Public Accountants.)*

all such indicators derive most of their factors from the balance sheet, a document we have now placed under severe criticism. Nevertheless, despite its limitations, it is the only source of data available to those outside the company.

We have said that the trend is the thing to watch, rather than absolute values. The overall business trend presented since 1980 by a great many American companies – and they are not alone, it is a worldwide symptom – is poor. There is a general air of malaise. For example, the current high interest rates are bringing companies who have a high debt into financial distress that will lead to failure, and there is little they can do about it. The debt cost as a percentage of cash flow has doubled in the last six years in the American corporate sector (see Fig. 20.2).

> Corporate liquidity and balance sheets are weaker than at any time in the last 30 years ... companies are overloaded with potentially volatile-cost, short-term debt ... the potential dangers are enormous. Companies must bring their debt down.

This alone can be a potent factor in company failure, so a growing or disproportionate debt burden is a warning signal.

As a result of high debt figures, the return on internal investment is naturally much higher, but this can be rather misleading. For instance, of the US$100 billion improvement in cash flow seen in US companies between 1981 and 1983, nearly half was attributable to new, accelerated depreciation rules. Business had *not* improved that much: this is an artificial improvement that peaks and then disappears. The movement is already slowing. A rise in write-off values of US$19 billion in 1983 was estimated to be only US$12 billion in 1984. Improvements

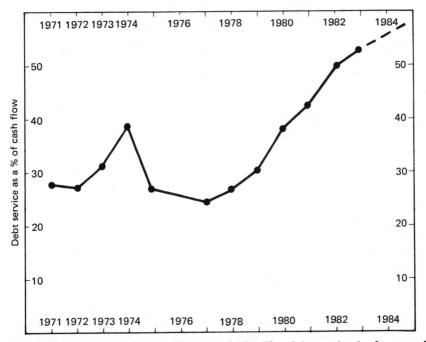

Figure 20.2 Corporate debt costs stay high. *The debt service is the annual repayment by non-financial companies of principal plus interest on their loans. This is compared with their retained earnings, plus depreciation and an adjustment for the change in value of inventories. (*Source: *Data Resources Inc.*)

in productivity and sales were also expected to be slower in 1984, with the result that the cash flow only increased in that year by some 14 per cent, about half the increase seen in 1983.

The problem is clear to see: money is expensive – and it is expected to remain expensive. This brings companies with heavy borrowing into trouble, and starts up a chain reaction. Companies have to borrow still more to stay where they are, and if they don't – because they cannot afford to – the economy is slowed down and unemployment starts growing again: a vicious circle. The only advice to those who would keep their companies in good health must be: limit borrowing. If the trend is to increase borrowing in today's economic climate, we have another, immediate warning signal. It should be going the other way!

The cost of capital

What we have just said relates largely to the USA. An exhaustive study sponsored by the American Business Conference points out that the very high cost of capital in the US, nearly four times that in Japan, may be the root cause of the problems now confronting so many US companies. The real cost of capital in the US as compared with Japan since 1961 is presented in Fig. 20.3. A ratio of 1.5 in 1961 widened to 4.0 by 1982. This gives Japan a considerable advantage in terms of manufacturing cost, so much so that the cost of a typical product in the US is said to be twice that in Japan. This cost difference has little to do with efficiency or productivity, but arises chiefly from the cost of capital.

The introduction and exploitation of new ideas, the source of all major growth, requires considerable capital investment. The high cost of such capital in the US makes innovation uneconomic there. This factor has a severe, adverse effect on the inherent ability of US companies to grow – it is as if they were born with a severe handicap. The lesson for us is that if innovation cannot be financed out of profits, then don't innovate. Accept the handicap and live with it, as so many in this sad world of ours have to do.

Summary

The only figures regularly available that will give us any indication at all of the health of a company are those conveyed to the public through the annual accounts and in particular the balance sheet. All such figures have their limitations, even when accurately presented. The problem is further complicated by what is termed 'creative accounting', whereby the figures in the balance sheet are designed to mislead – usually to disguise impending failure. Of the various agencies who should be preventing such misleading data being published, the auditor should play a powerful role.

When we look at the balance sheet in detail, we see that the cost of loans

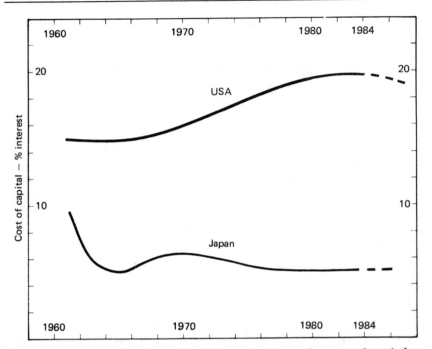

Figure 20.3   The cost of capital. *This graph shows the cost of capital to industry in the USA and Japan over the past decades. The difference is marked and seems likely to be maintained.*

is a growing problem. This means that the cost of capital is so high that innovation is being stifled, at least in the US. This we have likened to being born with a severe handicap. But, just as with us humans, there is nothing one can do but learn to live with such handicaps. The healthy company will recognize this.

References

1. Altman, E. I. (ed.), *Financial Handbook*, 5th edn, Wiley, 1981.
2. Taffler, R. J. and M. Tseung, 'The audit going concern qualification in practice – exploding some myths', *The Accountants Magazine*, 88, 263–9, July 1984.
3. Levin, D., *Buy Low, Sell High, Collect Early and Pay Late – The Manager's Guide to Financial Survival*, Prentice-Hall, 1976. Worthy, F. S., 'Manipulating profits – How is it done?' *Fortune*, 109, 34–8, 26 June 1984. .
4. Diance, R. R., 'How to diddle', book review for *Fortune*, 108, 155–6, 5 Sept. 1983.

21 Prospects for the future

Perhaps there is one thing certain when we look into the future: companies will continue to fail, go bankrupt, be taken into receivership and managers will continue to find life arduous. We have repeatedly warned that forecasting is an impossible task. Nevertheless we think it can be profitable to try and take a look into the future and assess what is likely to happen in relation to companies and business life in general. Are conditions going to get ever more difficult, worldwide, with the result that an increasing percentage of companies fail, or will things get easier in the years to come?

Global financial crisis

One forecaster warns of five crises to come, of which a global financial crisis is but one.[1] He points out that the worldwide financial structure is not sound: a number of third world countries are unable to service their debts, yet demand further aid to continue with their development plans. The obvious thing to do in such circumstances is to restrict exports to such debtor nations until they can meet their earlier financial obligations, but in this case that does not work. The debtor nation needs the capital goods he is buying to help him manufacture for export, in order to pay off his debts.[2]

It is unfortunate that the financial systems worldwide are so interlinked that a major default can disrupt the entire world banking system. For instance, nine of the largest US banks have loaned some 130 per cent of their equity to three Latin American countries. The problem is by no means limited to the US, however. In the UK the Bank of England had to take over the firm of Johnson Matthey, who ran a banking organization as an offshoot of its manufacturing activities, in order to avert a major crisis. The situation had gone unnoticed until events suddenly moved very fast indeed. The true state of affairs was only realized in September 1984, when lending losses by Johnson Matthey (US$186 million) exceeded their capital of US$126 million. Earlier, in June, there was a warning signal – we cannot call it an early warning signal in this case – when the 1983–84 pre-tax profits, as declared in the balance sheet, declined by 61 per cent as compared with the previous year. Apparently no one was watching, listening – perhaps they thought that banks do not need watching in the same way as do ordinary companies. However, while disaster was averted *because* it was a bank that was involved, it was the first such nationalization in ten years.

The Bank of England has now tightened up its financial monitoring systems. We wonder how? With industrial companies branching into banking it is interesting to speculate upon the future of the banks themselves. For instance:

> the (banking) system was expensive: people earned less on their money and paid more on their loans. Banks were important because they stored and judged information not easily available to others — but today information is cheap . . . and the practised ear can hear distant drumbeats. This is the twilight of the banks. It would be a more cheerful spectacle if we could envision the dawn of the institutions that will replace them.[3]

Future trends

While we assert, and history demonstrates, that forecasting the future is *not* possible, this does not deter the 'futurist' from pursuing his goals. In fact, despite the growing uncertainty and the failure of many established trends, activity in 'futurism' seems to be on the increase, if the volume of material being published is any guide. There is also a continuing succession of seminars on the subject. Let us look for a moment at a best seller whose futurist approach is based on the premise that new trends and ideas begin in the smaller cities.[4] Naisbitt[5] scanned some 6000 newspapers every month, mostly from the smaller cities, and analysed over two million local articles about local events. Based on this data, the kind of life to be expected by the year 2000 was depicted and it was asserted that the following trends are likely:

From	*To*
Industrial society	Information society
Institutional help	Self-help
Heirarchies	Net-working
Either/or situations	Multiple options

According to Naisbitt, a glimpse into the business life of the future shows that:

As our school system fails us, corporations will become the universities
In the US robots will replace operatives
The electronics, information and computer companies will replace the 'General Motors' and 'US Steels' of today
To be really successful, you will have to be tri-lingual: fluent in English, Spanish and the computer
You will tell your boss what to do. He will not tell you

It is said that the seeds for the future outlined above have already been sown. For example, the current robot population in the free world is estimated at around 60000 and this is expected to increase some three-fold by 1990. Japan is way ahead of any other country in this particular area of development. Most

Americans are seen as being engaged in the 'creation, processing and distribution of information', while the industrial production centres are moving to what we now call the developing world. The new leaders of industry are seen as facilitators, rather than as order givers (when we were discussing the qualities and attributes of the chief executive in Chapter 18, we spoke of him as a 'ferryman', responsible for the transfer of ideas).

While it is interesting to note such trends, we do not think that the situation will change as radically as is suggested. The basic assumption, which we challenge, is that 'all things continue as they are': that is, current trends will persist. But they do not, which is why it is impossible to forecast the future. An interesting recent example is the so-called 'oil crisis' of 1973, when some three to six months earlier the forecasts were for a continuation of abundant 'dirt cheap' oil for many years to come. The crisis caused a whole range of graphs that had been going steadily upward to collapse and change direction. The incidence of another crisis – we will not speculate on its nature, but merely assert that there will be one – will change it all once again. Our subject is corporate failure and what we are sure of is that companies will continue to fail, probably with increasing frequency, with the result that the role of management and the man will also increase in importance. The concept of the machine taking over is very far from the truth.

What will happen tomorrow?

We have been looking ahead some fifteen years, to the year 2000, but what is of much greater relevance is what is likely to happen in the intervening years. The developing countries, for instance, once thought as of no account on the international, multinational scene, are now becoming a force to be reckoned with. Examples of multinationals with their roots in the developing countries – if we may still call them that – are the Daewoo Corporation, active in trading and manufacturing, from South Korea: the Birla Group from India and the construction empire of Mendes Junior, based in Brazil. Although these companies do not have their headquarters in London, New York or Tokyo, they are now listed with multinationals such as Bechtel, General Motors and Mitsubishi and they operate worldwide.

The number of such companies or groups featured in the top 300 outside the USA has increased from 8 to 27 in the last decade and they now have some 2000 foreign subsidiaries, whereas just 10 years ago there were hardly any. This trend highlights the urgent need of the developing countries to export their wares, which they seek to facilitate by having a manufacturing base abroad. Such companies almost invariably begin by being owned by individuals or families, and have their origins and roots in countries where the regulatory machinery is loose and lax. This means, in our judgement, that there will be many more business failures in this area from now on than there have been in the past, in tandem with increased growth in this area.

At the same time, the earlier multinationals are changing in character: they are becoming what we will call 'global', for want of a better word. This step seems to be their answer to growing competition in the multinational field. A typical example would be Coca Cola. This was the first multinational to go global in its field, and that step has brought it significant cost and price advantages. There is also the advantage that there is what might be called a brand premium: the brand name becomes accepted as typifying the product worldwide. A good example of this is to be found in the field of disposable syringes. The company that pioneered the idea, but stayed national, now has a mere 6 per cent of the world market, whereas a late entrant, Universal Medical Supplies, with a worldwide business unit director and a cosmopolitan management, capable of adapting to local conditions, has won a third of the world market. While having a truly global strategy they have only three factories, each specializing in certain key components, and buy their raw materials cheaply because of the high volume discounts they receive. Since the risk increases with global operation, despite the initial advantages, one can expect the frequency of failure to grow in this field also. In other words, wherever we look, the immediate future for business seems to hold a steadily growing number of bankruptcies and other forms of company failure among both great and small.

Innovation through bankruptcy

This is the intriguing title of an article in *Business Horizons*.[6] Let us see what it means. We noted in Chapter 1 that bankruptcy laws worldwide were in general rather inadequate and that the dubious character of bankruptcy statistics has led to much faulty analysis. Future studies need to establish appropriate sampling techniques, survey tools and financial yardsticks that will enable an objective view to be taken of business failure. Otherwise the very fear of failure may well lead to the development of a corporate society, such as we have already in Japan, where the giant corporations dominate everything, leaving very little scope for the individual inventor. The bankruptcy laws need to be changed drastically, following a real understanding of the process of business failure: only thus will the individual and innovation be encouraged.

Despite the alarmingly high number of business failures in the US, ignoring for the moment the unreliability of the figures, the failure rate per 10000 new businesses is less than a third of that in the depression years of the early 1930s. In 1932, it reached an all-time high of 152 failures per 10000 'new starters'. The present so-called 'alarmingly high' rate of failure has caused some to call for a tightening of the bankruptcy laws, but this is liable to stifle innovation and mitigate against experimentation, an essential element in progress. Although various loopholes in the bankruptcy laws need to be plugged — at times there seems to be a premium associated with going bankrupt — yet initiative must not be stifled. A compromise seems called for.

It is perhaps ironic that the most successful business areas are those with the highest rates for both innovation and failure. The two seem to go hand in hand. For example, in the matter of new products: 'The investigation of corporate innovation leads to the conclusion that much uncertainty is ineradicable: despite enormous advances in the development and refinement of analytical and predictive techniques, far more products fail than succeed.'[7] If only the researchers could discover a link. Then perhaps it could be broken and we could have increasing innovation without the concomitant failure. Let it also be recognized, as we have seen time and again, that large corporations also fail. For instance, even Kodak, whose name has been synonymous with photography for half a century, is reportedly floundering.[8] In other words, there is not necessarily a correlation between size and failure, even if the statistics seem to point in that direction. After all, every business *starts* small, even if it grows tremendously later.

Let us suggest that the high rate of failure in the field of innovation is due to the fact that the innovator rarely has management skills *as well*. Those innovators who team up with a partner with such skills almost inevitably succeed, so we are back again with the thesis that *management matters*. This need seems to be recognized by the government agencies set up to encourage the small businessman, since they are prepared to offer him both finance and business expertise.

Strategies to the year 2000

Futurists seem to agree that further growth in developing countries will be higher than in the developed world. A major factor in this, if it is to occur, is the transfer of technology: and such transfer can be of benefit to both sides. So far this has been a trickle, but even so the results have not been necessarily beneficial. For example, in the Philippines the construction arm of the French Schneider Group, Spie-Batignolles, is being sued for selling inappropriate technology, while the beer producer San Miguel is said to have been 'taken for a ride' by another Schneider firm, Creusot-Loire, in a US$250 million joint venture to manufacture pipe fittings. Naturally enough, both sides have their own version of what has happened, but the debate can be most revealing to the listener. For instance, San Miguel claims that imported equipment was being used, and that many of the moulds supplied dated back to the 1920s. The French retort that the Filipinos had little idea as to what to order and made no effort to find out. Technology transfer?

For the transfer of technology to be successful, there must be a real and genuine desire on both sides to teach and to learn. Successful cases can be cited, such as the establishment of a project design and construction company in Indonesia, based on Kellogg know-how and now securing business worldwide.[9]

Turbulent times ahead

We have looked at some current trends that indicate a substantial shift and change in business patterns during the next few years. New terminology has crept in: the business world speaks of 'sunset industries', while the high technology innovative industries are not having it all their own way. What interests us in this is the fact that there *are* 'sunset industries': that is, industries on the wane, with all that is implied thereby. Yet the new industries are having to struggle to survive. Too many come on the scene, competition gets ever fiercer and many companies fail.

Turbulent times are ahead, for sure. We are not alone in our view: there is even a book telling us how to manage in such times.[10] Managers are told that if they are to ensure the survival of their company they must never deny, but rather face up to reality. You may think that obvious enough, but it seems that the obvious needs to be stated. Financial strength is essential when times are difficult, and care must be taken to assess the figures correctly. As we said earlier, figures can lie. For instance, failure to correct for the impact of inflation on the grounds that there is no foolproof way — as indeed there isn't — is to act like the physician who cannot decide what is wrong with a patient with a raging fever, and so declares him fit.

One interesting approach to growth and expansion in such times is said to be to lease rather than buy: a philosophy that seems to be taking hold.[11] Leasing is now seen as the 'neglected option', and it is asserted that it should now be used as an integral part of a company's financial resources. So little has management appreciated the significance of this particular tool that some companies have undertaken major leasing options far more casually than they would a loan of equivalent value.

Summary

Whatever else the future holds, there will certainly be many companies that fail, go into bankruptcy and need help, so we feel that the techniques we have discussed in this book will have a continuing value. Financial crisis is foretold, catastrophe is possible and turbulent times lie ahead for all of us. This only emphasizes the need for good management; which is the only sound solution. Management matters!

References

1. Neufeld, W. P., 'Forecasting potential crisis', *Futurist*, **18**, 7–19, April 1984.
2. Delamaide, D., *Debt Shock*, Weidenfeld & Nicolson, 1984.
3. Mayer, M., *The Money Bazaars – Understanding the Banking Revolution*, E. P. Dutton, 1984.

4. Hacker, A., 'A trendy view of the trends', *Fortune*, **108**, 119–20, 27 Dec. 1982.
5. Naisbitt, J., *Megatrends – Ten New Directions Transforming our Lives*, Warner, 1982.
6. Stacey, J. E., 'Innovation through bankruptcy', *Business Horizons*, **26**, 41–5, March–April 1983.
7. Foxall, G. R., *Corporate Innovation – Marketing a Strategy*, Croom Helm, 1984.
8. Chakravarty, S. N. and R. Simon, 'Has the world passed Kodak by?' *Forbes*, 5 Nov. 1984, pp. 184–7.
9. Stallworthy, E. A. and O. P. Kharbanda, *International Construction – and the Role of Project Management*, Gower, 1985.
10. Drucker, Peter, *Managing in Turbulent Times*, Harper & Row, 1980.
11. Hindon, R., 'Lease your way to corporate growth', *Financial Executive*, **52**, 20–6, May 1984.

22 Let's listen now

We think that we should bring this book to a close by taking stock and seeing where we have come in relation to the goal we set ourselves. At the outset we said that the subject we had chosen was not a pleasant one. Nevertheless, failure and bankruptcy are facts in the corporate world, facts that should be faced up to and dealt with. There is now a wide range of literature available on the subject, thanks to the efforts of both academic researchers and practising consultants in the commercial field.

Our objective is epitomized in our choice of title: *Corporate Failure – Prediction, Panacea and Prevention*. In our review of the available literature (we feel that many of the other approaches to the subject are either academic or purely sensational) we have sought to analyse the academic work and its findings, and then translate that into practical reality. It may well be titillating to read about the other people's troubles, but the purpose should be to listen and learn, so that similar mistakes are not made in the future. It may well be fascinating to develop a formula that allows you to predict that a company will collapse in some three years if nothing is done, but surely the real objective should be to prevent anything so drastic and so tragic ever happening at all. Let us see how our proposals meet that need.

The basic plan

In Part One, 'Basic concepts', we sought to set the scene. This approach was designed chiefly for the uninitiated, to let them see what is involved in corporate failure and its consequences: bankruptcy, receivership, the crisis and its causes. Those already familiar with the subject through working in this area, accountants, credit managers and the like, may nevertheless have found our overview helpful. The causes of failure are many, but we are certain that every time it comes back to mismanagement of one sort or another. Within management we find the man – the chief executive. With good management and the right chief executive, failure is most unlikely.

Then we considered actual case studies from around the world in various fields of business activity, starting with two classics, Penn Central from the US and Rolls-Royce from the UK. These both failed at around the same time, and brought home to the business world the fact that failure and collapse is by no means confined to the small business and that neither size nor reputation brings immunity. We called this part of our book 'Back from the brink?', since many of the cases we looked at demonstrated that final disaster could have been averted if the appropriate steps had been taken. In all we have taken some 25 case studies to illustrate the wide variety of ways in which a company can fail, or be on the road to failure, and we hope that we have demonstrated at the same time that failure is by no means inevitable, even when it is imminent.

We then moved on to the first of our three objectives, demonstrating that prediction is possible. The solution to any problem starts with a clear statement of the problem itself and quite often such a statement provides a direct clue to the solution. Better still, of course, if the problem can be seen looming ahead and action taken before it arrives. This possibility indeed opens out to us when we study prediction. While the prediction of failure is not easy, the pioneering work of several investigators has shown that it is possible. There is certainly no magic formula and, as we noted in Chapter 12, the best course is undoubtedly to use two contrasting methods of analysis. But we hope that you have realized that despite the immense amount of research that has gone into this subject around the world, the problem of prediction is by no means fully solved.

The prediction techniques available to us at the moment are of both the quantitative (objective) type and the qualitative (subjective) type. We have recommended that both approaches be used in combination for the certainty of successful prediction to be increased and that both *can* be used in the context where prediction is most appropriate: within the company at risk. We saw, too, that this combination of the qualitative with the quantitative approach is the basis of all good management. Of course, it is our view that the whole purpose of prediction is that one may have ample warning of impending failure and thus take preventive steps. But it is still possible for the warning to come too late. That leads us on to the 'panacea', dealt with in detail in Part Four.

Is there a panacea — a universal remedy? Yes, there is, if we accept that good management is the remedy. The difficulty that then confronts us is that bad management appears in all sorts of places within a company and has to be discerned if the remedy is to be applied. There is no standard approach to the problem and each case has to be taken on its merits and the remedy tailored to suit. The situation of each company is unique, just as each human being is unique. Diagnosis is the first essential: that *can* lead on to a remedy. But we came back again to the theme opened up in Part One, the crucial importance not only of management, but of the man. It is the chief executive, above all, who can and must set a company on the road to recovery. Recovery is not something that comes by accident: its course must be charted and followed. That led us to consider corporate planning and its key significance. A company without a plan is a company without a future. Through all this we sought to bring the subject alive by drawing your attention to practical illustrations of the points that we were making: case studies in miniature.

Finally, in Part Five, we examined the kernel of the matter, the *prevention* of business failure. It goes without saying that this is the best course of all, although it has not been the driving motive for all the research that has taken place over the years. That motivation has been rather the protection of financial interest. Nevertheless, the data is there and prevention is possible. While prediction can serve a turn in this, especially if employed by management itself, rather than by the outsider looking on, the real solution still lies in good management. The problem is that one can be blind to one's faults. Even when the fault becomes so apparent that it can be ignored no longer, the management can be very like the individual: the warning is ignored because its message is unpleasant. We felt that some of the commercial methods of appraisal ought to help in this area, if only they were used by companies to examine *themselves* as well as others. Perhaps an impartial warning might be heeded, but we wonder – human nature is very perverse. The logic of the situation may well be that while good management would heed a warning, it does not need it, whereas bad management, needing the warning, ignores it.

Our glimpse into the future gave us no cause to believe that things will get any better. Corporate failure and its concomitant, bankruptcy, is not only a fact of life but is on the increase. All the more reason, then, why you should listen to our message. Throughout we have sought to demonstrate the many tragic consequences of company failure: investors lose their money, the worker loses his job. The economy of the country and especially a region suffers, sometimes quite severely. And all because someone, somewhere, has failed. It is usually the management of the company concerned, but not always. Sometimes failure is precipitated by government policy, sometimes it is the fault of the workforce or the community in which the company has to operate. But the examples we have given should be warning enough: potential company failure is something that demands drastic action: it should never be ignored.

Management style

Who are we to tell managements around the world what is good for them? But we make no such claim: we merely examine the facts and point the lessons. We have reverted more than once to the importance – the vital importance – of good management, and went into detail in Chapters 3 and 16. We come back to it once again now because we cannot over-emphasize its value. Good management is crucial, and its absence brings failure sooner or later. We are convinced that good management can, more often than not, avert failure. Even when that is not possible, good management will most certainly minimize its traumatic effects.

What is good management? Looking around the world, we have seen various styles of management, of which the Japanese seems most successful, having brought that country from poverty to prosperity in some 30 years. Unfortunately you cannot just copy: it is not possible to transplant a management style from one country to another, when the cultural values, history and experience are all so very different. The essentials can, however, be assessed and the lessons applied: much good management is just plain common sense. This lesson was hammered home in a recent *Fortune* survey of the ten most successful plants in the US.[1] These ten turn out products ranging from shoes (E. T. Wright & Co.) to pick-up trucks (Nissan Motor Co.), from dishwashers (General Electric) to welding equipment (Lincoln Electric). Each of these companies was at the top of its particular line in terms of productivity or quality, or both. But there the resemblance ends. Their methods, when scrutinized, were seen to be neither American nor Japanese, but just common sense. However, it seems that such sense is not as common as it ought to be. The real point is that each case is so different that no rules can be laid down. These ten factories were vastly different from one another, even when one just walked through them, and the production techniques and management style had to be and had been adapted to suit the specific circumstances.

General Electric's brand-new dishwasher fabrication plant looked like a top-class hotel when one walked into it, whereas Lincoln Electric's long established, dimly lit workshops reminded one of a dingy hostel. Yet both had found ways to merge design, manufacturing, quality and automation to produce a product that the market accepted. They were both singularly successful in getting close to both their customers and their workforce. With Nissan it was somewhat different. When building their new facility their top executives doubted whether workers without experience in a similar facility could succeed in producing quality goods. But their Smyrna plant, now producing pick-up trucks, has surprised and perhaps humiliated the Japanese. The plant is entirely managed by Americans and 80 per cent of the workforce had no prior experience in building automobiles, yet customer surveys show that the Smyrna trucks are better than those made in Japan. To quote the plant manager: 'The Nissan executives find it a bit hard to take that their children are doing better than their parents.' The moral – and we do hope that you are listening – is that it is *not* the specific management technique, American or Japanese, that brings results, nor sophisticated equipment. What is wanted is common sense, hard work and integrity of purpose.

Do listen to outsiders

It is wise to recognize that the outsider, while not necessarily knowing your business all that intimately, can nevertheless often offer very sound advice. He has the advantage of an independent and impartial view of the business and its problems and can often discern a potential cause of failure that is hidden from those more closely involved. Typical of those in a good position to offer such advice are the non-executive director and the management consultant. An independent and objective view will always be of value, especially if those consulted are prepared to be frank and honest. To illustrate the real role that the non-executive director can play, let us quote:

> I think that in most firms the non-executive director can, and in fact does, play a useful part, because he is not dependent on anybody round the table. He can say what he wants, he's got the ultimate sanction of voting with his feet.[2]

His effectiveness, however, will depend upon the full-time directors. They either listen or they don't. So how does the outsider see his role?

> I expect to be *listened* to, but I don't expect my advice to be followed. That is entirely up to them and I would never look to see whether they had followed my advice or not. I wouldn't go back next time and say [especially if the company was failing], I told you that and you didn't do it.[2]

The emphasis and the comment is ours.

When, however, a consultant is called in for advice, especially in times of distress, his role is much more intimate than that of the non-executive director. To be effective the consultant, during the period of his assignment, has to be treated as an insider. Although a good management consultant is expensive (upwards of US$1000 a day plus all expenses) the benefit/cost ratio can be very high indeed. He is seen as a catalyst which although on the inside, does not take part in the reaction, although he will facilitate it and speed it up. His role can be vital to the growth and success of a business: 'Management consultants often have a talent, knack, skill, flair, call it what you will, of adjusting the pieces of a mental jigsaw into an order which creates a clear picture.'[3]

The consultant cannot, however, guarantee success: that is wholly dependent upon his client. The consultant can only bring about change if his client is willing to listen. In fact, we would go so far as to say that a consultant should not be called in unless the client has already resolved to listen and act upon the advice given. Unfortunately, many of the benefits resulting from the use of a consultant, being confidential, never see the light of day. Even when the press does mention that a consultant has played a role, the name is usually omitted. This is an integral part of the ethics of the profession of consultancy. Yet again, for many a client the need to engage a consultant is felt to be a confession of failure, and so secrecy is the order of the day. Quite often, as we have found for ourselves, the consultant has to advise his client that he should not proceed with a particular project or plan upon which he has set his heart. This may annoy him intensely, but the advice should be given if it is called for. Pet projects have been the death of many a company and we have presented you with case studies that demonstrate that fact quite clearly. Indeed, the book to which we have just referred quotes a case in point:

> A client (a technical enthusiast) in electrical and electronic engineering . . . saw that much of his electrical products were becoming obsolete with the trend for newer electronic technology. Of course, change to electronics . . . is a

formidable and expensive task. My contribution was to curtail my client's
enthusiasm – to point out that there was still several years life in the old
products and that he should not get bored with them too soon – particularly
as some of his competitors with an equal eye to the future were getting out
of the obsolescent market – leaving a greater share of it for my client. . .[3]

All consultancy assignments do not have such a happy ending. In the case of the
British company Bamford's, an agricultural machinery concern, the assignment
came too late to save it. A consultancy company was engaged in November of
1979 and a drastic rationalization with the injection of substantial extra finance
was recommended, but of course without any guarantee of success. The reaction
of the company's banker was to say: 'we cannot grant the additional facilities
which the board and its advisers believe necessary for the company to continue
trading'. In other words: no cash. In this case the writing had been on the wall
for some five years, for those with eyes to see. One of Bamford's main products,
a baler, was geared to haymaking, whereas agricultural practice had largely
switched to silage making. Even in the field of haymaking, the company had
been left behind by European developments in the field: drum mowers and
rotary star tedders. The end of the story? Bamford went into liquidation in June
of 1980.

Some consultants specialize in the turnaround of companies and one goes
so far as to call himself a 'company life saver'. Curiously enough, he actually
wanted to become a medical doctor, but thought the training period too long.

Go on listening

The non-executive director and the consultant can play a very helpful role as
critics of management. If they are heeded they can play a vital role in curing
sick companies. Their specialized knowledge of industry and expertise in good
management practice qualify them for the task. But it is still possible for laymen,
such as the enthusiastic journalist, to do quite a good job of sounding the
warning note at the appropriate moment. Much of what has been written borders
on sensationalism, but some of the writing on the subject is quite objective and
very refreshing to read. We would recommend, for instance, a book by two
reporters who have been eager and fast learners in this field. The title is dramatic
enough: *Life and Death on the Corporate Battlefield* but the treatment of the
subject is quite realistic.[4] Much of what they have to say makes fascinating
reading. For instance, they highlight and explode a number of myths, such as
the idea that in big business the executives know exactly what they are doing.
They don't! Geneen, whose management style we reviewed in Chapter 4, and
who propelled ITT to near the top amongst the multinationals, is quite clear
about this: 'Most chief executive officers today *don't know* how to handle their
jobs.'[5] The collapse of giants, of whom Rolls-Royce and Dunlop are typical,
is evidence enough of that. Senior executives, even in the biggest of companies,

are neither omniscient nor omnipotent. They are very human and will therefore put their own interest (such as preserving their job) above everything else.

Our two reporters interviewed several managers, entrepreneurs, financial experts and business school professors and tell their story using illustrations from real life. They show how large corporations have been outmanoeuvred by small companies or a single individual. They demonstrate that executives put their own interests first, citing the case of a recent takeover battle where Marathon executives preferred to be owned by US Steel rather than by Mobil. Why? Because that would bring them job security: the steel company had no experienced oil men to replace them! By the same token, managers are not for ever striving to maximize the return to the stockholders. Rather are they striving to increase the return to themselves. This is in line with the finding of a management theoretician, Herbert A. Simon, the only Nobel Laureate in the management field, although he received this award for economics. He declared that instead of maximizing corporate earnings, managers usually 'satisfice' – a word he invented to describe the maintenance of a minimum performance level which is sufficient to retain their own position or improve it. Wherever we look, those who write on this subject confirm our statement, made when we considered the course of action we recommend to avoid failure (Chapter 14), that ultimately judgement prevails over all the sophisticated techniques and detailed analysis. They often quote a former IBM executive charged with an important investment decision who said: 'Ultimately its a gut call. You can quantify all you want . . . but you can never replace the need for a judgement call.'

Then why all the fuss about numbers, tables and graphs? The executive went on to say: 'Companies – and managers – try to cope with uncertainty by seeking to protect themselves with numbers. . .they make statistical analyses and spend millions on market research until the numbers become a kind of security in themselves.' With that thought before you, we plead with you to listen, to heed and to follow the common-sense approach we have sought to advocate throughout. Do not let yourself be bemused with figures. Put them in their place and recognize them for what they are: useful but very fallible tools.

Summary

We have returned once more to the point that good management is the only answer, but that it is not something that can be described or defined in detail, because good management adapts itself to circumstances. It adapts itself, therefore, to the type of company and the context in which it has to work. Management can learn much from outsiders, if it will but listen. It is the good manager who will finally exercise his judgement and make the decisions that bring success. All the figures will ever do is sound a warning – and sometimes they are so manipulated that they fail to do even that.

References

1. Bylinsky, G., 'America's Best-Managed Factories', *Fortune*, **109**, 50–8, 28 May 1984.
2 Spencer, A., *On the Edge of Organization*, John Wiley, 1983.
3. Tisdall, P., *Agents of Change – the Development and Practice of Management Consultancy*, Heinemann, 1982.
4. Solman, P. and T. Friedman, *Life and Death on the Corporate Battlefield – How Companies Win, Lose, Survive*, Simon & Schuster, 1983.
5. Lubar, R., in a review of H. Geneen and A. Moscow, *Managing*, Doubleday, 1984, published in *Fortune*, **110**, 29 Oct. 1984.

Author Index

Subject Index